RUMOURSEXPOSED

RUMOURSEXPOSED

The Unauthorized Biography of Fleetwood Mac

LEAH FURMAN

CITADEL PRESS
KENSINGTON PUBLISHING CORP.
www.kensingtonbooks.com

CITADEL PRESS BOOKS are published by

Kensington Publishing Corp.
850 Third Avenue
New York, NY 10022

All Kensington titles, imprints, and distributed lines are available at special quantity
discounts for bulk purchases for sales promotions, premiums, fund-raising, educational,
or institutional use. Special book excerpts or customized printings can also be created
to fit specific needs. For details, write or phone the office of the Kensington special
sales manager: Kensington Publishing Corp., 850 Third Avenue, New York, NY
10022, attn: Special Sales Department, phone 1-800-221-2647.

CITADEL PRESS and the Citadel logo are Reg. U.S. Pat. & TM Off.

First printing: October 2000
First paperback printing: May 2003

10   9   8   7   6   5   4   3   2   1

Printed in the United States of America

Library of Congress Cataloging-in-Publication Data

Furman, Leah.
    Rumors exposed : the unauthorized biography of Fleetwood Mac / Leah Furman.
        p.   cm.
    Includes bibliographical references and index.
    ISBN 0–8065–2472–3
    1. Fleetwood Mac (Musical group) I. Title.
ML421.F57F87   1999
78242166'092'2—dc21   99-31799
[B]   CIP

For Mom

CONTENTS

ACKNOWLEDGMENTS

I would like to thank my agent, Giles Anderson, and my editor, Francine Hornberger, for the part they played in bringing this book to print. And I could never have done without the generous assistance of my mother, Mira, and my sister, Elina, and the extensive research of John Nikkah. Thanks also to Roman for listening to my many Fleetwood Mac stories. Thank you all.

RUMOURSEXPOSED

INTRODUCTION

ROCK OF AGES

The five musicians are gathered in the greenroom. Lounging on the dilapidated sofas, drinks and cigarettes in hand, the group appears the embodiment of relaxation. But they are enjoying the type of rest known only to those who have seen nine cities in ten days and have long since passed the brink of exhaustion. In fact, if anyone were to ask Stevie Nicks, Lindsey Buckingham, John McVie, Christine McVie, or Mick Fleetwood their home address, they'd need a minute to check their records before getting back with a definitive answer.

It's December 1975, and like a family of migrant workers in search of a paycheck, this band has been on the road for months. Instead of a spacious, amenity-laden tour bus—standard equipment for headliners on a concert tour—Fleetwood Mac's vehicles of necessity are a pair of rented Impala station wagons. Relentlessly spreading their influence from town to town, the band members are determined to break through their opening-act plateau and achieve fame, fortune, and everything that goes with it.

They may interact with seamless ease over the shared stash of drugs and booze that litters every surface of their backstage, but each is actually caught up in his or her own separate reality. There is scant need of the roadie announcing the minutes to showtime, as the crescendoing clamor of the anxious audience says it all. Many die-hard fans in the crowd believe they can guess what the musicians are feeling. It's the seventies, and love is all there is—especially for a band consisting of two couples and a happily married fifth man out.

What the audience doesn't know, but will discover within a matter of months, is that the Nicks-Buckingham relationship and the McVies' marriage have shattered over the road's many stumbling blocks. The details of these breakups will be revealed in the tabloid press, and the feelings behind them will be heard by over 25 million people worldwide in Fleetwood Mac's celebrated 1977 album, *Rumours*. But as Christine McVie observed, "If we'd all been getting on like a house on fire, the songs on *Rumours* wouldn't have been nearly as good."

The act is what kept these warring musicians together. And in retrospect, Fleetwood Mac looks to have made a solid case for its exacting work ethic. After all, relationships, they will come and they will go—but their songs will endure forever.

Rumours struck a chord, and in no time rocketed to Number One on the charts. It remained there for 31 weeks in the United States, went platinum within one month of its release, and proceeded to secure a position in rock 'n' roll history as the third top-selling album of all time. The music industry took note as well, awarding *Rumours* the Grammy for Album of the Year in 1977.

"Mr. Fleetwood, is there any truth to the rumors that Fleetwood Mac is breaking up?" is how the typical Fleetwood Mac press conference circa 1978 would open up.

The answer: "No."

A thousand times no. Fleetwood Mac would go on to release album after album, single after single. They would play all over the United States, Europe, Australia, and Japan. Their concert venues would expand from small auditoriums into expansive football fields and coliseums. Their music would spill out of weather-beaten Chevy Novas and posh Park Avenue parties on Saturday nights. Young men and women would take to outlining Nicks's and Buckingham's photos with red lipstick hearts and emulating the pair's hairstyles with ozone-depleting aerosol hair spray. Many of these same girls and guys would be inspired to pour their own hearts out in song, with the hope that maybe, just maybe, they, too, could touch someone like Fleetwood Mac had touched them.

––––––

Neither critics nor musicians shy away from paying homage to the supergroup that permeated radio waves worldwide and defined the sound of 1970s popular music. Even 1990s rock centerpieces such as the Smashing Pumpkins and Hole have covered "Landslide" and "Gold Dust Woman" with tremendous success. And in the middle of Fleetwood Mac's 1997 reunion tour, Mick Fleetwood was busy capitalizing on this new wave of Macmania by repackaging the classic *Rumours* as a tribute album.

The CD, titled *Legacy,* hit the shelves in 1998. Contributing artists included the Cranberries, Shawn Colvin, Elton John, Jewel, Matchbox 20, and Tonic. "I'm basically overseeing it," said Mick Fleetwood. "My wish and desire was to have them do their own full-on interpretations of the specific songs on the *Rumours* album."

As it turned out, the new generation of fans didn't need to have Fleetwood Mac's easy-on-the-ears music spoon-fed to them via a variety of modern artists. Whether by listening to classic rock radio stations or watching the MTV and VH-1 specials, generations X, Y, and Z have enthusiastically reclaimed the band's music as their own. One teenage fan from Arizona echoed the prevailing sentiment: "Fleetwood Mac is an excellent band mostly because of their distinct sound."

Current pop stars make no secret of their feelings for Stevie Nicks, the woman who came to embody the Mac's unique charm. "She had a huge influence on everybody, whether they admit it or not," said Courtney Love of Fleetwood Mac's frontwoman. Sheryl Crow elucidated the nature of Stevie Nicks's influence by explaining that "Stevie bridges the gap between the powerful rock singers of the sixties, like Janis Joplin and Grace Slick, and what's going on today."

Scores of female singer/songwriters are now forced to suffer the Stevie Nicks comparison. Jewel and Tori Amos are just a couple whom critics have branded "Nicksesque." While some may scratch their heads at the parallels, Stevie Nicks understands. "I look around at all the girl singers, and I think they're all my children . . . and they're all going to do this. . . . And, yes, maybe I inspired them because I did get through a lot, and I did have the same problems that they're going to have. You do have to give up a lot for it."

––––––

Fleetwood Mac is now being hailed as the band that brought arena rock to a new, much wider contingent of American society. The band's English faction, consisting of the McVies and Fleetwood, rode the momentum of the Great British Invasion, still going strong in the seventies with acid rock bands such as Pink Floyd and Led Zeppelin. Nicks and Buckingham, the Americans, were instrumental not only in songwriting but in satisfying the U.S. audiences' penchant for homegrown talent.

The band's female singer/songwriters played a crucial role in the changing zeitgeist. The singular voices of Stevie and Christine were recognized and supported by feminists all over America. Young women steeped in the rhetoric of the sexual revolution regularly showed up to Fleetwood Mac concerts wearing Stevie regalia: black chiffon and towering platform shoes. The enthusiasm of the female fans carried Stevie Nicks, along with Fleetwood Mac, into the forefront of pop-culture consciousness.

Justly or not, Stevie Nicks has received the lion's share of attention in the Fleetwood Mac revival. After all, it was she who first captured the imagination of millions more than twenty years back. The mention of a Welsh witch, a sparkle of crystal, and one sweep of her flowing gown was all it took to turn this young woman from Phoenix, Arizona, into a free creature of the enchanted forest. It matters little that she triumphed with the aid of two other songwriters and the best rhythm section in rock; audiences simply couldn't get enough of Stevie Nicks. They chanted her name, deified her voice, and followed her every romantic travail with voracious interest.

Years of *Rolling Stone* covers, heavy airplay, and MTV rotation would go by before Fleetwood Mac would buckle under the pressure of internal dissension. Solo pursuits, creative differences, and mass quantities of cocaine, to say nothing of the romantic turmoil, began to take their toll on the band as early as 1976, even though sales of later albums—*Tusk, Mirage,* and *Tango in the Night*—continued to peak in the multiplatinum range. Lindsey Buckingham would eventually take his leave after the successful debut of *Tango*. Christine McVie and Stevie Nicks would follow suit, and Fleetwood Mac would lie dormant for years before the waxing interest in classic rock would bring the individual members back into collaboration.

––––––––

"Don't stop thinking about tomorrow . . ." came blaring through television sets all over the world on January 19, 1993. Democrats and Fleetwood Mac fans everywhere were dancing in a haze of red, white, and blue confetti the night of Bill Clinton's Inaugural Gala. Yes, Fleetwood Mac played, live and with gusto, the very personal message of hope that Christine McVie had written for her former husband John.

That night, all five members were present and accounted for at Washington, D.C.'s Capital Centre. But those entertaining notions of an impending full-on, gang's-back-together reunion were in store for a major disappointment. At this juncture, the only Fleetwood Mac members willing to reunite were drummer Mick Fleetwood and bassist John McVie—the founders of the band and rightful owners of the Fleetwood Mac name. They had seen the band through thick and thin and were ready to take a bullet for the sake of their claim to musical immortality.

While not exactly a command performance, Fleetwood Mac played solely out of respect for the newly elected president. "My sense of musical growth is totally out of the realm of Fleetwood Mac," said Lindsey Buckingham. "At this point, I really wouldn't consider a reunion."

It had been years since the five quintessential Fleetwood Mac members had taken the stage together. And while reuniting would clearly have to wait until the wounds of the past had had ample time to heal, Clinton's request gave the favorite lineup a chance to put some of the bad feelings surrounding Lindsey's infamous 1987 desertion behind them.

––––––––

The last few years have seen Fleetwood Mac come out of retirement. And the timing couldn't have been more perfect. The individual musicians drifted back into the fold, one by one, just in time to commemorate the twentieth anniversary of *Rumours* and the thirtieth anniversary of Fleetwood Mac with their tremendously successful album *The Dance.*

Sliding into the Number One position on the Billboard pop charts, this new offering went quadruple-platinum less than a year after its release. Accompanied by an Emmy-nominated MTV special and followed by enough VH-1 coverage to give serious Mac fans a bad case of eyestrain, Fleetwood Mac quickly regained the ubiquity they let slip away back in the late 1980s.

To the band's enormous glee, the forty-city reunion tour brought enough fans out of the woodwork to make the three-month expedition the third highest-grossing tour of 1997. Show after sold-out show saw the band performing a notch above their former standard of excellence. Offstage, the entire fifty-something group appeared to have mellowed out substantially. Compared to the wild-bunch-goes-on-a-road-trip vibe resonating throughout the frantic 1970s concert tours, the 1997 tour was a pleasure cruise. Contraband had been swapped for the products of the General Nutrition Center, former rivalries had given way to mutual respect, and the great sense of anger and resentment that had once charged this pop supergroup had been supplanted by a peaceful acquiescence to their collective calling—fan gratification. This tour was a love-fest, and appropriately enough, reviewers responded with nothing short of public love letters.

———

It's a bitter cold Monday evening in Manhattan. The city streets are bustling with people desperate just to make it home before frostbite sets in. But those in the know are defying the elements to catch a glimpse of their favorite rock stars at the landmark Waldorf-Astoria Hotel. For tonight is January 12, 1998, the night that will witness Fleetwood Mac's induction into the Rock and Roll Hall of Fame.

The solid oak tables of the Waldorf's spacious ballroom are replete with music-industry luminaries. The Fleetwood Mac quintet is laughing and chatting it up like old friends who haven't a care in the world. All the insults and recriminations that they've publicly hurled at one another over the years have been transcended.

Among the honorees this evening are the Eagles, the Mamas and the Papas, and Santana. Fleetwood Mac's ties to their fellow Hall of Fame inductees are strong enough to raise eyebrows. Pure coincidence, or could there really be some truth to the legendary Fleetwood Mac karma? It was, after all, the Eagles that presented the biggest challenge to the Fleetwood Mac of the 1970s. *Hotel California* was the album to beat both on the charts and at the awards shows. Back in the day, the Eagles were also the men to date, as Stevie Nicks had evidenced, much to the dismay of her former inamorato Lindsey Buckingham. Of course, tonight there are no axes left to grind, as all the hatchets were buried ages ago.

Watching the induction of Michelle Phillips, John Phillips, and Denny Doherty of the Mamas and the Papas had both Stevie Nicks and Lindsey Buckingham waxing nostalgic. It was in San Francisco that "California Dreaming" first brought the pair together. Still in high school, neither was aware of the other's existence until both students showed up at the same party. Lindsey began to play "California Dreaming" on the piano. Struck by his good looks and voice, Stevie joined in. Two years later, and quite unexpectedly, Lindsey phoned Stevie with a request: Would she join his band? The rest, as they say, is history.

Get two such coincidences and you're humming the theme to *Twilight Zone;* get three and you've definitely entered the Mac dimension. With Santana's induction into the hallowed halls of rock 'n' roll fame, the coincidence theory goes out the window. Tonight has harmonious convergence written all over it. Those familiar with Fleetwood Mac's early work are undoubtedly aware of the debt that Santana owes the Mac. "Black Magic Woman," Santana's claim to enduring rock stardom, was actually a cover of the Fleetwood Mac original. Written by Peter Green back when the Mac was a supergroup of the British blues variety, "Black Magic Woman" figures prominently in the beginning of the Fleetwood Mac saga. And that's exactly where this story starts.

1

MEAGER BEGINNINGS

It's 1967, and London is in the grip of a social revolution. While the Houses of Parliament and the City are overflowing with stodgy hardliners intent on shaping policy and speculating their way to riches, London's West End is at the eye of the avant-garde cyclone that is currently changing the planetary landscape. The Mods, with their thigh-high minis and shaggy tresses, and the Rockers, spouting their angry antiestablishment messages, are transforming self-expression into a multimillion-dollar industry. Actors, artists, designers, models, and musicians have turned London into their own private playground. The whole of the world's vanguard, cockney and gentry alike, gathers in the same seedy nightclubs to catch a glimpse of what may be the next Big Thing. The Beatles are the undisputed kings of the swinging London scene, and the Rolling Stones aren't far behind. This anything-goes atmosphere is giving rise to the likes of Eric Clapton, Jimmy Page, Jeff Beck, and Van Morrison.

Blues is at the forefront of the nation's consciousness, and has been since Muddy Waters swept over England like a tidal wave in the 1950s. While racist booking practices had blocked the blues legends of the Mississippi Delta from gaining a foothold in the States—keeping them off the radio and on the black club circuit—British audiences have been quick to appropriate the new sound, making it their own in the process. Chuck Berry in America leads to the Beatles in England. Even as pop rock wins converts, Eric Clapton and John Mayall are just two of the blues purists who pick up the torch and run with it, spreading the word throughout the countryside. Finally, the music mushrooms into a national phenomenon, which comes to be known as the British Blues Boom.

Kids from provinces all over Britain are flocking to the capital for their shot at infamy. London's ever-proliferating number of bands cannot accommodate all the would-be musicians alighting from every incoming train, plane, and automobile.

———

One of these upstarts was Mick Fleetwood. Only fifteen years of age upon his 1963 London arrival, the six-foot, six-inch greenhorn came with a burning ambition to become a professional drummer. He was born into a Royal Air Force wing commander's family in Cornwall, England, on June 24, 1947. His father's career had the family traveling from one exotic post to another. Egypt, Cyprus, Norway: Mick had seen them all. But these carefree days would come to an end when young Mick was sent to a British boarding school for his dose of proper education.

Mike and Brigid Fleetwood had great plans for Mick and his older sisters, Sally and Susan. Like many parents, they wanted to give their children what they had never had—a chance to attend a university. But while the girls were doing just fine in school, Mick's academics fell woefully short of satisfactory. Hard as he tried, his exams were a series of disappointments. Of course, at the time no one had heard of dyslexia, the learning disability that was keeping Mick from reading, and consequently impeding all of his attempts at academic achievement. "I was absolutely hopeless in classes," Mick admitted. "I still don't know my four times tables. And I'm pushed to repeat the alphabet."

One of the few things that gave Mick any pleasure was banging away on anything he could find, pretending to play the drums. He was so enamored with drumming that his father bought him a drum set when Mick turned thirteen. Without so much as a single lesson, Mick soon became proficient by drumming along with his Everly Brothers LPs. Here, finally, was something at which he could excel.

London, with its rocking music scene and his now-married sister's apartment, was Mick's land of opportunity. In 1963, when all hopes for a higher education had been effectively quashed, Mick set out for the big city.

———

The year of Mick's arrival was also a banner year for a young bassist named John McVie. Born in Ealing, West London, on November 26, 1945, John was a bass player by default. He and a bunch of guys from the block had formed the Krewsaders while still at school. "We had jackets, a logo, the whole deal," John recalled. "We played weddings and parties, those kinds of things."

The only point of contention was that everyone was jockeying to play lead guitar. Modest and unpretentious by nature, John wasn't one to let pride get in the way of his band's ascent. He reined in his ego and graciously resigned himself to the background. Pulling the top two strings off his guitar was all it took. Voilà, a bassist was born.

The son of a sheet-metal worker, John had never counted on a career in music. His levelheaded, rational plan included a job in the tax office as a fallback position. Luckily, John wouldn't have to content himself with the life of a bureaucrat for too long. The day that John began his career in civil service was the same day that he embarked upon a collaboration that would eventually lead to bigger and better things.

John's participation in the small-time Krewsaders came to an end in January 1963 when he was invited into John Mayall's band. Mayall had yet to distinguish himself as "the Father of British Blues" when he first met McVie, in 1961. Having come to London a few years back, he was a commercial artist by day, an up-and-coming blues musician by night, and his goal was to create a solid blues band.

Originally, Mayall had wanted another bass player, Cliff Barton, in his band. But Barton, who lived near the McVie family, was already in a prominent British blues ensemble. He turned down the job, but not before offering a referral: "I know this boy of fifteen, give him a chance."

Upon meeting McVie and hearing him play, Mayall realized that John was not ready for the Bluesbreakers. But he liked the kid nonetheless and wanted to guide him in the right direction so he gave the aspiring musician B. B. King and Willie Dixon records to learn from. Two years later, right around the time that Mick Fleetwood was first setting foot on London soil, Mayall completed his John Mayall and the Bluesbreakers ensemble by inviting the seventeen-year-old John McVie to join.

Of course, it would be some time before John could bid the daily grind adieu. No band could command a king's ransom when first starting out. "My first show was in Acton—they paid me ten shillings—in a pub at the Uxbridge Road," recalled John.

John McVie would go on to pay homage to his first mentor, stating: "I believe that John Mayall was fundamental in exposing blues music to the world."

––––––

Of course, neither Fleetwood nor McVie had any inkling that one day their names would be forever intertwined. Already, though, they did have one thing in common: Both spent much of 1963 working mind-numbing day jobs, John in the tax office and Mick at a department store.

Mick Fleetwood's dyslexia followed him to this first job. It was a desk job and required reading, which Mick had never quite mastered. "I don't read books: I've read two in my life," he said. *"Sherlock Holmes,* I remember I had to read that one for class. And *Alice in Wonderland."*

Every morning Mick dreaded coming in to work, fearing that his illiteracy would be discovered. His attitude was so negative that when the ax finally fell, he was overcome with relief. Had he lived on his own, the issue of money might have had Mick drumming a different tune. But as he was still living with his sister and brother-in-law, he used the extra free time to practice his drums.

The constant noise must have irritated many of the residents who shared his sister's quiet street. But one day, when the beating of the drums wafted over to Peter Bardens, the young keyboardist was curious. Following the sound all the way into a neighbor's garage, Bardens found Mick pounding away on the professional drum set his father had given him as a going-away present. The two got to talking, and when it came out that Mick had never played with a band, Peter was ready to lend a hand.

Within a few months Bardens put together a blues band with Mick as the drummer. The Cheynes, as they called themselves, signed with the Rik Gunnell Agency, the same agency that represented the Bluesbreakers.

———

John Mayall and the Bluesbreakers became a hot act very quickly after recruiting a young blues guitar prodigy in 1965. Eric Clapton was drawn to the blues, and when his own band, the Yardbirds, abandoned the blues for their chance at pop stardom, he found a comfortable home with the Bluesbreakers.

The band would play at British pubs and back up the great American blues players who were pouring into England. They were playing so much that it took them less than a month to record their first album, *John Mayall and the Bluesbreakers With Eric Clapton.* "It was done at Decca Studios in West Hampstead, England," said McVie. "We'd just go in and do takes live, with no overdubs. And as soon as the session was finished, we'd be out to gig."

The results of this hasty effort received great accolades from British blues fans. Eric Clapton was suddenly saddled with the appellation of "God." And John McVie was enjoying every minute of his newfound success. No longer in need of his fallback job, he quit the tax office just as he was nearing his wit's end. Always partial to a spot of lager, McVie also began his enduring love affair with the bottle around this time. "When I joined Mayall the drinking was part of the scene," McVie said. "I met a lot of people who drank, and it snowballed until I'd be drinking half a bottle of spirits a gig." And while the continuous binge-drinking drove Mayall to distraction, the bandleader appreciated McVie's music too much to let him go.

It was also around this time that Peter Green, a fan of Clapton's work, came into the picture. "After the album came out a strange situation developed, because this upstart guy named Peter Green started playing with John. There were guitar style wars going on between them—all the stuff about 'Clapton is God' being sprayed on the walls was real!" recounted McVie.

Battle lines were drawn after Mayall asked Green to fill in for a meandering Clapton in the fall of 1965. While most followers remained loyal to Clapton, a few were quickly won over by Green's passionate guitar style. Several months later, when Clapton defected to form Cream, "Green is better than God" became the new rallying cry.

————

Despite the rivalry, Peter Green was actually a loyal disciple of Clapton's guitar playing. Born Peter Greenbaum on October 29, 1946, he grew up in a working-class London neighborhood. At an early age, Peter took to taking apart his guitars and record players, trying to figure out what it was that made them tick. "I did end up back at the shop once or twice when things didn't work out!" he admitted.

Peter came from a poor Jewish family from London's East End, who couldn't afford to provide their son with an upper-crust public school education. But that was just fine with the lad, who had never nurtured any dreams of becoming a barrister. Music had always been the one thing that stirred his soul. After making his way through ten years of perfunctory schooling, Peter found himself a blue-collar worker at fifteen years of age. Although his free hours were spent playing bass in a number of unsigned and unrecorded pop bands, he was earning his daily bread as a butcher's apprentice, and then as a television-cabinet polisher. "There's a great skill to it," said Peter. "I had to clean up old telly cabinets, fill in the chips and scratches, then polish it all over and spray it with lacquer."

While his proficiency at manual labor provided some measure of financial security, it was hardly a point of pride with Peter. In fact, he cursed his fate and planned his grand exit on a regular basis. He dreamed of a day when he could drop the *a* from *avocation* and make playing music a full-time gig.

Nearly four years passed in this fashion. At last, Peter happened upon Clapton playing guitar with the Bluesbreakers in 1965. From that moment on, pop music was a thing of the past—and so was the bass. The blues spoke to Peter like no other form of music ever had. And "God's" lead guitar echoed in Peter's head for days after this initial encounter. Aimless no more, Peter knew what had to be done.

Peter threw himself into a crash course on the Kings of blues. He studied Albert King, B. B. King, and Freddie King with a fervor bordering on the fanatical. After hearing Clapton sing for the first time, vocals also began to interest him. He and his friend Rod Stewart worked on their blues singing voices together.

As his self-confidence swelled, Peter started scouring the music-industry trade papers. When he answered an anonymous ad for a blues guitarist, he had no idea which band he would be seeking to join. One night, while Clapton was off traipsing around the Greek isles, Peter received a phone call from one of his British blues heroes, John Mayall, who needed a guitarist—a temporary Clapton replacement. When the two met at a Bluesbreakers gig later that night, Peter knew that it was now or never. He was sure he could put in a worthy performance. Mayall had never heard of Green before, but with Clapton down for the count and several untenable replacements behind him, he was willing to try anything or anyone.

Impressed with Peter's soulful technique, Mayall allowed Clapton's anonymous protégé to fill in until the frontman's return. When Clapton came back, Peter was out—but certainly not down. While he was dissatisfied with the brevity of his role as a Bluesbreaker, the confidence he gained from being admitted to the band spurred him on to pursue the life of a bluesman.

The Bluesbreakers gigs were significant for yet another reason: They brought Peter Green into contact with John McVie. While the ice between the two had yet to be broken, this meeting was a sign of things to come.

———

By the time Peter Green met Mick Fleetwood, the latter had already gained a reputation in London's musical circles as the Cheynes' fierce drummer. His band had released three singles and was quite a hot number when Peter Bardens decided to leave to join Them, which also featured Van Morrison, in the spring of 1965 and the Cheynes disbanded.

During his two-year tenure with the Cheynes, Mick had moved out of his sister's house and into a London flat with Bardens. They often played host to a bevy of London music scenesters, John McVie among them. The drummer had also begun dating one of London's more prominent models, Jenny Boyd, whose older sister was seriously involved with the Beatles' George Harrison. But gallivanting around town with this group and paying his half of the monthly rent required a serious income. So when Mick suddenly found himself out of a job, he didn't waste any time in placing an ad in London's music weekly, *Melody Maker.*

The Bo Street Runners, an R&B group that had once won a televised battle-of-the-bands-type contest, came to Mick's rescue. It was his primary meal ticket until Bardens presented him with another opportunity in February 1966. Bardens had just formed an instrumental act called Peter B's Looners (soon to be whittled down to the Peter B's), and Mick jumped at the chance to join him.

With Dave Ambrose on bass and Mick on drums, the only thing missing from Barden's new ensemble was a guitar player—the same position Peter Green was looking to fill when he showed up at the Gunnell Agency, which represented the Peter B's. Upon hearing Green talk of his limited past experience as a bassist, Mick grew incredulous. Green's bravado grated on the unassuming drummer's nerves. Mistaking his pluck for arrogance, Mick wondered what it was that made this arriviste think he could just up and play lead guitar.

Fortunately, Bardens didn't entertain any such doubts. He admired Green's moxie and dedication and put him on the payroll. "He had a great 'sound,' as they say," Mick told *Mojo* magazine, "but me and Dave didn't think he knew enough about the guitar. He only played a couple of licks, variations on a theme, Freddie King. And to Peter Bardens's credit, he pulled me aside and said, 'You're wrong, this guy's special.' "

The great strides Green made right after joining the Peter B's were a testament to Bardens's foresight and forced Mick to revise his initial impression. In fact, the guitarist's tremendous talent soon had Mick looking to him for approbation. "He's my mentor, and he's the reason Fleetwood Mac became what we became," Mick would later tell the *Los Angeles Times*. "We owe Peter a lot; he's a heavyweight—the B. B. Kings and Eric Claptons all recognize Peter as being a major, major talent. I'll always set my guidelines by Peter Green."

Green became the main attraction in a matter of months. After a vocal section was added, in the form of his old friend Rod Stewart and accomplished songstress Beryl Marsden, the band was renamed Shotgun Express. The move away from pure instrumentals made the group more fashionable than ever.

Unfortunately, being the local favorite does not always a successful band make. And since Green's role in Shotgun Express was destined to be short-lived, the band would soon fold. But it wasn't his lack of commitment so much as his way with women that was really at the root of the outfit's undoing.

Green's fancy guitar work and quiet confidence found no shortage of female admirers. So it came as no surprise when the lovely Miss Beryl Marsden took a fancy to the gifted lead guitarist. Since Marsden was rooming with Mick's girlfriend, Jenny, the two couples spent many hours together. Mick and Peter bonded during this period. Mick related to *Mojo* that "as young men we had an incredible friendship. I was basically . . . in love with him. We roomed together. When it was cold we slept together. I knew this man."

All good things come to an end, and Green and Marsden were no exception. Their relationship fizzled out after a few months. Green had jumped the gun in search of commitment, only to learn that his girlfriend wanted nothing more than to remain footloose and fancy-free. "It soon felt right to get married," he said. "A bit later she turned me down." With the ensuing breakup getting uglier by the day, Green was forced to quit the band to get away.

Fortunately, leaving Shotgun Express in July 1966 was no big sacrifice for the ingenious guitarist. He was already in contact with John Mayall and was Mayall's first choice to replace Eric Clapton. And weighing the personal travails of Shotgun Express against the all-star status of the Bluesbreakers, Peter was only too happy to take Mayall up on his offer.

———

While the lads who were one day to combine into Fleetwood Mac were engaged in carving out their respective careers, a young woman fresh out of art college was also busy earning the status of British blues-circuit veteran. She was none other than Christine McVie, or, as she was known at the time, Christine Perfect.

Christine was born into a highly musical atmosphere on July 12, 1944, in Birmingham, England. Her father, Cyril, was a violinist with the Birmingham Symphony, and her mother, Beatrice, had also at one time been a musician. Moreover, Beatrice was a zealous practitioner of faith healing and the occult, eradicating her daughter's wart with the touch of a finger and even curing a family friend of leukemia. "Her strange talents and interests used to concern me, because she belonged to these psychic research societies and would go off ghost hunting." Christine told *Rock Lives* author Timothy White.

Christine learned how to sing and play guitar at an early age. Feeling the pull of the stage at sixteen, Christine and a friend harkened to the call of London's many musical talent agencies. But all plans were foiled when their parents showed up to take the itinerant daughters home. Christine acquiesced to the demands of her elders and began to study for "a completely useless degree in sculpture" at art college.

Here, the then-portly teenager met Spencer Davis during a meeting of her folk music club. "We'd meet every Tuesday night, above a pub somewhere, and drink cheap beer," she told *Rolling Stone.* "Whoever could, would play a folk song or violin, whatever they could do. Anyway, one night in strolls this devastatingly handsome man, who was from Birmingham University. It was Spencer Davis. I just fell in love with Spence. I swore I would get thin and go out with him." True to her word, Christine eventually got her man—albeit more in a musical capacity than a romantic one. At the time, Davis was teaching German at Birmingham University and singing in a jazz band with Christine, but he would soon team with Steve Winwood to form the renowned Spencer Davis Group.

Through her friendship with Davis and Winwood, Christine was able to understand the gratification of playing for an appreciative audience. "Boy, they were so hot," she told *Rolling Stone.* "Nothing was like that. Stevie Winwood played like I'd never heard anybody play before. It just gave me goose bumps. They were just a blues band, but a really, really great blues band. He could yell the blues. A fifteen-year-old boy. No one could believe it. The nineteen-, twenty-year-old girls would have the hots for him." But following the band from gig to gig also allowed Christine to experience the downside of a life on the road; the late nights, the lugging of heavy equipment, the poor lodgings, the shrewd and unscrupulous club owners. So Christine knew exactly what she was getting into when she decided to play keyboards for another local band, Sounds of Blue.

After Christine graduated from college in 1965, she headed for London with a head full of glamorous ideas about the life of a career girl. Young, single, and well educated, Christine had no trouble finding a job as a window dresser at one of the city's most dapper department stores. It sounded like a dream job, but the young college graduate soon understood that reality doesn't always live up to expectations. Working at the store proved thoroughly dissatisfying, and she began to grow nostalgic for her days in Sounds of Blue.

Fortunately Christine only had to endure the workplace ennui for a year. In 1966, a former Sounds of Blue member telephoned her with an offer to join his new blues band, Chicken Shack. Christine Perfect did not need to be asked twice. She hit the stores in search of blues piano greats to emulate and developed a style all her own within a matter of months.

———

In the great tradition of cosmic balance, just as Chicken Shack was beginning to establish a footing in London's music industry, Mick Fleetwood's Shotgun Express, along with what there was of his personal life, was falling apart. No sooner had Peter Green announced that he would be taking his leave than Jenny Boyd put the kibosh on their relationship after nearly two years. After Mick had failed to bid her farewell before a modeling trip to Rome, Jenny felt free to do as she pleased and began dating another man. Upon her return to London, she chose to tell all—breaking Mick's heart and ending the relationship in the process.

As if to add insult to injury, Green's departure had heralded the beginning of the end for the struggling Shotgun Express. And when Rod Stewart left to join the Jeff Beck Group in February 1967, the remaining band members retired their act. Mick Fleetwood turned in his drumsticks for a paintbrush, pushed up his shirtsleeves, and took to painting walls.

Departures like Green's were a sad fact of life in the music business. A band could nurture a talent, polish it until it shone so bright that it would cast the brilliance of the spotlight over the entire outfit, and then, with no warning, the bomb would drop—usually in the form of a prominent band looking for a new musician or a label executive pushing to back a solo venture. That's when the goose who laid the golden eggs would fly the coop. Such maneuvers were so common in the dog-eat-dog world of the starving musician that they rarely resulted in hard feelings.

Mick held no grudges against Peter Green for skipping Shotgun Express in favor of an act with national stature. After all, what was a band if not a stepping-stone to greater fame? Peter's renown did indeed escalate as a result of the well-timed move. As a replacement for Eric Clapton, he was, by all accounts, superb. Luckily, he wasn't the type to hoard the wealth. Within a matter of weeks, he had Mick off the paint fumes and back in the drummer's seat.

It was April of 1967, and John McVie, Mick Fleetwood, and Peter Green were playing in tandem for the very first time as John Mayall's Bluesbreakers. "When Mick came in the band, something did click," recalled Mayall. All three shared a highly emotive technique but never sought to cramp their bandmates' styles. While this exalted form of give-and-take secured the trio's friendship, it was not enough to please their exacting bandleader.

Mayall's fans simply didn't take to Mick like they did to Peter. When Mick replaced Aynsley Dunbar in the Bluesbreakers, fans of the superlative drummer were disappointed. During Mick's first gig with the band, the audience members jeered and demanded the return of their favorite beat-keeper. That night John McVie took Mick under his wing by stepping up to the mike and commanding the audience to listen. "I loved John McVie from that moment on," wrote Mick in his book *Fleetwood: My Life and Adventures in Fleetwood Mac*. Soon John adopted Mick as his partner in Scotch-swilling, and the two quickly became inseparable.

But Mayall's hands were already full with McVie's shenanigans. The last thing he needed was another cutup throwing off his band. What's more, Mick's musical range was called into question. He simply lacked the technique to perform up to Mayall's lofty standards. Thus, Mick was dropped from the lineup in May after only a few weeks of playing.

———

Contrary to all expectations, this expulsion didn't faze Mick in the least. He had been ready to get the boot all along and was only surprised that it didn't happen sooner. In hindsight, it was Mick's discharge that sealed the fate of Fleetwood Mac.

The idea for the band was first conceived while Mick was still playing alongside Green and McVie. Months before, Mayall had presented Green with a birthday present of recording time at the Decca Studios. When Mick joined Mayall and the Bluesbreakers, Green, quick to recognize the strong groove between him and his bandmates, decided to put Mayall's present to good use by going in and recording as a trio. The chemistry among the three was so palpable that, in a show of affection, Green prophetically named one of the resulting tracks "Fleetwood Mac," after Mick Fleetwood and John McVie.

After Mick was fired, McVie and Green carried on as the Bluesbreakers, but for Peter Green the band had ceased to be a source of pleasure. Within a month he was out the door. The jazz-inspired direction toward which Mayall began to lean didn't suit the guitarist's proclivity for traditional blues. As it was generally understood that the differences between Peter and Mayall were confined to the creative sector, the parting was amicable. "He always let me enjoy myself and put my interpretations on whatever it was we were doing," Peter later told *Guitar Shop* magazine.

Green wanted to play the blues and had even toyed with the idea of going to Chicago to jam with some of the genre's masters. But the Bluesbreakers' producer, Mike Vernon, had other plans for the up-and-comer. Vernon had launched a blues record label, Blue Horizon

Records, and was eager to sign Peter. He'd been following the guitarist's career with great interest ever since he made his recording debut with the Bluesbreakers, at Decca Studios. "Me and Gus Dudgeon were looking across at him and thinking, 'Who the hell is this? Where's Eric [Clapton]?' " he later recalled in *Mojo* magazine. "John Mayall just said, 'Oh, he's Eric's replacement.' I hadn't even heard that Eric had left the Bluesbreakers. John said Peter was as good as Eric, which was a bit hard to believe at first until he actually plugged in, and then we thought, 'Ummm, he can play a bit!' "

Booking agent Clifford Davis of the Gunnel Agency had also had his eye on the ax man for some time. He had represented Green's bands ever since his days with the Peter B's and had never been shy about voicing his willingness to represent Green should he ever decide to go solo. Davis's and Vernon's persistence paid off after their prized musician decided to form Fleetwood Mac, signing with the Blue Horizon label and installing Davis as band manager a few months later.

By the end of June, nearly all of the elements for a four-piece blues band were in place. Peter had brought Mick out of seclusion at his sister's house to play drums. He had even taken on another guitar player to better offset his own signature chops: Jeremy Spencer, eighteen years old, with a wife of three years and a coarse sense of humor. He was a one-trick pony whose primary claim to fame was an uncanny Elmore James impersonation.

Mike Vernon had heard Jeremy play at Decca Studios as part of an unsigned group and suggested that he meet with Peter Green upon learning of Fleetwood Mac's search for yet another member. Once Peter heard Jeremy do his thing, the search was over. He had yet to hear anyone play Elmore James's electric blues with Jeremy's flourish. "I thought he played slide with conviction," said Peter, "and looking at him I could tell he was a villain." Spencer was hired on the spot.

John McVie was also approached. And while London's favorite blues bassist was loath to give up his long-running collaboration with Mayall, Peter nevertheless decided to call his newly formed band Peter Green's Fleetwood Mac. With a little persuading, he knew, John would eventually come around.

———

Of course, the band couldn't afford to sit idly in wait for the coming of John McVie. They needed to find a bass player in a hurry. That's when Bob Brunning came stumbling into the picture. Brunning's audition was scheduled after he responded to an ad in *Melody Maker*. Since the publication had misprinted Peter's phone number, Bob was one of the few people to reply, having tracked down the correct number by calling the magazine.

In spite of this advantage, Bob managed to make a bad first impression. When he met Peter at the audition, he asked the bandleader whether he'd ever heard of *the* Peter Green. "I made a complete fool of myself," said Bob.

While it was painfully obvious that Bob was no John McVie, time was one commodity Fleetwood Mac couldn't afford to squander. Peter, a great bassist in his own right, figured that with a little tutelage Bob would do just fine. As Fleetwood Mac's debut performance was scheduled to take place at the Windsor Jazz and Blues Festival a month later, band rehearsals began immediately.

Forty thousand die-hard blues fans were expected to come out for the festival, and the band knew they had to sound tight. As the centerpiece of the band, Peter held the reins—and he had no problem alternating between snapping the whip and acting the den mother. His first priority was to put on a great show, and he did everything within his power to make that possible. When any band member was out of line, one word from the leader would let him know it. Yet, with both Mick and Bob feeling insecure about their abilities, Peter also knew how to lay on the moral support. Mick attests that Peter "saw what I had a long time ago, and it was not what people normally see, because I'm not horribly technical. I'm an emotional player, and he read that and made me really strong."

Finally, and not a moment too soon, Peter Green's Fleetwood Mac Featuring Jeremy Spencer was ready for action.

By virtue of sound alone, the Fleetwood Mac of today could never be mistaken for the Fleetwood Mac of 1967. Fans of the pop supergroup would be hard pressed to identify the scrappy gang of guys who took their first bows at the Seventh Annual Windsor Jazz Festival under the moniker of Fleetwood Mac. In fact, few people knew what to make of the band the night they astounded their maiden audience.

It was a great day for listening to the blues, and thousands of fans had arrived at the festival to do just that. This last day of the seventy-two-hour event featured a veritable who's who of British blues rockers. But as the Jeff Beck Group, John Mayall and the Bluesbreakers, and Cream were busy waiting to cap off the evening, Peter Green's Fleetwood Mac Featuring Jeremy Spencer took to the stage and warmed up the audience faster than they could say "What's Peter Green's Fleetwood Mac Featuring Jeremy Spencer?" And so on August 13, 1967, Fleetwood Mac was born.

———

While the elements of the original Fleetwood Mac were just beginning to fall into place in England, the finishing touches were coming together clear across the Atlantic, in San Francisco. By the mid-sixties, the Bay Area was already considered the epicenter of America's "turn on, tune in, and drop out" counterculture. Acid tabs were up for grabs on any corner of the Haight-Ashbury district courtesy of Dr. Timothy Leary. Ken Kesey and his band of Merry Pranksters were riling up the immediate environs and slowly but surely diffusing their influence throughout the nation via rock and roll.

While the powers that be were waging war on the red menace in some godforsaken corner of the globe, music was quickly becoming the foremost means of civil disobedience. Seemingly overnight, California turned into a hotbed of brooding and self-destructive talent. Janis Joplin, the Doors, Jefferson Airplane, Bob Dylan, the Grateful Dead, and countless others were retaliating against the Man by striking a blow for individual freedom.

It was in this context that a brief but memorable meeting took place between two teens who would one day save a beleaguered Fleetwood Mac from the depths of obscurity. One night in 1966, at the height of the Mamas and the Papas' popularity, a clean-cut high school junior named Lindsey Buckingham set out for an after-school shindig. Upon his arrival, he made a beeline for the prominently positioned piano, sat down, and proceeded to play "California Dreaming."

The young man was already counting the days until he could form his own professional band. Unlike his two brothers, Lindsey wasn't planning on going to college or taking over the family business. Born on October 3, 1948, the youngest son and resident black sheep of a coffee-growing dynasty, Lindsey only wanted one thing—a career in music. His obsession with the guitar began when he first picked up the instrument in second grade. "I was one of the tons of guys who ran out and got a guitar when Elvis came along," he told *People*. But, said Lindsey, "I can remember drawing guitars when I was about five. I used to spend hours and hours in my brother's room listening to 45s."

Lindsey's father, Morris, taught his three sons to swim at the family country club. Pretty soon, their constant presence in the communal pool earned them the title of the "Swimming Buckinghams." But while his brother Greg trained for the Olympics—he would go on to win a silver medal at the 1968 games—Lindsey devoted most of his free time to perfecting his signature finger-picking technique. He experimented with a wide range of musical styles and instruments. "I owned a banjo when I was [about] twelve," said Lindsey. "That was '62 and the Beatles hadn't come along, Elvis wasn't making great records, and folk music was the fresh thing. I'm one of the few people who admit they were a big Kingston Trio fan."

At least one of the Menlo-Atherton High School students present at the party that night watched Lindsey's performance with something more than casual interest. A senior and a recent transfer student who was already wildly popular, Stevie Nicks had no qualms about approaching the intense pianist and singing along. "He was sitting in the middle of this gorgeous living room playing a song," Stevie remembered. "I walked over and stood next to him, and I just started singing with him."

———

Stage fright had never been a problem for the diminutive runner-up to the throne of Menlo-Atherton Homecoming Queen. As soon as she was old enough, Stephanie "Stevie" Nicks's country-singing grandfather was already grooming her for a life in showbiz. A. J. Nicks was an outlandish country crooner who "wrote music his whole life" and saw nothing wrong with hoisting his four-year-old granddaughter up on stage to warm up the saloon audiences.

As Stevie's parents appeared to tolerate these stunts with—all things considered—a surprising degree of equanimity, A. J. began to plan a future of performing with Stevie by his side. When the time came for him to go out on tour, he had no idea that his son and daughter-in-law would deny him the pleasure of taking Stevie along. It would take two years for A. J. to get over the disappointment and visit his son's house again.

Stevie was distraught over the loss of her grandfather and her hobby. The perpetual relocation brought about by her father's constant promotions didn't help matters any. Over the course of his career, Jesse Seth Nicks was an executive vice president with Greyhound and the president of both Armour Foods and General Brewing. "Our father would always be getting promoted and transferred, so we never grew up in any one place," Stevie's younger brother, Christopher, told *Rolling Stone.*

"Just as we were making friends, Dad would come home and say, 'I got promoted!' " continued Christopher. "Stevie had it pretty bum with all the relocation." Born in Phoenix, Arizona, on May, 26, 1948, Stevie would pass through New Mexico, Texas, Utah, and Los Angeles before finally ending up a student at one of the San Francisco metro area high schools her junior year.

Not long before that move, Stevie's parents presented her with a guitar. "It was my sixteenth birthday," she recalled, "and I wrote a song the day I got it." The song was called "I've Loved and I've Lost, and I'm Sad but Not Blue." It was about the heartbreak of yearning for a popular boy who didn't know she existed. "I realized right away I could write songs because I could have experiences without ever having them," Stevie said. "I'd run to the guitar, and I'd cry, and my parents would leave me alone because it was like, 'Don't come in the door, a great artist is at work here.' "

Soon after, she followed in her hero Bob Dylan's footsteps by starting a folk-rock band, which she called the Changing Times. Although the many transfers were difficult for Stevie and her brother, they did teach the would-be singer/songwriter how to reach out to others through her songs. Music became Stevie's constant companion at a time of chaos and upheaval and helped to bridge the gap between the "new kid" and her peers.

The ploy worked so well and for so long that she inevitably began to identify acceptance with the musical spotlight. By the time Stevie's family moved to San Francisco, she had the routine down pat. "She first arrived at my school when I was a junior, and she just kind of flew in somewhat flamboyantly and became popular at school," recalled Lindsey in an interview with *Guitar World.* "I think she was working on being a bohemian type even then, with the poetry and all of that."

Yet the unbelievable success presaged by their "California Dreaming" duet would have to wait. While both students were impressed with much more than one another's harmonies, the casual circumstances kept each mum on the subject of mutual attraction. Stevie would later reveal her first impression of Lindsey—"he was so beautiful"—but that evening she wasn't willing to lay her cards on the table. When their performance ended, the future dynamic duo parted ways, not to reunite for another two years.

2

UP AND AWAY

After Fleetwood Mac descended from the stage at Windsor, critics and audiences were brimming with great expectations and lavish praise. With John Mayall heading into jazz territory and almost everyone else embracing a progressive, psychedelic groove, Peter Green's outfit distinguished itself on the basis of playing blues, pure and raunchy. Here finally was a band to satisfy British fans' rampant hunger for rambunctious blues performers in the old Chicago tradition.

High on their victorious debut performance, feeling that success was imminent, Fleetwood Mac celebrated by watching the festival wind down. Among the acts crowding the bill of the Jazz and Blues Festival was Chicken Shack, a band also signed with Mike Vernon's Blue Horizon label. Its frontwoman, Christine Perfect—saucy, attractive, svelte, and in possession of a soulful and resonant voice—was the group's most striking feature. Christine's charms were not wasted on either her audiences or her fellow blues musicians. As Chicken Shack strutted their stuff, John McVie, Peter Green, and Mick Fleetwood were all taken with the fetching blond singer, who also played keyboards. "She was a killer blues pianist, just a phenomenon!" recalled John.

———

In 1968, not long after John McVie first set eyes on Christine Perfect, thereby laying the ground work for future Mac lore, Fleetwood Mac's most riveting backstory was brewing in the States. When last they met, Stevie Nicks and Lindsey Buckingham had shared a moment that in two years' time would lead to a lifetime of attachment. Since neither had declared their romantic interest back in the Menlo-Atherton High School days, Lindsey's sudden phone call to Stevie came as a complete shock to the young coed.

"He called me and asked me if I wanted to be in his rock 'n' roll band, which I didn't even know existed," Stevie told *Spin* magazine. But, at the very least, Lindsey was confident that his phone call to Stevie wouldn't automatically end with the words "Lindsey who?" As he told *Guitar World*, "She was aware that I played guitar, and I was aware that she played guitar and sang. We had some rapport, but that was about it."

Having graduated high school, Stevie was now studying speech communications at San Jose State University. Lindsey, on the other hand, had eschewed his parents' carefully laid plans in favor of a career in rock music. Staying true to his dream, he began playing bass for a band called Fritz because, as he told Paul Zollo in *Songwriters on Songwriting*, "the guy who played lead guitar had all the gear. That was pretty much the logic back then." To be fair, Fritz may have had a better reason for sticking Lindsey with the bass. In his own words, "I couldn't go whoo-whoo at all. I couldn't play screaming lead."

Since he last spoke to Stevie, Lindsey had, on a number of occasions, thought about the remarkably petite young woman who had once joined him in song. With many a popular local rock band being fronted by women such as Grace Slick and Janis Joplin, Lindsey was willing to give Stevie a try.

While talking to Stevie on the phone, Lindsey was all business. Nonetheless, she was quite taken aback by his unexpected show of interest. But when he revealed the purpose for his call, Stevie was delighted with the prospect of performing and quickly put aside all reservations. "I had been playing guitar and singing pretty much totally folk-oriented stuff," she told *US* magazine. "All of a sudden, I was in rock 'n' roll." She accepted the offer and later recalled that "within two or three months we were opening for Jimi Hendrix, Janis Joplin, all the San Francisco bands."

It was at one of these shows that she first grasped what it meant to connect with an audience. After opening for Janis Joplin's Big Brother and the Holding Company, Stevie stood in the wings and watched as the legendary singer's unparalleled energy shocked the audience into dumbfounded submission. She never forgot how Joplin held sway over the audience, seeking to emulate it with every successive show. "We opened for her in Santa Clara," Stevie told *Goldmine* magazine. "She walked onstage and for an hour and a half my chin was on the floor. You couldn't have pried me away with a million-dollar check. I was absolutely glued to her, and that is what I learned a lot of what I do onstage. It wasn't that I wanted to be like her, because I didn't. But I said, 'If ever I am a performer of any value, I want to be able to create the same kind of feeling that's going on between her and the audience.' "

Watching Janis clearly gave Stevie something to which she could aspire. But it was at another Fritz gig that she was visited by a vision that helped her to define her personal style. "I saw this woman walk by, and she was wearing a mauve chiffon layered midiskirt and high platform cream-colored suede boots," she told *US.* "I thought: I want to be her."

With irrepressible thoughts of music obscuring her original goal of becoming a teacher, Stevie dropped out of junior college and joined Fritz as a full-time member—just one semester shy of earning her degree. "That did not amuse my parents too much," she told *Rolling Stone.* "They wanted me to do what I wanted to do. They were just worried I was going to get down to eighty pounds and be a miserable, burnt-out twenty-seven-year-old."

Luckily, Lindsey brought out only the best in Stevie, and vice versa. Keith Olson, who would become the couple's friend and record producer, remembered that "there was a timbre that happened when the two voices would join that was unique. You never heard that before, and I don't think you've heard it since. Those two voices sing like that and sound like that for a reason. They were meant to sing together."

Their days in the San Francisco rock band saw Stevie and Lindsey's relationship solidify and evolve. Although ostensibly the two were just bandmates, much was stirring beneath the surface. Because romance played no part in the band's plan for widespread recognition, members of Fritz made a point of observing certain boundaries around their lead singer. "If anybody in the band started spending any time with me," Stevie later told *Rolling Stone*, "the other three would literally pick that person apart. To the death." As a result, the special bond that grew out of Stevie and Lindsey's working relationship was to remain platonic for some time. But neither would be able to resist the magnetic pull of chemistry for very long.

First smitten by Christine Perfect at the 1967 Windsor Jazz Festival, John would spend months putting off the daunting task of professing his undying devotion. He was never one to jump headlong into any decision; it even took him a few months to join the band that already bore his name.

In the meantime, Fleetwood Mac was on the fast track, steamrolling their way to stardom. However, tooling around the countryside in their used vans left precious little time for recording their first album. "We spent virtually every night of our lives driving up or down some horrid British motorway," Mick told *Creem* magazine.

Somehow, the nascent band did manage to record a single, "I Believe My Time Ain't Long," one of Jeremy Spencer's infinite tributes to Elmore James, with Peter Green's "Rambling Pony." Recording was easier said than done, since Mike Vernon had to sneak the band into Decca Studios on the sly in order to pony up a demo tape for the scrutiny of CBS Records executives.

After the demo received a stamp of approval, and the single was released in November 1967, Fleetwood Mac was in for a disappointment. Their success on the bar circuit had led everyone to believe that a single would make an impact on the charts. Yet the consumer market showed no interest. Of course, this didn't deter the young men from plowing on.

By this time, Bob Brunning was no longer a Fleetwood Mac fixture. Less than a month after the band stepped out for their first performance, John McVie was ready to enlist. The pivotal moment came in early September, at a John Mayall and the Bluesbreakers rehearsal.

"At the time, John [Mayall] had horn players in the band," McVie told *Bassplayer* magazine, "and we were rehearsing at some club when John [Mayall] turned to one of them and said, 'Okay, just play it free-form there.' I said, with typical blues snobbishness, 'I thought this was a blues band, not a jazz band!' I immediately went across the street, called Peter, and asked if he still wanted me to join up." That was all it took.

In September 1967, John McVie turned his back on Mayall, the man who had never ceased threatening to fire him, and joined Fleetwood Mac, a band whose first performance he had labeled boring (most likely in a display of sour grapes) a month earlier. Ironic as this seems, Fleetwood Mac was at last complete—but what about Bob?

Fortunately, Bob had harbored no illusions that his role in the band was anything but temporary. He knew full well who put the Mac in Fleetwood Mac, and was only glad that Britain's leading bass player was taking his place instead of some hack.

With John McVie in tow, the mates were ready to tackle the task of putting together their first album, *Peter Green's Fleetwood Mac,* which took only three days to record. The time it spent on the U.K. album charts was considerably longer—seventeen weeks in the top ten, and nearly a year on the charts.

————

After its February 1968 release, the album was embraced all over Europe and even managed to elicit a warm, albeit subdued, welcome in the States. *Melody Maker* pronounced *Peter Green's Fleetwood Mac* "the best English blues LP ever released" and dubbed Peter "the toughest and meanest of the guitar heroes." Suddenly, the band was the toast of swinging London and riding a wave of popularity not unlike that of the Beatles and the Rolling Stones.

Although "Black Magick Woman," Peter's new single written for his girlfriend Sandra Elsdon, wasn't a smash hit, it commanded hours of airplay on England's fledgling pop music radio station, Radio One. This, along with a constant presence in the music press and on the pub circuit, helped spread word of Fleetwood Mac throughout Europe. Manager Clifford Davies was working overtime just to keep pace with the overwhelming demand. He was quick to up the band's asking price, as well as the size of their venues. In a matter of weeks, the band could boast international appeal and a fully booked European tour.

On their home turf, the band that had started as a gimmick-free blues purist's dream let the shock-rock rip. "We were very crazy in those days," John told *Di Gitarist* magazine. "Jeremy had this enormous dildo, called Harold, with which he got the public excited." They pulled no punches onstage, spewing invective and swinging "Harold" at the audience. It was just one such stunt that got them barred from London's hottest venue, the Marquee Club. One night, during a Marquee gig, instead of simply brandishing the sex toy, Jeremy actually affixed it to his gaping fly. Half the women left, escorted out by their boyfriends. Branded criminally obscene by the management, the Mac was banned from the premises.

While the guys' United Kingdom stage show had already morphed into something much tawdrier than anything ever done by Benny Hill, the band rarely ventured into objectionable territory while touring Europe; how many members of a German-speaking audience could really appreciate their limey gutter humor anyway?

In spite (or because) of the controversy, Fleetwood Mac was at a point where they could do no wrong. Having conquered the United Kingdom and Europe, it was time to make like other British musicians and invade the States.

———

Fellow Blue Horizon recording artists Chicken Shack often shared the bill with Fleetwood Mac. Christine Perfect was well on her way to becoming the leading lady of the testosterone-laden British blues scene. As busy as both she and John McVie were at the time, the blues circuit just kept on pushing them together. "I remember going to see Fleetwood Mac before I ever joined it," said Christine. "I used to trail them around because I thought they were so great." Mike Vernon had even asked Christine to sit in on piano for Fleetwood Mac's second album, *Mr. Wonderful.*

But John had yet to muster enough courage to ask the celebrated singer/songwriter for a date. Believing the bass player to be betrothed to another, Christine hadn't the slightest clue as to John's feelings. In fact, she was busy sizing up Peter's romantic potential when John finally expressed his interest.

"He asked me if I wanted to have a drink and we sat down, had a few laughs, then they had to go onstage," Christine recounted to *Rolling Stone*. "All the time I was kind of eyeballing ol' Greenie. After the concert was over, John came over and said, 'Shall I take you out to dinner sometime?' I went, 'Whoa . . . I thought you were engaged or something.' He said, 'Nah, 'sall over.' I thought he was devastatingly attractive, but it had never occurred to me to look at him." On the heels of this first date, the couple was a hot item, and Christine forgot all about Peter.

In light of this budding romance, it was with a happy heart that John prepared to take on California. And while Mick may not have known it at the time, his love life was about to come out of remission. He and Jenny Boyd were about to reunite after a long-term separation. The fan adulation he found with Fleetwood Mac was a poor substitute for real intimacy. Cliché as it was, Mick was lonely at the top. Despite a surplus of suitors, Jenny had not been any more successful at forgetting her first love. Donovan had even written "Jennifer Juniper" as an ode to her, but all the songs in the world couldn't help her move on.

While staying with Mick's (and Jenny's) friend Judy Wong in San Francisco, the band became tight with her pals the Grateful Dead. The jam-masters had heard of Peter Green through his work on the Bluesbreakers' *Hard Road* album and were glad to befriend the fellow musicians. Fleetwood Mac was quickly inducted into the many mysteries of the hippie culture. It was only a matter of time before Owsley, the renowned creator of the electric Kool-Aid acid test, would offer the young Brits a taste of his high-grade LSD.

The boys weren't quite ready to dabble in mind-altering experiences, and since they didn't know the first thing about acid, they were wary. They politely declined Owsley's generous offer by taking a raincheck—the redemption of which would have disastrous consequences for Peter Green.

———

During this first visit to the States, Jeremy Spencer's perverse wit knew no bounds. The fact that the lad was a devoted husband and father who never left home without his trusty Bible jarred with his loud and bawdy persona. By all accounts, Jeremy appeared to be in the throes of acute Jekyll-and-Hyde syndrome. While his Christian upbringing had instilled in him a fear of sexuality, the discipline was not rigorous enough to keep him in line. Jeremy's transgressions usually happened late at night, when his resistance was at its lowest. And since resolve is never so strong as after a night of excess, Jeremy would be a model family man until it was time to head off for the night's gig.

At first, his obsession with sex and such was a constant source of amusement to his bandmates. "Jeremy was very much a mimic with a beautifully sarcastic sense of humor," recalled John. But eventually, Jeremy's crude quips and gags began to turn everyone off. His degenerate behavior during the band's stay in San Francisco made the normally mellow and tolerant Judy Wong rue the day she ever agreed to open her doors to the visiting ruffian. (For example, he would draw pictures of spread-eagled women and leave them in Judy's refrigerator.)

It was Jeremy's depraved brand of humor that got the band declared taboo by the Marquee in the summer of 1968. After that debacle, it was only a matter of time before Fleetwood Mac's sick and twisted musical sideshow would receive a cool reception from most of England's prestigious concert halls.

While Mick, John, and maybe even Jeremy could have bowed to the pressure and cleaned up their act, Peter was vocal about not compromising the integrity of the show, saying, "If I want to say *fuck* then I will, because if I say it normally in my speech then I'm going to say it onstage too, at least until I get arrested." The rest of the band echoed their fearless leader's sentiments. Who needed those stuffy indoor venues anyway? Summer was a time for music festivals, and Fleetwood Mac played them all.

As for John and Christine, the couple became engaged soon after John returned from the States. But Christine and John's now-infamous ten-day engagement was attributable less to their impulsive constitutions than to the failing health of the bride-to-be's mother. Since Beatrice Perfect was not expected to live much longer, it was for her benefit that the couple decided to expedite the nuptials. Thus,

Christine Perfect would take John's surname and become Christine McVie by summer's end. "I thought it was extremely romantic," Christine said. "Obviously a little bit of the glamour of what Fleetwood Mac was in those days rubbed off. It was almost like someone marrying a Beatle. You married one of the links in the chain and you were part of them."

––––––

Mr. Wonderful, the follow-up to *Peter Green's Fleetwood Mac,* was released that summer. The debut album had been a runaway critical and commercial success, but *Mr. Wonderful* didn't measure up to its name. The situation might have turned dire had Peter not been planning his *coup de maître.*

The addition of Danny Kirwan helped recharge Fleetwood Mac's early career. Just like Jeremy Spencer, Danny Kirwan was already a member of a subpar unsigned band when he was recruited into Fleetwood Mac. The eighteen-year-old from Brixton, England, was opening for Fleetwood Mac the night his guitar hero rescued him from mediocrity.

Peter couldn't believe his ears when he heard Danny play. To Danny's delight, Peter asked him to join in a jam session that very evening, and the two soon became chums bound by a passion for the blues. At first, Peter took it upon himself to find the young man a band that could better showcase his formidable talents. He encouraged Danny to go out on his own as a professional musician. He even arranged auditions for the guitarist's new band, but since everyone who tried out came up short, plans for Danny's new group were scrapped. Instead, he was accepted by Fleetwood Mac as one of their own.

Danny's presence made Fleetwood Mac the only band in England at the time with three lead guitarists. Audiences were pleased with the novelty, but Peter had more substantial reasons for celebrating Danny's arrival. While Jeremy Spencer's homages to Elmore James and his raucous onstage parodies of everyone from Elvis to John Mayall were certainly entertaining, there was more to the music business than fun and games. Jeremy didn't like to rehearse, he didn't write his own songs, and his range of styles was stunted by the Elmore James fixation. And although Mick supervised the interpersonal aspect of the band, and John was simply one of the best bass players in England, Peter was the only one in charge of the band's creative output. He needed help.

For Fleetwood Mac's next album, Danny Kirwan would take care of one half and Peter the other. Danny may not have expected to pick up as much slack as Peter had left, but his performance showed he was prepared for the job. "Jigsaw Puzzle Blues," one of Danny's first contributions, was a stellar track heavily influenced by Django Reinhardt. "Those were the types of records I'd buy down at Dobell's near Charing Cross. I worked out 'Jigsaw Puzzle Blues' from that stuff," explained Danny.

Danny provided a perfect sounding board for Peter's ideas, added stylistic texture to the band's sound, and moved Fleetwood Mac away from pure blues through his up-tempo rock 'n' roll leanings. His assumption of creative responsibility also freed Peter to concentrate on the band's next single, "Albatross." The haunting track was unlike anything Peter had ever produced before. Although it was completely devoid of lyrics, Peter sensed it was going to hit big.

The ethereal instrumental was far and away the most commercial Fleetwood Mac song to date. And as expected, the band's blues fans were incensed at their favorite ensemble's decision to penetrate the mainstream. With one of the most successful proponents of blues turning commercial at the tail-end of the British Blues Boom, the future of the genre looked bleak. Many of the Mac's English fans never got over this betrayal.

"Albatross" turned out to be the first of what Fleetwood Mac would one day term the Big Four—four monster hit singles compliments of Peter Green. With the success of their first album, the band had only needed to make good on one single to get their name on the map. "Black Magic Woman" and "Need Your Love So Bad" had been valiant but doomed efforts to bring the blues to a larger audience. To the chagrin of their blues following, "Albatross" would abandon the struggle, but would launch Fleetwood Mac into the stratosphere of British rock bands.

Its name partly inspired by the slain bird in Coleridge's poem "The Rime of the Ancient Mariner," "Albatross" perched atop the British charts less than five weeks after its November 1968 release. "It was a complete accident that it was a hit," Mick admitted to *Rolling Stone*. "The BBC used it for some wildlife program, and then someone put it on *Top of the Pops* and it was a hit." The exquisite composition hit the charts the following week, ascending every week thereafter until finally arriving at Number One just in time to bring in the New Year.

―――――

Word of "Albatross" spread so fast through their native land that the touring Fleetwood Mac were actually the last to hear about their new-found rock stardom. Without a notion of their imminent success, the band had left for a full-scale U.S. tour only a couple of weeks after the release of the single.

On the road, thousands of miles away from home, the guys had ample time to brood over their personal problems. With Danny Kirwan and Peter Green taking to the ladies like stallions put out to stud, and John McVie and Jeremy Spencer both happily married, Mick Fleetwood was left to confront his lingering feelings for Jenny Boyd. During a stint in San Francisco, Mick poured his heart out to Judy Wong, who convinced the forlorn drummer to write Jenny a letter explaining how he felt. Mick got right to the point and asked his ex-girlfriend to marry him.

For Mick, this first major U.S. tour would forever remain a symbol of auspicious new beginnings. Conversely, the trip would also be the first tentative step in the painfully slow undoing of Peter Green. The tour dates in San Francisco marked the beginning of Peter's experimentation with acid. Owsley was still imploring Fleetwood Mac to try his mind-expanding concoctions when they opened for the Grateful Dead. Surrounded by acid-trip veterans on all sides, the bandmates shed their apprehensions. However, because they were trying a new drug in an unfamiliar country, they decided to hole up in their hotel room before indulging in Owsley's wares.

The decision proved a smart one. Prodigious amounts of liquor and weak, vintage-1960s grass had done nothing to prepare the friends for their first trip. As none of them had tried LSD before, they couldn't turn to each other for help in understanding what was happening. Luckily, they got through to Owsley who assuaged their fears. This would be the first of many LSD trips for Peter, who would one day fall victim to the drug's most severe side effects.

Meanwhile, there was no way this gang of blues bandits was going to leave the States without attempting to link up with at least a few of their influences, and their tour schedule could not have been more advantageous for the purpose. Their January 1969 stop in Chicago had them as the opening act for their idol, Muddy Waters. From here, the city's world-renowned Chess Studio, home to such icons as Otis Spann, Buddy Guy, and Willie Dixon, was just a step away. The next thing they knew, they were in the recording studio cutting tracks with the legends of blues. "At that point in time, I didn't know how famous they were," Buddy Guy recalled in an AOL Live Chat. "I was just invited to play with them, and it was great." The resulting *Blues Jam at Chess* album would provide a lasting testament to the band's blues prowess, as well as close the lid on Fleetwood Mac's career as a British blues band.

The platinum success of "Albatross" that greeted the band back in London, coupled with their new stature as a household name, would ensure that rock 'n' roll would become Fleetwood Mac's mainstay.

———

Now that he was a big-money star, Mick was ready to face Jenny Boyd. He tracked her down at a commune, where she was involved with another man. The two had a serious discussion and decided to give their relationship another try. Soon they were engaged and living together in Mick's sister's flat.

While Mick wanted to get married, and had said as much in his letter to Jenny, his first love had always been his music. But it wasn't the drumming itself that motivated Mick. Unlike his bandmates Peter and Danny, Mick wasn't driven so much by creative forces as by his need to succeed. His early shortcomings in the English public school system haunted him into adulthood, forcing him to prove to himself and others that he was someone special—and destroying many of his most vital relationships along the way.

John McVie had a completely different cross to bear. Ever since his

Bluesbreaker days, liquor had held the bass player in a viselike grip. It was the young man's intelligent and introspective side—the side that had led him on countless trips to the London Zoo to take photographs of the displaced penguins—that had won the heart of Christine Perfect. After they married, "I was in Chicken Shack for another six months," she told *Crawdaddy,* "and it worked out that John and I were meeting each other on the doorstep with suitcases in hand. He'd be coming back from a tour just as I was leaving—or vice versa."

Since their courtship had gone by so quickly, the couple was still getting to know each other several months into their marriage. Although this process was often obstructed by the grueling touring schedules of John and Christine's respective bands, the long separations did have one bright side: Since John was never around long enough to make his drinking problem felt, Christine was able to focus on his innumerable attractive qualities.

By the time Fleetwood Mac returned from America, Christine was growing tired of her bohemian lifestyle. Ever the homebody, she wanted only to retire and keep house for her husband and herself. Of course, Mike Vernon of Blue Horizon wasn't having any of it. He wasn't going to let the main attraction of one of his most popular bands go—not without a fight. Vernon held out the promise of a solo career for Christine, and she eventually consented. With John away so much of the time, home-making for her solitary enjoyment hardly made sense anyway.

Christine's decision was based in part on the fact that Fleetwood Mac was back on the road mere weeks after their triumphant London landing. *English Rose* had just been released in the States in lieu of the ill-fated *Mr. Wonderful.* The band's Stateside audience had yet to be built, but it had always been the band's motto that if the fans don't come to the music, the music would have to come to the fans. With a new album to promote, the United States beckoned yet again.

The guys would remain in the States well into April of 1969. The group dynamic had seen a lot of changes since Danny Kirwan's arrival less than year before. Whereas Danny had then played Peter's faithful disciple, he was now often at odds with the bandleader. More than twenty-five years later, Danny would succinctly delineate the alliances within the band, clarifying his role and revealing a possible reason for Jeremy Spencer's enduring inclusion in the Mac.

"I always liked Mick Fleetwood—he was like family. John McVie was the cleverest person, and I could see that at the time. A nice bloke and highly intelligent, he was like my best friend in the band for a time," Danny told *Guitar* magazine. "Although I used to get on with John and Mick, it got very cliquey. The thing with rock bands is that they get very interested in themselves and their own relationships with each other. Spencer and Green, for instance, knew each other well and were . . . mischevious."

———

The second of Peter's Big Four singles, "Man of the World," spoke frankly about the artist's disenchantment. "I was stuck on how successful I was," Peter has since said. The guitarist just couldn't let himself believe all the hype. Encountering a lovestruck new audience right on the heels of playing with the likes of Buddy Guy and Otis Spann made Peter wonder whether he truly deserved the accolades. Together with his exorbitant intake of LSD, this attitude dimmed Peter's enthusiasm. "I went through a stage for about three years when I did feel I was going through the motions," Peter later summed up his last years in Fleetwood Mac. All his dreams had come true by the age of twenty-two, yet Peter could not have been more unhappy. This inability to enjoy his fame and substantial fortune came tumbling out in the single.

But even the dirgelike tone of the piece couldn't keep "Man of the World" from rising to Number Two on the U.K. pop charts. Released in April of 1969, it reinforced the band's preeminence in the British market and created an air of expectation for Fleetwood Mac's next album. "We had all the Number One hits and the screaming girls," Mick said about the period of early success. And while many of today's Mac fans remain completely unaware of these previous achievements, it was this initial blaze of glory that would prepare John and Mick for the triumph of the *Rumours* album eight years hence.

Stardom would have the opposite effect on Peter. The more success followed him, the more despondent he became. His first fame-induced moral dilemma emerged when the band was forced to leave Mike Vernon and his Blue Horizon label in the spring of 1969 because of a financial dispute between Vernon and the band's manager, Clifford Davis. Peter had been happy with Blue Horizon and felt very uneasy about shopping around for a new label just for the sake of netting more money. The promotional work was also a constant source of anguish for the much-too-candid-for-the-camera frontman. "Santana has the right idea," he said in an interview with *Guitar Shop.* "They don't do any interviews; they just go onstage and play their music."

Personal travails aside, in 1969 everything Fleetwood Mac touched turned to gold. That spring, the band toured the United Kingdom with one of their favorite bluesmen, B. B. King. "Oh Well," the two-part single released in the fall of that year, turned out to be the third of Peter's Big Four. Just like "Man of the World," it was Number Two on the charts before so much as a month had passed. That year's album, *Then Play On,* was their most successful to date, reaching Number Five in England and going gold in the States. Now their shows were finally being seen by great crowds of people—and pulling in unprecedented sums of money. Appropriately enough, at year's end Fleetwood Mac was voted 1969's top progressive group by *Melody Maker* and the best band by readers of the *New Musical Express.*

None of this good fortune could shake the steadily deteriorating Peter Green out of his funk. As he grew more and more morose, the rest of the band members began racking their brains trying to figure out how to help. But it was too late—LSD had already done its worst. In September 1969, the bandleader was prepared to exchange all his worldly possessions for a life of the spirit. It was only the thought of his bandmates in need that convinced Peter to remain. As the band's prize guitarist/songwriter, Peter felt the pull of responsibility too strongly to decamp without hesitation. "I was the writer of hits for the group," he said. "I was the sole writer—at least it felt like I was."

———

By the time Fleetwood Mac began preparations for a European tour in support of their latest LP, *Then Play On,* Christine McVie, still known as Christine Perfect to her fans, was busy working on her self-titled solo album. But for all her efforts, she could not get enthused about the prospect of her name in lights. Christine had always been able to feed into and off of the energy of a band and was almost sorry to have committed herself to a solo venture. "It was a disaster," she told *Crawdaddy.* "I hadn't written any material and didn't have a band. But I got one together and recorded the LP in about a month. The two or three songs I wrote weren't very good. I was such a novice."

Just as Christine was coming to terms with her distaste for solo work, Peter Green was indirectly laying the groundwork for bringing her into Fleetwood Mac. No one truly believed that Peter would remain in the band for long. As much as his bandmates wished for the return of the old, ambitious Peter, no one had much confidence in that happening. For the most part, the guys had hope but lacked faith. So even as 1969 witnessed Fleetwood Mac outselling the Beatles and the Stones, there was a palpable feeling among the Mac that the success couldn't last.

Even before the launch of the 1970 European tour, LSD had pushed the normally introspective frontman to extremes. Desperately searching for quick answers to life's eternal questions, Peter became caught up in a web of his own delusions. The reality of the band's situation was now far beyond his reach. He began spouting wild ideas, such as demanding that the band donate all their proceeds to charities. As Mick told the *Los Angeles Times,* "Peter basically ceased to see the light with Fleetwood Mac and had aspirations of playing for nothing in strange places."

The straw that broke the band's frontman came during the winter's European tour. After a Fleetwood Mac concert in Munich, Germany, Peter was swept off to a wild acid party thrown by a group of rich, German hippies. "They had a mansion, a great big place it was," Peter later told *Mojo* magazine. "I went back with one of the road managers. He gave me some LSD. . . . Then I just sat around thinking and thought about everything. I was thinking so fast, I couldn't believe how fast I was thinking! And I ran out of thoughts. I must have been thinking solid for about an hour."

Although the band's road manager didn't remember giving Peter any LSD, insisting that their drinks had been spiked by their radical hippie hosts, neither he nor Peter retained a clear recollection of what went on during the twenty-four hours they were at the mansion. "I'll never accept that it was just me," Peter later tried explaining to *Guitar*

Shop. "I've always known that someone made it happen to me, some-one mucking about with me."

Although it appears no one will ever know what actually happened that night—rumors have run the gamut from brainwashing to black magic—one thing is certain: The amount of acid Peter ingested at that party had a pernicious influence on his already fragile psyche. He would eventually be diagnosed with schizophrenia, one of the drug's most heinous long-term side effects; the immediate result of the Munich trip was to hasten Peter's departure from his band.

After the party, Peter wanted nothing more to do with Fleetwood Mac. He told his fellow band members that he wished to remain with the Germans. "It was a freedom thing," he told the *Los Angeles Times.* "I wanted to go and live on a commune in Germany. . . . I had to get away. Acid had a lot to do with it."

But the drug was only a symptom of a larger problem. "People thought I left Fleetwood Mac because of the LSD, but it wasn't just that," he told *Guitar Shop.* "The whole fame thing was just dragging me down." The gifted guitarist had always been an idealist. He spurned the material trappings that both enticed and helped to ground Mick Fleetwood and John McVie. Seeking to discover the meaning of life through acid trips, Peter wound up mentally alienated and com-pletely alone. His long relationship with Sandra Elsdon came to an end because of her refusal to put up with Peter's drug use, and his true friends and bandmates were forced to muddle through without him.

———

Peter gave his notice that March, while still in Munich. He was com-mitted until May 25, but that was it. John McVie called the Munich in-cident "Trauma City"—not so much for Peter, but for the rest of the band. Peter had been to early Fleetwood Mac what Stevie Nicks would come to mean to the band in five years' time. To continue the band without him posed a great challenge, and no one knew whether they'd be able to surmount it.

In the two months preceding Peter's departure, he wrote "Green Manalishi," the last of the Big Four. While the single would peak at only Number Ten, it would always be Peter's favorite composition. "I think 'Green Manalishi' is the most interesting," Peter said. "It's all about having too much money, and all the harm it does." As the song revealed, fame wasn't Peter's only problem; his money would also have to go. Although he never did make it over to the German commune, he freely disposed of the vast majority of his assets and was swindled out of the rest. Finally, he would lose his passion for music and lead the aimless existence of an acid casualty for the better part of twenty-five years. "He made several interesting albums after he left, then basically took a left turn in terms of his psyche," said Mick. "He pulled out of the mainstream and chose to stay at home."

Late in the spring of 1970, while Peter's search for God was being blown out of all proportion by the press, fans of his former band were becoming skeptical. To most people, Fleetwood Mac sans Peter Green was as misconceived a notion as a romantic comedy without a leading man. Thus the star's much-ballyhooed exit concerned Fleetwood Mac as much as it did the perpetually misquoted and misunderstood Peter Green.

Mick, John, Danny, Jeremy, and their manager, Clifford Davis, all knew that no one expected the group to carry on much longer. While Peter's name had been dropped from the official appellation years ago, the band had never ceased to be Peter Green's Fleetwood Mac. According to the naysayers, the only thing left for the broken band to do was to follow the lead of their main man and dismantle. Of course, all such prophecies of doom would forever remain unfulfilled.

3

NEITHER HERE NOR THERE

Peter Green's parting was the first in a long series of blows that would strike Fleetwood Mac. Its impact left the band reeling, but as John McVie and Mick Fleetwood would go on to prove time and again, it would take a lot more than losing a headliner to tear this band apart. "It's never been, 'Oh, we're breaking up,'" Mick told Amy Hanson of *Goldmine* magazine, "it's always been, 'Well, who's next?'"

While Mick's nonchalant attitude may belie the fact, picking up the pieces had never been easy. With Peter gone, Danny and Jeremy were overcome by anxiety. The guitar players were expected to take over for a departed genius at the height of the band's fame. All eyes were on them, and as Mick recalled, "they felt so stripped of the security that Peter had given to them . . . they especially felt very naked."

"When Peter left the band, a lot of people went, 'Ahh . . . forget Fleetwood Mac . . . because Peter Green was Fleetwood Mac,'" explained Christine McVie.

Something had to be done. For the first time, Mick stepped into Peter's shoes and took total control of the band's affairs, engineering their relocation en masse from London to the provinces. Even

Christine, who had withdrawn from show business a short while ago, was present and accounted for.

Having recently released two hit records, one with Chicken Shack and one solo, honored by *Melody Maker* as Female Vocalist of the Year in the process, Christine Perfect shocked the world of music by retiring. To the public, quitting on such a resounding high note seemed a sacrilege. But to Christine it was long overdue. She had known all along that if she was going to follow music, she would have to sacrifice everything else. A homebody at heart, she made a clean break, turning her back on her career for the sake of life, love, and family.

"I quit and returned to life as a housewife," Christine proudly asserted. But in two months' time, she would subvert her homemaker status by joining Fleetwood Mac's front line. Living in their rented communal abode in the small town of Alton, Christine witnessed the band's travails firsthand. No matter how well they played or how skillfully they wrote, nothing worked quite like it had in Peter's day. With Britain's first lady of blues living in their very house, it was only a matter of time before the band sought out her help. Fortunately for Fleetwood Mac, Christine agreed to do what she could. And so began one of the longest-running careers in the history of the band.

———

By the time the Mac moved into Kiln House, as they christened their rural farmhouse, Mick and Jenny were ready to tie the cans to the fender and say their I do's. The couple went legit as Mick and Jenny Fleetwood not two weeks after Peter left. Although Mick had asked for Jenny's hand over a year ago, his band's unexpected success had deterred him from setting a date.

Jenny had not been unsympathetic to her suitor's plight. Her sister, Patty, had gone through the same thing with George Harrison and would go on to repeat the performance with Eric Clapton (who later wrote "Layla" to plead for Patty's heart). Jenny understood Mick's point of view and was secure enough in the relationship not to pressure him.

Since Peter was the "main draw" for the band, his desertion freed up Fleetwood Mac's schedule for the next several months, creating an excellent window of opportunity for Mick and Jenny to marry. A honeymoon, however, was one luxury the pair couldn't afford. The rest of the spare time had to be used to cut a new album. And to prove that Fleetwood Mac was still a viable commodity, the new release had to be good. So after the simple wedding ceremony, Jenny settled into Kiln House's idyllic life of peace and quiet, while Mick Fleetwood and the band worked overtime to put out an LP worthy of their celebrated name.

Aptly titled *Kiln House,* the new endeavor was widely regarded as a strong effort. Although it would not make it to the top of the charts, it was nonetheless a victory for the band that had been ready to throw down their instruments only a few months ago. The addition of Christine on keyboards bolstered their sound, while Danny's guitar arrangements were impressive as always. Even Jeremy Spencer had taken a leap of faith by writing "One Together," his first non-parody song, for the album. In view of the circumstances surrounding its production, the album was a smashing success.

Even after *Kiln House* was in the can, the guys were still wary of asking Christine to join the band as a full-fledged member. Knowing that she harbored no regrets about having traded a strong solo career for a domestic lifestyle, none of the band members wanted to put Christine on the spot by requesting that she resume the life she'd left behind. But eventually, necessity won out over scruples. The band needed Christine—and with a U.S. tour looming on the horizon, they needed her fast.

Luckily, the powerful singer didn't need to be asked twice. "I had to decide; either I'll be lonely or I'll damn well adapt enough to be like big sister, to be with the guys and still retain that respect," was how Christine explained her long-standing status as Fleetwood Mac's only female member and resident mother figure. "I mean I love to be with men, generally more so than women."

She and her husband knew how to have fun together. Both were tour veterans, and the prospect of hitting the States as a team filled each with delight. Christine joined Fleetwood Mac and toured with John McVie from that point on. But not Jenny. She was without instrument and *with* child. The band's touring schedule kept her husband on the road most of the year, and the young bride justifiably feared that Mick would never amount to much of a family man.

Later in life, Mick would reflect upon the sacrifices he made for his band and regret the moments he missed with his family. But at the time, he believed that Fleetwood Mac needed his help more than anyone else. As the one constant that would see him through life, the band was Mick's baby. Nobody cared as much or worked as hard to keep it healthy. He was willing to do whatever it took to make sure it stayed strong and viable.

————

Fleetwood Mac toured to promote *Kiln House* from August until December. Phase one of the tour took place in the States and saw Christine's first performances with the band. Her participation turned Fleetwood Mac into a somewhat kinder and gentler stage act. Dealing with the new addition brought no growing pains or adjustment difficulties. Ever since her first Fleetwood Mac show at the Warehouse in New Orleans, Chris fit right in. What's more, her nurturing instincts and skillful piano playing helped the struggling artists get over the loss of their leader both personally and professionally.

The second phase of the tour took the band to Europe. It was scheduled to begin only a few days after the completion of the first. When all was said and done, although the European fans missed Peter Green, the tour proved successful. But Fleetwood Mac's work, it seemed, was never done. No sooner had they returned to Kiln House from Europe than they were back on the road for a U.K. tour.

The short period of time between tours saw the band scrambling to move out of Kiln House and into Benifold, a huge estate located on several acres of Hampshire land, complete with its own tennis court and servants' quarters. The band's new digs contrasted sharply with the tiny Kiln House.

On the whole, the band was pleased with their new investment. For Mick especially, it was the beginning of a long-standing (and often financially ruinous) interest in real estate.

Benifold was surrounded by an aura of landed gentry that brought a sense of easy country life into the hard working lives of the touring musicians. It also provided Jenny, and Jeremy's wife, Fiona, with the ideal locale to nurse their newborn babies. Sadly, the two women had little else in common. Whereas Jenny was worldly and sophisticated, Fiona was simple and down-to-earth. The band, who divided their time between music, booze, and drugs, didn't offer Jenny much in the way of a common denominator, either. So while days spent at Benifold were heaven on earth to Mick, to Jenny they seemed stifling and endless.

In spite of his wife's complaints, but true to his first priority, Mick was intent on staying at the country mansion. The band had bought Benifold as a group, and Mick believed that the band that lives together stays together. Their next U.S. tour confirmed the notion that even the most copious precautions are not guaranteed to ward off disaster.

———

The tour kicked off at the Fillmore, Fleetwood Mac's old San Francisco stomping ground. After the encores, everyone agreed that if this show was any indication, the winter 1971 U.S. tour would be a colossal coup. L.A. was the site of their next performance.

The night before they were scheduled to disembark at LAX, a powerful earthquake rocked Los Angeles. Everyone on the tour was taken aback by the news, especially Jeremy. Ever the god-fearing Christian, he was convinced that Los Angeles had just been visited by the First Horseman of the Apocalypse and was unwilling to follow his band into Babylon. Finally, Mick was able to coax him into making the flight. What happened next is the stuff of Fleetwood Mac legend.

After arriving at their hotel, Jeremy casually said that he was going to step out. "I'll be right back," he told Mick. Everyone presumed that he meant only to stretch his legs before that night's show. When Jeremy missed the concert altogether, manager Clifford Davis went directly to the authorities. Jeremy may have been lazy, and he may have pulled some crazy stunts, but in the four years he'd played with the band, he had never blown off a show. Although Jeremy had vociferously predicted that no good would come of going to L.A., no one guessed that he would be the victim of his own prophecy.

At the time, the city was crawling with fringe-religion missionaries, handing out pamphlets, preaching their gospel, and employing brainwashing tactics wherever there were lost souls to be saved. When Fleetwood Mac showed up at the police station, they were told that

Jeremy had probably fallen in with such a cult. He might not want to return, the police warned the agitated band.

Regardless, Fleetwood Mac spared no expense in their three-day search for Jeremy. The bandmates had grown fond of one another over the years; they couldn't pick up and leave without knowing what befell their friend. Perhaps even more important, the future of Fleetwood Mac depended upon finding the guitarist. While there may have been warm feelings all around, there was never any question as to why this disparate group of people suffered each other's company for so long. Their band was both their livelihood and raison d'être—but it was only as strong as its weakest link.

By now, half of the stage show relied exclusively on Jeremy's parodies. His send-ups of Elvis, Jerry Lee Lewis, and other golden oldies had elicited such a consistently enthusiastic response from audiences that his role in the act was expanded. By the time this U.S. tour rolled around, a show without Jeremy would be like no show at all.

Fleetwood Mac frantically scoured the streets in search of their lead guitar player. Given the myriad of L.A.-based cults, it was like looking for a contact lens on the floor at a rock concert. Finally, they were led to the secret stronghold of the neo-Christian Children of God. "When we found him," Christine explained to *Crawdaddy,* "he was surrounded by about four hundred kids chanting prayers." Dennis Keen, the band's road manager, recalled that "everyone could see [he] had been totally brainwashed, and, in my opinion, brainwashed for the better. Jeremy looked a lot worse before he went and then looked alive afterwards: You could see he'd found what he'd been looking for."

"He went out for groceries and ended up quoting the Bible," the taciturn John McVie summed up in a *Newsweek* article.

Jeremy had renounced his life of vice and dissolution, sent for his wife and kids, and left his colleagues in the lurch. Nearly twenty-five years later, Mick would tell the *Los Angeles Times* that "Jeremy's alive and well, he has nine children, and he lives in Rio de Janeiro. He's been all over the world with the Children of God. . . . The man's happy, he's doing what he wants to do, and so be it." But back in 1971, he was singing a different tune. Jeremy's journey into a blissful and God-fearing existence had Fleetwood Mac looking at potential bankruptcy.

———

Stevie and Lindsey's act wasn't faring any better. Having begun auspiciously enough in 1968, opening up concerts for many a San Francisco brand-name band, Fritz finally found a manager in 1971. But when recording-contract offers failed to follow, the band disintegrated within a few months. According to Stevie, the breakup was typical. She and Lindsey found themselves heartbroken at having to "tell the three guys in the band that nobody wanted them, only us."

On the positive side, Lindsey and Stevie were now free to please themselves, both personally and professionally. They formed an eponymously titled folk-rock duo, Buckingham Nicks. Pretty soon, they were also a couple. "Stevie and I kinda got selected out of that group as the ones who were perceived as having the most potential," Lindsey told *Bam*, "and when Fritz broke up, we kind of got together on a lot of different levels." The union was the happiest and most fruitful either of them had ever known. Besides arranging Stevie's powerful lyrics, Lindsey also began to write songs, something he'd had little interest in before. Meanwhile, Stevie worshiped her talented boyfriend. "I did everything I could do to make him happy," she said in a later interview.

Soon they were ready to try their luck in Los Angeles. That's when mononucleosis took Lindsey out of commission. For nearly nine months he was too weak to perform, and the trip had to be postponed. Stevie used the time to write songs, while Lindsey rehearsed for his future role as a consummate lead guitarist and record producer. "We spent a year writing all those songs and making those demos and going out to Lindsey's dad's coffee plant and working all night, every night," Stevie recounted in a *Rolling Stone* interview. "All the people leave the plant at six P.M.; we went up there at nine P.M. We rocked all night long until six in the morning, five days a week. It was so scary up there that we locked ourselves in the room where we were and didn't go out, ever, because it was a big warehouse, you know, a coffee plant. So it was very scary. So we would stay in there all night, and if we heard things, we would just, like, stay in there and keep the door locked."

By the time Lindsey's convalescence was complete, the hard work had paid off. The pair was now a fine-tuned act ready for the big time. It was still early in 1972 when Buckingham Nicks hit Los Angeles.

Unfortunately, to say that they took the capital of the music industry by storm would be a bald-faced lie. "I didn't understand nor did I like this world in Los Angeles," Stevie would later reveal in an interview. In fact, the singer had little reason to feel otherwise, since her act took its lumps just like the thousands of other unsigned bands who were making the L.A. scene back in 1972.

After arriving in Los Angeles, they moved in with record producer Keith Olsen. As Stevie told *Bam*, when she and Lindsey first laid eyes on their friend's recording studio, Sound City, they "thought it was the most fabulous big, huge, incredible rock 'n' roll studio. We had never ever been in such a big studio before. We'd only been in little tiny ones in San Francisco." And as Olsen busied himself with trying to find the couple a record contract, Stevie was working overtime trying to support Lindsey and herself. She waited tables to make ends meet. "I was a good waitress," she told *HP de Tijd*, "I ran from one side of the restaurant to the other. I probably had a better physical condition then than today."

In fact, Stevie was pulling most of the weight in the couple's relationship. She was used to assuming responsibility—as a young girl, she had helped her mother take care of Christopher, five years her junior and the baby of the family. With Lindsey being both younger and emotionally more fragile than Stevie, reverting to the childhood pattern was effortless. Many was the time that Stevie came home from a hard day's work only to find Lindsey and his friends passed out in the living room.

"I didn't want to be a waitress," she told *Spin* magazine, "but I believed that Lindsey shouldn't have to work, that he should just lay on the floor and practice his guitar and become more brilliant every day. I never worried about not being successful; I wanted to make it possible for him to be successful. And when you really feel that way about somebody, it's very easy to take your own personality and quiet it way down." That, of course, suited her music-obsessed boyfriend just fine—he needed a strong woman to patronize his artistic endeavors. Having grown up the youngest in a three-son household, Lindsey took the attention and coddling for granted.

Notwithstanding this inequitable division of labor, Lindsey and Stevie's relationship was at a high point. Just starting to make their way in L.A., with no band and few prospects to back them, it was

Buckingham Nicks against the world. "Our relationship was great," Stevie told *Rolling Stone.* "We had other problems: didn't have a lot of money, alone in L.A., didn't have our families, no friends, didn't know anybody. But we had each other. I knew that we were going to be somebody."

———

The sense of being alone in a hostile universe also descended on Fleetwood Mac. When Jeremy found his calling, the band was at a total loss for a suitable replacement. They were hard pressed to choose between two evils: canceling the rest of the tour or putting on a series of drab and disappointing performances. Either option would tarnish their reputation beyond repair.

There was but one solution to their immediate problem, and it rested in the hands of Peter Green. Fleetwood Mac's repertoire was still dominated by Peter's songs, and he would have had no problem replicating Jeremy's parts. But judging from Peter's *End of the Game,* the entirely instrumental, acid-jam-packed solo album he'd released after defecting from the band, Fleetwood Mac and its founding father had precious little in common. After wracking their brains for an alternative, though, the band decided to put their reservations—and pride—on hold and summon Peter.

Characteristically, Peter took pains to exacerbate an already difficult situation. Instead of giving the band the simple yea or nay they were looking for, he presented a set of impossible demands. The worst of his stipulations was that Fleetwood Mac play none of their hit songs, none of the *Kiln House* material, and not even anything from their former albums while Peter was with them. He would play only "Black Magic Woman," and jam the rest of the time. The predicament was a Kafakaesque nightmare for Fleetwood Mac, who were now left with three evils from which to choose.

In the hope that Peter would change his mind upon arriving in the States, Fleetwood Mac agreed to his conditions. But the reinstated lead guitarist wasn't budging; he knew he had the band by the throat and planned to take full advantage of his position. As Nigel Watson, a bongo player who accompanied Peter on this Fleetwood Mac tour, recalled in *Peter Green: Founder of Fleetwood Mac*: "His attitude was 'If they want Peter Green, they'll do the music I now want to do.' "

In spite of his antagonistic stance, Peter did manage to save the band. His skillful jams brought down house after house of drugged and hallucinating audiences. While concerts packed solid with instrumental jams weren't Fleetwood Mac's idea of a good time, they appreciated Peter's participation during the remaining six weeks of the tour. Danny Kirwan alone found nothing for which to feel grateful. Peter's constant showboating completely usurped Danny's standing as the lead guitarist, a role the young man had worked hard to master after Peter's spur-of-the-moment departure. "We played well together, but we didn't get on," he told an interviewer. In fact, Danny was so angered by Peter's antics that after one show he hurled a beer bottle at Peter's head.

Thankfully, the tour was over before any real bodily harm befell its participants. In fact, Mick would later refer to it as Fleetwood Mac's "best tour ever." But returning to the U.K. filled the musicians with dread. Last year Peter had gone; now Jeremy was down for the count. With so much succession going on, it was becoming increasingly more difficult to shrug and say, "Well, who's next?"

———

When the band returned to their country manor, relaxation was again not in the cards. An imminent British tour meant that Fleetwood Mac either had to cancel and disband altogether or find someone to take Jeremy's place. Whether from a burning desire to keep on playing or from simple inertia, the musicians decided that they would remain a team.

Auditions got underway almost immediately. But as one guitarist after another failed to play up to the band's elevated criteria, the anxiety began to mount. The threat of dissolution hanging over the band began to take its toll on personal relationships. Danny's artistic temperament flared; John's alcoholism began driving his wife of three years to distraction. As she explained to *Rolling Stone,* "The strain of me being in the same band as him started to take its toll. When you're in the same band as somebody, you're seeing them almost more than twenty-four hours a day. You start to see an awful lot of the bad side 'cause touring is no easy thing. There's a lot of drinking. . . . John is not the most pleasant of people when he's drunk. Very belligerent. I was seeing more Hyde than Jekyll."

Jenny Boyd's feelings of abandonment also had fertile ground in which to breed as more and more of Mick's time went to putting out professional fires. The situation was getting desperate when Judy Wong, the woman who had played Cupid for Mick and Jenny, and was now a frequent visitor at Benifold, suggested that her ex-boyfriend Bob Welch try out for the slot.

Bob was an American expatriate living in Paris when he got the call from Judy. A cynical, sharp-witted man of twenty-six, Bob would be the first Yank in Mick Fleetwood's court. Bob had been brought up in Beverly Hills, steeped in the glamor of Hollywood's golden years. His writer/producer father, Robert Welch, worked for Paramount Studios and produced such films as Bob Hope's *The Paleface.*

When Bob was eight years old, his father awoke within him a life-long passion by buying him a guitar. Raised on the prose and verse of Jack Kerouac and Allen Ginsberg, Bob decided to travel to Paris after high school. His goal, as he told *People* magazine, was "ostensibly to study at the Sorbonne, but I mostly smoked hash with bearded guys five years older. Sitting in the Deux Magots café turned out to be as revolutionary as a Honda Civic."

When the epiphany of his own triteness came upon him, Bob high-tailed it back to his native land, where he enrolled in UCLA and joined the Seven Souls. He played with the eight-piece R&B band for six years before they broke up in 1969. During this period, the act became a local favorite, touring with the likes of James Brown and Ike and Tina Turner, but consistently failed to break out of the small time. After the band dispersed, Bob played a key role in an offshoot group called Head West. They relocated to France and enjoyed a modicum of success before a falling-out with their manager left them destitute, "living on rice and beans and sleeping on the floor."

When Judy Wong called with the news of Fleetwood Mac's emergency, Bob was in no position to be choosy. He packed his demo tapes and hopped the next flight to London. Bob was charmed by the sight of the band's cooperative digs. Wives, kids, girlfriends, and a steady stream of visitors from town combined to make Fleetwood Mac a tight-knit family. The setup made a favorable impression on the vagabond guitarist. In turn, the band was pleased, and not a little surprised, by the American's dry-as-the-Sahara wit and unassuming personality. With the tour drawing nigh, there was no time for hesitation. In under a month, and just in the nick of time, Bob was installed as a permanent fixture in the band.

"My era was the bridge era," Bob Welch told the *Plain Dealer.* "It was a transition. But it was an important period in the history of the band." As yet another of Fleetwood Mac's triple-threat singer/song-writer/guitarists, Bob was bound to change the band, in both style and substance. And nowhere was this change more palpable than on *Future Games*, the follow-up to *Kiln House.* Never had the band sounded so far from the original. With Bob, Christine, and Danny—each a full-fledged songwriter in his or her own right—all making considerable contributions, the blues were all but imperceptible. Due largely to Bob's California-inspired influence, *Future Games* was Fleetwood Mac's definitive step in the West Coast pop direction.

––––––––

The band's British fan base remained uncompromising in their intolerance for anything outside the realm of pure blues and were not amused by Fleetwood Mac's change of tune. Neither did the European audiences roll out the welcome wagon for what they viewed as a band whose time had clearly come and gone. But the lack of respect and their diminished stature couldn't keep the troupe from plodding on. They were still getting paid to play, which in their book still beat working for a living. Whereas the group's musical leanings would soon drive them out of the United Kingdom altogether, for the time being Fleetwood Mac was content to take only their touring westward.

It was American hospitality that saved the band from the ravages of disappointing record sales. The States had been the group's last chance to stay on amiable terms with their record company. Unaware of the impact that the British ensemble's changing personnel was having on the home front, and nurturing no overwhelming yen for blues, U.S. audiences took to the band just as they had in the early days.

"What I can't understand, especially when we're in England, is that people keep on asking us about Peter Green," Christine McVie would later tell *Hit Parader.* "Over here they haven't had that attitude, and they were a lot nicer about it and figured that the music was good, and so Fleetwood Mac just carried on to greater and greater heights." And while America's Mac appreciation had never rivaled the all-consuming passion of their British blues fans, its constancy helped the band weather the four-year slump that set in with Peter Green's departure.

Fleetwood Mac's *Future Games* U.S. tour kicked off nearly a full year on the road. The survival instinct was in high gear as the ensemble pushed themselves past exhaustion to score in the consumer market. Since middling record sales also called for the band to cut another album, Fleetwood Mac was forced to juggle the responsibilities of recording and touring.

The songs for the next album, *Bare Trees,* had to be written and recorded on the go. Released in spring of 1972, the album was an homage to melancholy and homesickness. Its cover photo showed leafless trees, and its final cut wasn't a song but a poem, "Thoughts on a Grey Day." The unifying theme of *Bare Trees* could be summed up as the winter of our discontent. But despite the instrumental and lyrical strength of this output, the Old World and the New displayed a vast disparity of response yet again. While Europe and Great Britain relegated the Mac to a warm-up act, U.S. engagements had the band headlining bills and packing them in at midsize venues.

This period saw Fleetwood Mac morph into a touring machine. Under so much pressure, something had to give. As it turned out, that thing was Danny Kirwan. Ever since the exodus of Peter Green and Jeremy Spencer, Danny had been the weakest link in the chain. He had indulged in drink, grass, and psychedelic drugs, doing nothing to avoid his fate and everything to hasten it.

Danny's behavior had become untenable by the time the American *Bare Trees* tour rolled around in the summer of 1972. According to Jenny Boyd in *My Life and Adventures in Fleetwood Mac,* "Danny suddenly started having these total outbursts and tantrums that had no grounding to them at all—a side of him would just kick in and be totally inappropriate to the situation. I think drugs and alcohol got Danny totally nuts in the end. He was just too sensitive a soul." And while it was painfully obvious that he was cracking, the sympathy he inspired in his bandmates was obscured by their general resentment.

The situation came to a climax on a muggy August night, when a trifling disagreement drove Danny to literally bang his head against the bathroom wall. He then turned his anger on his guitar, smashing it against the floor. Finally, he turned on his band by refusing to join them onstage. It was clearly a cry for help. Unfortunately for Danny, he had long since exhausted his bandmates' reserve of tolerance.

Had Danny simply responded to Mick's pleas to go onstage, or even walked off in a fit of anger, maybe the consequences would not have been so severe. But sticking around to watch, with tears of laughter streaming down his face, as Bob Welch struggled unsuccessfully to replicate his lead guitar parts, was just too much for the exasperated musicians. Everyone wanted Danny out, and it fell to Mick, as the band's leader, to deal the final coup de grâce.

4

IDENTITY CRISES

The loss of yet a third mainstay shook the band to its very foundation.
Danny had been a powerful guitarist, as well as the last remnant of
Peter Green's inaugural front line. But while Danny would go on to
record three albums, only to end up a homeless drifter, Fleetwood Mac
would soon rally. No strangers to the sudden departures of their bandmates, the remaining band members were, by now, well equipped with
the coping skills necessary to manage. For Fleetwood Mac, this was
simply another case of "who's next?"

The answer came in two parts: one part a cocksure lead singer, the
other a deft lead guitarist. Following the advice of Clifford Davis,
Fleetwood Mac looted the talent pool of Savoy Brown, a band they had
opened for on countless occasions, to secure a wild, eye-catching frontman, Dave Walker. While Walker's personality was far from a perfect fit,
he had just the sort of larger-than-life stage presence the group was looking for. What's more, the band members hoped to see some of the success Walker had had with Savoy Brown rub off on them. In fact, even
John Courage, who would become Fleetwood Mac's longtime friend and
road manager, was purloined from Savoy Brown around this time.

Part two of the band's new equation arrived from Long John Baldry's ensemble in the form of Bob Weston. He was an adroit and confident guitar player, with looks and attitude to match. While Dave Walker was something of the odd man out from the get-go, Bob Weston quickly managed to maneuver his way into everyone's good graces. Even the reticent Jenny Boyd found a friend in the affable Weston. So, within two months of Danny Kirwan's adieu, Benifold had adopted three new recruits and a completely different aspect.

Of course, more did not always mean merrier. After the fall 1972 tour, which took the sextet all over Europe and the States, it was time to cut another album. Invited to participate was Peter Green, who had retreated to the periphery of the music industry and had spent time on a kibbutz and working as a cemetery caretaker. Nonetheless, he consented to play uncredited on Bob Welch's "Night Watch." It would be Peter's last musical endeavor for six years.

Bob Welch and Christine were now the only songwriters onboard, and for the first time in Fleetwood Mac history, the composers were required to customize their chords and lyrics to the frontman's vocals whereas each songwriter in the band usually sang his or her own songs live. As their sensibilities clashed so thoroughly with those of their lead singer, Chris and Bob's attempts to furnish him with material were at best half-hearted. Carousing seemed to be Walker's main interest, and he found favor only with the equally inebriated John McVie.

The product of these January 1973 recording sessions was called *Penguin,* in tribute to John McVie's abiding fascination with the flightless bird. The title and accompanying penguin cover art continued the trend begun by John in *Future Games* (the cover of which featured a photo of a penguin where John should have been). The penguin would soon become the band's trademark.

As the recording sessions wore on, Fleetwood Mac's discomfort with Walker's star turn was made readily apparent by the bit part he was consigned to play on *Penguin.* In an unorthodox move, the LP featured only two songs sung by the so-called lead vocalist. After the misadventures-filled *Penguin* tour—at its low point, the band and the spectators were tear-gassed by the police at a ballpark music festival in California—Fleetwood Mac politely handed Dave Walker his walking papers.

It was the summer of 1973, and Fleetwood Mac was hard at work on their next album, *Mystery to Me*. After Dave's exit, it seemed as if a huge load had been lifted off the band's conscience. Truth was, everyone knew that bringing in Dave had been a mistake. Even in the days of Peter Green, Fleetwood Mac had always been more an ensemble than a star vehicle. Now that things were back to normal, the creative juices could flow freely. The resulting *Mystery to Me* album had all the makings of a megahit, and the band was braced for their second go-round in the spotlight.

The winds of fortune were also working their magic in Los Angeles, where a timely record contract helped Buckingham Nicks sail through the "as-yet-unsigned act" doldrums. "Buckingham Nicks signed to Dave Swaney Productions in Hollywood" read the "Signings" section of the December 16, 1972, issue of *Billboard*. And while the label may have been a small one, its size bore no correlation to the magnitude of Stevie and Lindsey's relief. The couple was overjoyed.

They set to work immediately, laying their tracks at Keith Olsen's recording studio, Sound City. Here they met and befriended a young recording engineer who would later play a crucial role in turning Fleetwood Mac into superstars, Richard Dashut. In *Modern Recording*, Richard remembered that on his "second day of the job there was a gentleman standing in the corner with his girlfriend smoking a joint, and because I like smoking joints myself, I went and joined them and we became instant friends. That couple was Lindsey Buckingham and Stevie Nicks."

Hitting it off famously, the threesome decided to rent an apartment together. Although staying at Keith Olsen's house had been cheap and convenient for the struggling artists, they were wearing out their welcome. Keith proposed that Stevie put in a few hours a week as his cleaning lady, in return for which he was prepared to offer her $250 per month. Stevie's financial straits were such that this was one offer she couldn't refuse. "I did an incredibly good job," she said. "And with that $250, I paid for Lindsey's and my rent."

Lindsey and Stevie were still recording their debut album when the partners of Dave Swaney Productions went separate ways. Suddenly, Buckingham Nicks's label was kaput, and their contract in limbo. Disaster was averted when Polydor Records offered one of the original Swaney partners a contract, taking Stevie and Lindsey along for the ride. The *Buckingham Nicks* album was still on track.

What was in some danger of derailment, however, was the couple's romantic relationship. It was becoming increasingly tempestuous with each passing day. As Stevie explained to *Playboy*, "My relationship with Lindsey was tumultuous and passionate and wild and we were always fighting, so I was never happy." Crafting their songs side by side also brought out their fiercely competitive natures and shed light upon their respective shortcomings. Lindsey and Stevie needed each other to succeed, but neither was willing to admit it. Years later, in an interview with *Circus*, Stevie would look back on this time and say, "We'd been trying to break up, off and on, for years."

They would continue trying for some years to come. In the meantime, there was a record to be cut. *Buckingham Nicks* was several months in the making. Dedicated to Stevie's grandfather and early mentor, A. J. Nicks, the album was a solid first effort with definite chart possibilities.

The cover, which featured a provocative photo of the attractive couple naked from the waist up, was not the savvy piece of self-promotion it appeared. The fact of the matter was that Stevie had spent the last of her money on a very expensive new blouse, only to find that Lindsey hated it. "I didn't like the *Buckingham Nicks* cover," she divulged in an interview. "I didn't like the fact that I had to sit there with Lindsey with no blouse on. I spent my last $111 on this blouse. Right? I didn't eat for days because of it."

Stevie's tears of protest met with Lindsey's stern disapproval. "I was crying when we took that picture. And Lindsey was mad at me," Stevie recalled. "He said, 'You know, you're just being a child. This is art.' And I'm going, 'This is not "art." This is me taking a nude photograph with you, and I don't dig it.' " Despite her displeasure, once the album was ready for release, the duo prepared to reap the rewards of stardom. But as is so often the case, the label executives didn't share in their enthusiasm. Polydor Records decided to go short on the promotional budget. What a setback! Scant advertising meant little awareness, and the end result was nothing short of widespread disinterest.

Without a touring band to back them, Buckingham Nicks's attempts to promote their LP via live performances met with about as much applause as their album. Oddly enough, while the duet couldn't even get arrested in their native Los Angeles, people in Birmingham, Alabama, of all places, were wild about their album. Despite this regional success, Polydor Records soon decided that Buckingham Nicks were a one-city-wonder.

In VH-1's *Stevie Nicks: Behind the Music* special, Stevie described her and Lindsey's feelings of despair at the time: "We have had a taste of the finer things. We have recorded in a big recording studio. We have been introduced to fabulous musicians. We have met a lot of people. We are very proud of our record, and it just gets dropped, and we're back to square one."

The company released the act from their contract just as they were beginning work on their second LP. Lindsey and Stevie were starting again, as destitute as ever—but no longer having the time of their lives.

———

Unlike *Buckingham Nicks,* the release of *Mystery to Me* was greeted by all the propitious signs of a hit generator. Fleetwood Mac was ready to pull out all the stops to make sure the album made good on its promise. While they had always looked upon rock 'n' roll as more a labor of love than money, everyone felt that this LP deserved much more than moderate success. As American audiences helped take the album to Number Sixty-seven on the *Billboard* charts, a four-month U.S. college tour was quickly arranged, and Fleetwood Mac was ready for action.

Inexplicably, this particular road trip included Mick's wife and two daughters. While the tour hardly provided the most opulent of accommodations, Jenny was intent on seeing Mick play, and the drummer couldn't have been happier. After all, it was just a few months ago, during the spring's *Penguin* tour, that he had missed the birth of his second daughter. Togetherness seemed to be just what this family needed.

If only it had been that simple. Time together could not heal the wounds that Mick's sustained withdrawal and Mac-absorption had inflicted upon his marriage. Jenny was there as the band played to one eager audience after another, but more often than not, it was somebody other than Mick whom she was watching. When this fact surfaced, it brought about Fleetwood Mac's third near-downfall in a span of three years.

Jenny's affair with Bob Weston had begun at Benifold a few months earlier. Having won Jenny once, it had never occurred to Mick to keep on trying. And while his wife was struggling with her dissatisfaction, Mick was too caught up with his band to grasp that all was not well with his world. To Jenny, it had seemed as if Weston was the only one at Benifold who took any interest in her. With Mick always looking the other way, it was only a matter of time before her friendship with Weston reached its eventual level of intimacy.

Even as their relationship progressed, Mick never once suspected the truth. It was only on tour that he was made aware of the situation by an irresponsible bystander. In his autobiography, Mick recalled being asked how he felt about his wife's affair with Bob Weston. At that moment, he didn't know what to believe, but as all the pieces began to fall into place, he had to wonder how he could have failed to notice. Of course, Weston must have been the reason behind Jenny's sudden interest in going on tour. And after Jenny admitted as much, Mick was left with a choice: He could end the marriage, fire Bob Weston, stop the tour, or take refuge in denial.

The decision was not an easy one. Whether it was because Mick had to learn about the affair through a stranger, or because Bob Weston had become a close friend, or because Jenny didn't appear to regret the adultery, the transgression could not have been more painful had Jenny deliberately planned to hurt him. Mick felt he was being supplanted by Weston in his own family. It was almost too much to bear. After trying to put his feelings aside for the good of the album and the tour, Mick finally broke down at the sight of Weston reading poetry to his wife and daughters.

On every previous occasion, it had been Mick who argued that individual differences and turmoil should not interfere with business. Mick was the one who tried to convince Peter and Jeremy to remain in spite of their misgivings, and it was he who held out the longest when Danny's volatile personality turned the rest of the band against their lead guitarist. Now, in an unprecedented move, Mick brought an end to the tour by demanding that Bob Weston be fired.

After Bob Weston was removed, Bob Welch called Clifford Davis back in England to notify him of Fleetwood Mac's decision to postpone the remaining leg of the tour. Davis hit the ceiling when he heard the news. According to *My Life and Adventures in Fleetwood Mac,* Davis's last words to the band he'd seen through thick and thin were "I fucking own Fleetwood Mac, and the sooner you get that through your heads, the better."

On that note, the band decided to show Davis who was the boss by taking an extended leave of absence from music. But, in all fairness, it was hard to blame Davis for flipping his lid. Here was a man working hard to run a business by arranging logistics and finding bookings for his clients. Backing out of scheduled performance dates would mean alienating quite a few bread-and-butter concert promoters. And after all the travails that accompanied the Jeremy Spencer imbroglio of 1971 and Danny Kirwan's last stand in 1972, Davis was worried about his plummeting reputation.

When his warning to the band went unheeded, Davis was consumed with rage and righteous indignation. So while the individual members of Fleetwood Mac—Mick Fleetwood in particular—were trying desperately to put their lives in order, Davis was hatching the revenge that would forever cast him as the villain in the Fleetwood Mac saga.

After sending the band a threatening letter to no avail, Davis decided to commandeer Fleetwood Mac by claiming ownership of the band's name and hiring musicians of his own choosing to make up the ensemble. In a frantic attempt to achieve some semblance of legitimacy, Davis decided that he would use the musicians who were recording with Danny Kirwan at the time, along with Dave Walker and Bob Weston, to pose as the New Fleetwood Mac. Having assembled his ménage, Davis quickly dispatched them to the States to complete Fleetwood Mac's aborted *Mystery to Me* tour.

Even as the band's former manager was doing his worst, the real Fleetwood Mac, ignorant of Davis's clandestine goings-on, kept on assuring him that they would regroup after their hiatus. The band members scattered in different directions in spite of their manager's scurrilous admonitions. Mick went all the way to Africa to seek out clarity, while Bob paid a visit to his hometown of L.A.

The McVies also made good use of their free time. The constant to-getherness and the many ordeals of the road were taking a heavy toll on the couple's relationship. Christine was trying her best to get John to stop drinking so heavily—and failing miserably. The truncated tour presented the pair with a perfect opportunity to put several thousand miles between them. While there was no talk of divorce, separate vacations were in order. John flew off to Hawaii, and Christine returned home.

Much like her husband, Jenny was also desperately trying to decide upon the right course. While Mick was immersing himself in Zambian-style asceticism, Jenny consulted a psychic who helped her come to the conclusion that all was not lost. She telegrammed Mick in Africa, asking him to come back. Considering his children, his unflagging love for his wife, and his distaste for both the ascetic and the tomcat lifestyles, Mick gladly agreed to give his marriage a second chance.

When he returned to Benifold, Mick found himself confronted with chaos. With Jenny still visibly unhappy and his band's future up in the air, his family, his band, his entire life was poised on the precipice of ruin. Another man might have crumbled, but Mick held strong.

The New Fleetwood Mac was performing to American audiences who, upon realizing that they were the victims of fraud, would turn into angry mobs every time. There were Clifford Davis–originated stories throughout the press about how John and Bob had quit the band. Davis had even lied to the band's booking agency, telling them that Mick and Christine were still in cahoots and expected to perform with the new musicians. As the band's longtime manager, Davis had more than enough power to sink the band. It was his voice that the Warner Bros. Records executives recognized and his name that was signed at the bottom of the agreement, so even Fleetwood Mac's recording contract was under his control.

To get out of this mess, the band would need an army of attorneys and money to burn. As they had neither, losing the rights to their band name began to seem like a distinct possibility.

It was Bob who first discovered and eventually foiled Davis's scheme to destroy the Mac. After Mick returned from Africa, lawyers were hired, and an injunction stopping the New Mac from performing was issued. But the morass of documents and issues involved in the lawsuits would mean that Fleetwood Mac would be cut off from all funds, as well as the right to perform, until a decision was handed down.

Bob's was a simple yet amazingly effective solution: Relocate to Los Angeles, buddy up to Warner Bros., and win back the record contract. "I'm the one who brought the band to Los Angeles from England," Bob revealed to the *Plain Dealer.* Coming to terms with saying goodbye to the motherland took some time. While they were hardly the queen's most loyal subjects, Fleetwood Mac still had ties binding them to jolly old England. There was their country home, their families, and the culture they all knew and loved. But as the savings began to dwindle, there was no disputing the logic of Bob's proposal. It was either repair to L.A. or dismember the band altogether.

———

By the time Fleetwood Mac came to the unanimous decision to give L.A. a trial run, it was already April 1974. They had been out of work for five consecutive months, and the pressure to scare up business was on. Years later, Bob Welch would testify to the Mac's distress, saying, "I saw the band through a whole period where they barely survived, literally."

While it may sound hard to believe of a band that had consistently moved approximately three hundred thousand units per album release, Fleetwood Mac couldn't even afford to buy a property upon relocating to L.A. The Fleetwoods rented a small house in Laurel Canyon, while the McVies were forced to set up shop in a postage-stamp-size three-room apartment in Malibu. The group sank their last converted pounds into retaining a lawyer; their only chance at survival was in the hands of their record label. A new era had dawned, and nobody was sure what the future would bring. As Mick Fleetwood told *Rolling Stone,* "There's always full potential of either great things happening or totally disastrous things happening." One thing soon became evident: Whatever happened would have to happen in Los Angeles.

At the very least, the days of hired managers were over. "Mick and I comanaged the group for years," said Bob Welch. Fleetwood Mac had been badly burned, but they did learn a valuable lesson: Trust no one.

Since neither of the McVies showed any inclination toward running the business side of Fleetwood Mac, Bob and Mick rose to the occasion. They formed their own management company, calling it Seedy Management in tribute to Clifford Davis.

According to Christine McVie, this arrangement would work out most favorably for several years to come. "Our success only started when we got rid of all the leechy managers," she would go on to tell *Hit Parader*. "Mick knows everything that a good manager knows anyway. He has good intuition, good timing about things. I suppose the things that prospective managers would tell us would be the usual old bull, that we don't have the time because we have to concentrate on the music. . . . But none of us want that."

Yet the band's identity crisis was far from being resolved. The mere fact that they were self-managed worked against them. No one had heard of an act of Fleetwood Mac's considerable caliber managing their own operations. It was simply not done. If there was anything music-industry executives agreed upon, it was that musicians are right-brained artists, with no head for the pesky details of business. But at every meeting and negotiating session, there were Bob Welch and Mick Fleetwood, ready to do business with the big boys.

Clifford Davis was also reluctant to let go of the group. Knowing perfectly well what his ex-clients were up to, Davis was tenaciously checking them at every turn. Even when it came down to recording their first post-Davis album, he was right there, demanding that an injunction be issued against the "spurious" use of the Fleetwood Mac name. The manager was out for blood, and had Fleetwood Mac not made the savvy decision to move to Los Angeles, Davis would certainly have seen the band fold in 1974.

Fortunately, Warner Bros. was quick to recognize the real deal. After meeting with Fleetwood Mac's people and hearing them out, there was no denying that Clifford Davis didn't have a leg to stand on. New Fleetwood Mac or no New Fleetwood Mac, Davis wasn't the one who could create an album worthy of the *Billboard* 100—only the original Fleetwood Mac could do that. So, within a few months, the record company had inked a new deal, and Fleetwood Mac was back in the studio recording their next album, the aptly titled *Heroes Are Hard to Find*.

———

Throughout these lean times, Bob Welch had stood by his band. Polishing up his lead guitar and writing many of the songs on the *Heroes* album he could handle, but negotiating contracts, finding attorneys, and managing the band took a lot out of him. With his second marriage in a state of perpetual disarray, and no end in sight to the Mac-related turmoil, an overwhelming sense of wanderlust was beginning to set in.

But to leave a displaced band at this stage would have been tantamount to stabbing a friend in the back, so Bob set aside his personal problems and poured everything he had into the album. As always, Christine's contributions, such as the pop treasure "Come a Little Bit Closer," were full of positive vibrations and bounce. Peaking at Number Thirty-four on the *Billboard* charts, the result was, by early Fleetwood Mac standards, a smash in the United States.

When time came to release the album and mount a tour, Clifford Davis resurfaced. As the small matter of the band's name was still undecided, Davis was damned if he was going to let Fleetwood Mac earn a living without a fight. But with the support of their record label, the band was able to beat off his court order and bring their new music to the fans—both on vinyl and in person.

While winning this legal battle by no means ended the war, the victory considerably brightened the group's outlook. In spite of their exacting tour schedule, hope once again reigned supreme. *Mystery to Me* had leveled off somewhat early in the charts, but Fleetwood Mac attributed the disappointment to the disastrous tour. Surely, they figured, had the show remained on the road, or had they even been allowed to postpone their tour, the album would have broken through into the coveted top ten. Since the band was convinced *Mystery*'s success had been unnaturally stifled by the shenanigans of Clifford Davis, their faith in the current LP's future as a runaway hit was unshakable.

Much to their dismay, they would soon learn that in the music business, as in the rest of life, there are no sure things. Despite their best efforts and a bustling tour schedule, *Heroes* never made it past Number Thirty-four, and the "Heroes Are Hard to Find" single died in obscurity. Although the album was far and away the band's most respectable American outing, the sales figures fell woefully short of the great expectations. Worse still were the vastly diminished performance fees Fleetwood Mac had to settle for in order to prove their mettle after the debacle of the last tour.

No one knew what to make of the disappointing turnout, which should have been better given the touring, a favorable feature in *Rolling Stone*, and the quality of the product. The band could make out no method in the madness of the record-buying public. Not that they didn't have ample time for reflection; in an interview with *People*, Bob would voice his hard-learned wisdom, saying: "Hit singles tap what Jung called the collective unconscious. No one can predict what'll be accepted—not producers, artists, or executives. And not icons, incantations, or voodoo."

———

When it came to setbacks, Fleetwood Mac had nothing on their now-fellow Angelenos, Stevie and Lindsey. The former was once again reduced to the drudgery of waiting tables and cleaning house for producer Keith Olsen, while the latter had found a steady, albeit sketchy, gig as a home-based advertising salesman for a sham business-products directory. Their four-year relationship had long since turned volcanic and was a source of pleasure for neither party. All in all, life was having its way with the onetime up-and-comers, and according to Lindsey the duo was "trying to figure out what to do next."

Contrary to all assumptions, the couple received little assistance in the way of cash from their wealthy relations. "If I wanted to move back home, then they would support me," Stevie assured *Rolling Stone*. "If I was gonna be here in L.A. doing my trip, I was gonna have to do it on my own." Neither was Lindsey's family any more eager to pay his way in L.A. Back in the days of Fritz, he had inherited a tidy sum from one of his aunts. Much to his parents' chagrin, instead of socking it away, Lindsey blew the whole wad on an Ampex four-track tape console. On rare occasions, the parents would contribute to the couple's starving-artist fund, but it was hardly the type of money that would enable the musicians to quit their day jobs.

Although their families refused to bankroll their creative endeavors, Lindsey and Stevie proved that princes make the best paupers. As

Stevie told VH-1, "We were on a mission." Truly, madly, and deeply in love with the idea of making beautiful music together, the couple cared little for their lack of material wealth. While they may have covered the gamut of odd jobs to tide themselves over until the next break came along, selling out their talents was never an option.

Opportunities to lower their standards were ample. Pounding the pavement in search of a new record contract yielded a bumper crop of offers to revamp their act into a top forty cover group and plug into the family restaurant circuit—hardly the creative outlet the duet was looking for. Even in the face of menial labor and near starvation, Stevie and Lindsey wouldn't allow their artistic integrity to fall by the wayside for a mere pittance. Instead they gave up their own place and crashed at the apartment of their friend and former roommate Richard Dashut.

No doubt, much of their self-confident attitude, along with the success to which it would lead, was attributable to their privileged backgrounds and general freedom from deep-seated financial concerns. Nonetheless, hard work for little pay proved to be a demoralizing way of life. Stevie was fast becoming the incredible shrinking woman, losing weight and looking increasingly fragile by the day. Her parents were terrified lest she should fall prey to the hard-knocks life of a music-industry survivor. No way was their little girl going to live out her life praying for a miracle and barely making ends meet. When she paid her family a visit in September 1974, her father saw that she was miserable and wasting away. "He said, 'I think you better start setting some time limits here,' " she told *Rolling Stone*. "They saw, I really think, shades of my grandfather A. J. He was unhappy, trying to make it. He wanted to make it very badly. He turned into a very embittered person, and he died that way."

To complicate matters even further, Stevie's father had recently been rushed to the hospital for open-heart surgery. For a while, nobody knew whether he was going to make it. "From that day onward, I was never, ever the same," an overcome Stevie told *Rolling Stone*. "It was such a horrible thing for me and [my brother] Chris and my mother; Chris passed out. Nothing else mattered; Lindsey didn't matter, music didn't matter, songs didn't matter, nothing mattered more. I said, 'Dear God, I would give everything up if you would just let me keep him for a little while.' "

Stevie took her father's advice to heart and put a six-month limit on her quest for a record deal. At the time, she and Lindsey were still writing songs and recording their second album on a deferred payment plan, courtesy of Keith Olsen. With this six-month deadline hanging over their heads, the couple decided to sojourn to Aspen, Colorado, for a change of pace and a boost of inspiration. "We went to somebody's incredible house, and they had a piano, and I had my guitar with me," recalled Stevie during VH-1's *Storytellers.* "And I went into their living room looking out over the incredible Aspen skyway, and I wrote 'Landslide,' and I also wrote 'Rhiannon.' "

The compositions were intended to appear on the follow-up to the *Buckingham Nicks* album. But as luck would have it, the future held bigger things.

————

When it became evident that *Heroes Are Hard to Find* was not going to be Fleetwood Mac's breakthrough LP, they too began to think about their next record. On a break from the fall 1974 tour, Mick was already scouting potential studios. It was at this time that he was referred to Keith Olsen's Sound City.

"The producer Keith Olsen played me a demo he'd been working on, just to demonstrate the sound of the studio. It turned out to be 'Frozen Love' by Stevie and Lindsey. At that point Lindsey put his head around the door, and we nodded to each other," Mick recollected for the *Independent.* "I remember Lindsey's gorgeous curly hair. He was very handsome."

That day, Mick also saw Stevie and was equally impressed by her beauty. But little did he know that his band would soon be on intimate terms with the two head-turners. In fact, had Fleetwood Mac hit it big with *Heroes,* or had Bob Welch's second marriage not crumbled in the wake of comanaging the Mac, Buckingham Nicks and Fleetwood Mac might never have found a reason to meet.

All "what if?" games aside, as things stood, Fleetwood Mac was balanced on the brink of immortality. Bob Welch was unhappy with the band's stalled progress and with being solely responsible for the lion's share of work. As he would explain to *People,* his state of mind was such that he simply had to quit. He didn't even feel capable of making a worthy artistic contribution to the Mac's next album. Although Christine and the other members assured Bob that he was "such a big part of this band," there were no two ways about it. He said he was "pissed and disgusted and at the end of my rope emotionally. I had no juice or chutzpah left." *Heroes Are Hard to Find* had been Bob's last hoorah with the band he'd called his own for nearly four years.

Of course, the significance of the guitarist's departure in the grand scheme of things escaped his bandmates, who had come to rely upon his friendship and inestimable songwriting skills. But when Bob left the Mac, a long, stagnant period in the band's history went with him. As the clock ticked off the last hours of 1974, the stage was set for a major climax.

5

HARMONIC CONVERGENCE

While most people were going about their holiday shopping, mulling over their resolutions, and counting the days until their New Year's Eve parties of 1979, Stevie Nicks was in a heated race against time, trying to record the Buckingham Nicks LP that would put the duo on the map. With her six-month grace period fast on its way to expiration, every day was of the essence.

Lindsey was also feeling the pressure. While his relationship with Stevie had become almost excruciatingly complicated, they remained very committed. "Stevie and I were not married," Lindsey said, "but we were as good as married." If his girlfriend ever decided to quit the music business, their status as a couple might very well have crumbled. But Lindsey needed Stevie by his side too much to take that chance. After everything they had been through together, any rift in the romance would have horribly painful consequences. Both musicians were running themselves ragged to make sure nothing like that came to pass.

It was only when time came to ring in the New Year that the pair put their worries to rest for the evening. Celebration was in the air,

Keith Olsen was having a soirée, and the night was ripe with possibility. Who knew what the next three months would bring?

As it turned out, an act of divine intervention plucked Stevie and Lindsey out of oblivion right there at Keith Olsen's party, and it came in the form of a simple phone call. It was Mick Fleetwood who, as always, wouldn't let his band take a backseat to something as trifling as New Year's Eve. "When he heard my guitar something obviously clicked in his mind," Lindsey told the *Independent*, "because after the guitarist Bob Welch left, I got a call from Mick asking if I wanted to join Fleetwood Mac."

"We oohed and aahed, and laughed and cried, and said 'We'll call you back,' " recalled Stevie on *Storytellers*. Much was still left to be decided. Did this invitation extend to Stevie? What could Fleetwood Mac do to augment the sound of Buckingham Nicks? Could Buckingham Nicks really help Fleetwood Mac out of its present scrape? Did they even want to? All these questions would have to be answered in the affirmative for the couple to consider joining forces with the Mac.

But on that fateful evening, all Stevie and Lindsey knew for certain was that they still had a fighting chance. During the course of their conversation, Lindsey told Mick, in no uncertain terms, that he and Stevie were "a package deal." All that was left now was to decide whether they wanted to join.

————

"Mick came back and said he'd found this fantastic guitar player," recalled Christine. "We didn't know who the girl was . . . 'cause it was really only the guitar player we were interested in at the time." But Fleetwood Mac has always operated on the go-with-the-flow philosophy, so making room for two proved as easily said as done. Mick wasted no time in relaying Lindsey's sole condition to John and Christine. Foremost in his mind were Christine's feelings on bringing another woman into the band.

Fortunately, Mick's fears proved unfounded. While Christine may have preferred the company of men, she shared her husband's infamous penchant for the sidelines. As she told *Crawdaddy*, "I'm the keyboard player, which keeps me out of the limelight. I enjoy it because

I'm not an extrovert." Once Mick was certain that Christine was in no way averse to sharing the spotlight—be it with a man or a woman—he had all the information he needed to officially incorporate the struggling Buckingham Nicks into his well-established outfit.

Trusting his sharp intuition, he didn't even need to hear the pair play and sing in person. According to Stevie's testimony in *Goldmine* magazine, "He never said, 'Do you want to audition,' or 'Do you want to come over and we'll get to know each other,' or anything. Right from the beginning, it was 'Do you want to join?' " Having given the "Frozen Love" demo more than a casual listen just six weeks earlier, Mick didn't need further convincing. He was absolutely certain that Lindsey and Stevie were exactly what the band needed. "Even though we were looking for a guitarist at first," said Mick, "we found that Stevie and Lindsey came as a duo. Their loyalty to one another was apparent; they were very much a couple, and a powerful package."

As for the would-be recruits, they had no idea what they should do. Aside from Fleetwood Mac's big hit, *Then Play On*—to which Lindsey had listened while trying to learn lead guitar back in the early seventies—the couple had been totally out of the loop where the post–Peter Green Fleetwood Mac was concerned. All that changed when Mick declared his interest. "I went out and bought all the albums," Stevie told *Trouser Press*. "Actually, I think I had asked Mick for them because I couldn't possibly afford to buy them—and I sat in my room and listened to all of them to try to figure out if I could capture any theme or anything. What I came up with was the word 'mystical.' There is something mystical that went all the way from Peter Green's Fleetwood Mac straight through Jeremy, through all of them: Bob Welch, Christine, Mick, and John. It didn't matter who was in the band; it was always just there. Since I have a deep love of the mystical, this appealed to me. I thought this might really be the band for me because they are mystical, they play wonderful rock 'n' roll, and there's another lady so I'll have a pal."

Hence, when Lindsey asked Stevie for her opinion, her immediate response was "I think we can add something to this band." But as the couple was still a bit ambivalent about their newfound prospect, it would take a meeting of the bands to close the deal. "Stevie and I weren't ecstatic about Mick's offer to join Fleetwood Mac," Lindsey once admitted, "because we really believed in what we were doing with our second record." With songs such as "Landslide," "Monday Morning," and "Rhiannon" all worked out, Buckingham Nicks's optimism was hardly unfounded.

In spite of these minor misgivings, Stevie and Lindsey were honored by the offer. When one of their friends, a heavy-duty Mac devotee, told them about seeing the band leave one of their shows in "big black Cadillac limousines," Stevie could hardly believe their luck. "There I was in my waitress's outfit and white nurse's shoes, going 'Oh my God!' and imagining those limos," she told *Goldmine.*

Ultimately, they had no choice but to take a meeting with Fleetwood Mac. The fivesome got together for dinner and casual conversation—no stuffy boardrooms, no business suits, and no legal mumbo jumbo. In classic Mac style, this was the one and only audition Buckingham Nicks would have to pass before gaining entry into Fleetwood Mac. As the three Brits were sizing up the two Americans, and vice versa, an aura of consonance and goodwill enveloped the group. Everyone felt the sense of symmetry inherent in a band featuring two couples and a manager. The chemistry was electrifying. There could be no denying that this was one of those beginning-of-a-beautiful-friendship moments. As Lindsey has since remarked, "When we went up to their house to meet them, that clinched it right there. You could just tell, the five of us in that room, that there was something happening."

By the time dinner was over, there was no question, on either side, whether Stevie and Lindsey were the right people for the job. According to Stevie in *HP de Tijd,* no formal invitation was even necessary. "No one ever said, 'Okay, join us.' At the end of the evening it just went like, 'Next Wednesday we're rehearsing there and there.'" The merger was officially complete, and Fleetwood Mac was now a British-American quintet.

While Stevie and Lindsey may have hemmed and hawed at the outset, in retrospect, Stevie told *Circus:* "It's a good thing that happened right then. Without Mick's offer I think we would have had some serious problems."

All that was left to do now was to see whether this high-voltage rapport translated into the same electricity when it came to actually playing as a group. The outcome was better than anybody could have expected. According to Lindsey, "As soon as we started rehearsing, there was a certain effortlessness." After hearing Chris, Lindsey, and Stevie harmonize, it was clear that Mick's intuition had served the group well yet again. The amalgam of hard-driving rock 'n' roll rhythms and the smooth vocals of the new additions were proof positive that Buckingham Nicks and Fleetwood Mac were meant to be together.

Of course, at the time, nobody in the band had the slightest inkling that this new lineup would immortalize the Fleetwood Mac name. While Stevie and Lindsey seemed dedicated enough, no one suspected that they would remain with the band for over fifteen years, much less that this revamped Mac would soon make the existence of Peter Green's Fleetwood Mac a hazy memory. Chris, John, and Mick had grown used to the constant overhauls in their band's sound and vision. To them, the new front line signified little more than a favorable change in the weather.

And as far as Lindsey and Stevie were concerned, Buckingham Nicks had yet to run out of steam. A few days into the power couple's tenure with the Mac, their Birmingham, Alabama, constituency "called out of the blue and asked us to headline a show there," Lindsey told *Crawdaddy*. "Stevie and I had gone there twice in the previous year to open shows, and apparently our album had sold very well there. So we went to Birmingham and discovered we'd sold out an auditorium. Just blew our minds because we were totally unknown in L.A., couldn't get a gig at a club or anywhere. And here were six thousand people out there going NUTS! We played three dates around there, the great 'Buckingham-Nicks inaugural/farewell tour.' We announced we were joining Fleetwood Mac, and everybody went 'Whaa?' I dunno, we had no idea what we were getting into."

Neither Stevie nor Lindsey had ever been privy to the type of unbridled adulation they encountered in Birmingham. The couple finally felt as if they had accomplished something as a duo: While they may have been considered "nothing" and "nowhere" in the music industry, they were bona fide stars in Birmingham, Alabama. These final shows furnished Buckingham Nicks with an ideal form of closure. As Lindsey told *Rolling Stone*, "We went out in style."

———

When the conquering heroes returned home to their newly adopted bandmates, it was time to plan the forthcoming album. After deciding to entitle the album *Fleetwood Mac*—in order to assert the permanence of the band despite the changing configurations—the musicians immediately buckled down to the task of recording. "We rehearsed for about two weeks and then just cut the LP," Lindsey told *Rock Guitarist.*

Christine McVie was at the ready with her contribution, which included "Say You Love Me" and "Over My Head." And much to the original Mac members' pleasant surprise, all the work Lindsey and Stevie had put into their scrapped second album was perfect for inclusion on *Fleetwood Mac.* "Everything was already worked out. Everything," stated Lindsey.

Going into rehearsal, they had eight album-worthy songs ready for the studio. To round out the record, Stevie suggested that "Crystal," a song that had appeared on the Buckingham Nicks album, be reworked for *Fleetwood Mac.* With only a couple more tracks required to complete the LP, Christine and Lindsey began collaborating on "World Turning." "Christine and I somehow had a common foundation, even though she was trained and I was not," Lindsey explained. "And even though her background was in the blues, we had a very similar musical sense, a very similar melodic sense."

Although Lindsey and Christine were thrilled with the unexpected musical compatibility, someone was feeling hurt and shut out by their camaraderie. In *Spin* magazine, Stevie remembered "getting very upset with Lindsey one night when I realized that he and Christine had written 'World Turning.' I had been with Lindsey all those years and we had never written a song together. Plus, I walked into the studio and they were singing it together."

Lindsey's role had always been to arrange Stevie's songs, but they had never written together. "He just knows how to interpret her," Mick explained in *Goldmine.* "She respected and trusted what Lindsey would do. That was their partnership. Lindsey and Christine had a different relationship, because theirs was much more of a musical one, because she's a player." Despite such strong rationales, Stevie's artistic insecurities must have been triggered by the sight of her boyfriend working with another woman. Deep down, Stevie probably understood that her self-doubts were unsubstantiated—that she was no less a songwriter simply because Lindsey preferred to work with someone else—but this one action of his brought out many of the same feelings that would normally accompany an adulterous affair.

––––––––

While Stevie was trying to get a grip on the new group dynamic, Lindsey was also experiencing his fair share of difficulties. Back in the days of "Buckingham Nicks against the world," it was Lindsey who had held the reins as the uncontested leader and resident creative genius. Now, he was thrown into a situation that was as different from Buckingham Nicks as it was from Fritz, or anything else he had ever encountered. "There's been a lot of adapting to do," he admitted. "When I first joined the group, I had to go and play Bob Welch's songs and all this strange stuff that had nothing to do with me or me growing as an individual." What's more, Lindsey was initially asked to forgo his usual fingerpicking in favor of a flatpick. "I said, 'No, I don't think so.' This is what I do," he told *Guitar World Acoustic.*

As the new kid on the block, the guitarist was often exasperated. He could bring so much to the recording process if people would only try to understand. But with five individuals in the mix, he couldn't always have his own way, and he was unaccustomed to being second-guessed. His main gripe was with John McVie. The two would invariably butt heads whenever one tried to direct the playing of the other. Lindsey was especially angry because of what he saw as John's obtrusive bass playing; John could hardly believe his ears when he heard the rookie trying to steer him in the so-called right direction. "He had very fixed ideas," John later told *Bassplayer,* in response to which, John would only dig his heels in even further. "I would say, 'Look, this is how I feel it.' " Lindsey's natural impulse was to bridle at such staunch opposition, but fuming was about all could do about it.

"I'd think John's playing was too busy, there was too much going on," he later explained to the *Independent.* And while he may have grown to admire John's musical prowess as the years progressed, back in 1975, Lindsey felt pushed into the background and uncertain of his new role in the band. "I had mixed feelings during the first album," he told *Crawdaddy.* "There were things important to me I'd given up for the sake of playing team ball."

Fortunately, personal style didn't figure into Lindsey's list of sacrifices. "There was never any conscious effort to try to fit into their styles other than, say, doing their songs onstage. But even so, I didn't listen to those records and try to copy what was on them. We just started playing, and that was what came out," he told *Rock Guitarist,* adding, "Maybe one of the reasons Fleetwood Mac has been able to survive for so long is that they've been able to change."

The often painful adjustment process did have its rewards. "We really went from nothing to getting two hundred dollars apiece a week, and then in four weeks, four hundred dollars," Stevie told VH-1's *Behind the Music.* While the money was hardly what Stevie and Lindsey considered their raison d'être, it did enable the pair to move into a more spacious apartment and buy some swanky new clothes. Now that she had the means to do it, Stevie was especially interested in putting together a signature style.

The chiffon-draped look with which Stevie would emerge was not the only enduring Fleetwood Mac staple to come out of the first heady months of the Buckingham Nicks–Fleetwood Mac collaboration. It was during the recording of the *Fleetwood Mac* album that cocaine also surfaced in the group. The mid-seventies took a light view of the drug; if everyone was doing it, it couldn't be addictive, much less dangerous. Musicians with no time to spare and money to burn thought of the white fairy dust as a gift from the gods and used it accordingly. Fleetwood Mac was no different. "The subculture of drugs really was considered to be the norm in the circles that we traveled in," said Lindsey.

The impeccable California-pop sound of *Fleetwood Mac* greatly outweighed any drawbacks the new union may have presented. "We did not consciously alter our sound," Christine told *Bam,* "but at the same time, I thought, 'Hmmm. I think this is something special we have got here.' " Certain of their impending good fortune, the band was all set to hit the road when disaster struck.

The completed master tapes of *Fleetwood Mac* had somehow been misplaced. Whether anyone got fired over the gaffe remains undetermined; what is certain, however, is that the band nearly lost their minds searching for their masterpiece, ransacking their studio top to bottom. The tapes were finally found—and just in the nick of time. They had been stashed with a pile of tapes headed for the garbage.

After this close call, there was nothing to keep Fleetwood Mac from going on tour. As usual, the new members did not impede the band from performing their entire repertoire. "We could tell by the first concert we ever did it was going to be good," Christine said in *Stage Life.* "That first show went down like a storm. There was something about the combination of people on the stage that was very special." Ever the quick study, Lindsey skillfully adapted the varied material to his own distinctive fingerpicking style. But it was Stevie who began to blow audiences away. Relating her own spiritual quest to the mystical stylings of Fleetwood Mac past and present, she threw herself into the role of black-caped sorceress—top hat and all. In *Rolling Stone,* Stevie described the look as "my combination of Natalia Makarova and Greta Garbo and the elegant rock and roll that I love."

Swept up by the whirl of her imagination and the twirl of her gossamer, the audiences went wild. She was beautiful, a vision in black. While all this Stevie-directed attention could have irritated her bandmates, they understood that she was both a natural and an asset. "Stevie's a show woman and she loves it," said Christine. "Nobody contrived for Stevie to be a foxy chick. It just emerged. She moves and dances purely because she likes dancing." The performances also made Lindsey look upon his live-in love in an entirely new light. "The kind of role that, say, Stevie and I had towards each other in Buckingham Nicks as compared to what happened six months after we joined Fleetwood Mac—I really had to turn around," he told *Musician Player and Listener* magazine. "It was a very good thing to happen. I gained so much more appreciation for Stevie that way. I had to reevaluate the whole thing."

After spending nearly two months trumpeting their upcoming album to audiences country-wide, Fleetwood Mac headed home satisfied with the effect of their stage show. The new LP was slated for a July release, and the band was in need of some rest before the real touring began.

———

But there would be no rest for Mick Fleetwood. Managing and playing with Fleetwood Mac was much more than a full-time job; it was a lifestyle. After the Clifford Davis trauma, Mick was certain that if he wanted something done right, he would have to do it himself. As he told *Creem,* "I don't really trust anybody. I don't assume that anyone will do anything right. So I'm a compulsive worrier—even if something doesn't go wrong, I'll still be worrying about it."

With this attitude, Mick set about ensuring the success of *Fleetwood Mac*—and the failure of his marriage. Instead of spending time with his wife and two daughters, he embroiled himself in a scheme to secure a big future for the new Mac. A few weeks before the album's release date, Mick had sounded out the executives at the record label. Put off by their lukewarm response to the issue of promotion, the drummer decided to take matters into his own hands. In hopes of orchestrating Fleetwood Mac's first hit single in five years, he hired an independent contractor to sell the radio stations on the LP. But culling a single from the album turned out to be quite an elaborate process.

First to be addressed was the question of which song to choose. "Monday Morning," "Say You Love Me," and "Rhiannon" appeared to be the strongest contenders, but at the last minute, and much to the surprise of the composer, it was decided that Christine's "Over My Head" was going to get the honors. "It was the last track we ever thought would be a single," she told *Goldmine.* Then another producer had to be brought in to create a more radio-friendly version of the song. The finished product had the polished, easy-on-the-ears groove that was ideal for radio exposure.

Finally, the radio stations were biting. The LP was showing robust sales figures. And soon Fleetwood Mac was back on a thirty-five-city tour, enjoying the validation of ever-increasing audiences. "We played constantly and everywhere," said Stevie, "places like Casper, Wyoming, and Normal, Illinois. And people were so wonderful and gave us such good vibes." Everything was going according to the grand plan, and no one could believe how well all the members were getting on. In other words, all hell was about to break loose.

(*Above*) A young
Mick Fleetwood
doing what he does
best, circa 1965
(Photofest)

(*Right*) "Fleetwood"
and "Mac" together:
Mick Fleetwood
(*right*) and John
McVie in 1977
(Photofest)

(*Left*) Mick
Fleetwood all
grown up, 1976
(Photofest)

(*Below*) Mick
Fleetwood in
concert, 1977
(Photofest)

(*Above*) A publicity still for Warner/ Reprise in 1976 (Photofest)

(*Right*) Fleetwood Mac with their new Grammy, 1978 (Frank Edwards/ Fotos International/ Archive)

THE MANY INCARNATIONS OF FLEETWOOD MAC...

(*Above*) *Left to right*: Danny Kirwan, Mick Fleetwood, Jeremy Spencer, John McVie, and Peter Green in 1968 (Photofest)

(*Below*) *Left to right*: Bob Welch, Christine McVie, John McVie, Mick Fleetwood, and Danny Kirwan in 1970 (Photofest)

(*Above*) *Left to right*: Bob Welch, Mick Fleetwood (top), John McVie, and Christine McVie in 1974 (Photofest)

(*Below*) And the final lineup (*left to right*): Mick Fleetwood, Stevie Nicks, John McVie, Christine McVie, and Lindsey Buckingham in 1978 (Photofest)

(*Above*) Stevie Nicks and Christine McVie at the 1978 Grammy Awards (Frank Edwards/Fotos International/ Archive)

(*Left*) Mick Fleetwood and then-wife Jenny at the Palladium in 1976 (Frank Edwards/Fotos International/ Archive)

Stevie Nicks leads the USC Trojan Marching Band during halftime festivities in 1980
(Archive)

(*Above*) On her own:
Stevie Nicks during
her first solo HBO
Special in 1982
(Photofest)

(*Right*) A shaven,
shorn, and solo
Lindsey Buckingham
in 1984 (Photofest)

———

Turning thirty had not mellowed John McVie. If anything, the perpetually changing front line and the constant pressure to make ends meet
had only aggravated his drinking problem. "I drink too much, period,"
he told *Rolling Stone*, "but when I've drunk too much, a personality
comes out. It's not very pleasant to be around."

On countless occasions Christine had implored her husband to lay
off the bottle. For years she had put many of her own needs aside to
minister to her husband, but he had taken all her care for granted. In
spite of his great love for Christine, he continued to disregard her pleas.
Finally, she could take it no more. It was either stay with John and
grow to hate him, or leave her love intact by ending the marriage.

With months still left to tour, Christine had to summon all her resolve to do what she knew to be the right thing. "I broke up with John
in the middle of a tour," she explained. "I was aware of it being rather
irresponsible. I had to do it for my sanity. It was either that or me ending up in a lunatic asylum."

"Being on the road, for a start, and living together, and seeing everybody at their best and their worst, literally their worst, she said, 'That's
enough,' " John explained. "We talked about it and made the decision."
While the legal divorce would take some time, the McVies' marriage
was beyond repair. "I still have a lot of love for John," Christine would
tell *Rolling Stone* two years later. "Let's face it, as far as I'm concerned,
it was him that stopped me loving him. He constantly tested what limits of endurance I would go to. He just went one step too far."

John's anguish at losing Christine was not lessened by the realization that he had no one but himself to blame, while watching the man
she loved descend into depression pained Christine to no end. "It was
awful," John said, "because you're told by someone you adore and
love that 'I don't want you in my life anymore.' " In spite of the emotional fallout, all signs were pointing toward professional success, and
the show had to go on for the sake of all involved. Through sheer force
of will, and with a lot of help from their bandmates, the couple managed to persevere in spite of their personal torment.

———

All things being relative, Mick Fleetwood was the lucky one. At the very least, he could say that he didn't work with his wife. But he could add that he didn't live with her either. Too much togetherness was partly to blame for the downfall of John and Christine's marriage, and a paucity of shared moments had had the same effect in the Fleetwood household.

Predictably enough, the drummer had no clue that his marriage was coming apart. "I was basically having a ball being crazy and being socially how I wanted to be," Mick told VH-1. With his band's popularity on the upswing, he was more Mac-obssessed than ever. Stevie and Lindsey's presence added a youthful vitality to the old-time British blues band, turning Fleetwood Mac into something akin to party central. As John put it, "It seemed we were sort of traveling in this bubble called 'us.' " But while the successful debut of *Fleetwood Mac* gave the band a new lease on life and helped Mick attack his management duties with renewed vigor, his family could go for months without seeing their busy breadwinner.

Angry with her dream-chasing husband, yet unable to vent her feelings, Jenny was at an impasse. It would take a near nervous breakdown for her to express all the bottled-up rage and resentment she had been feeling. "It happened at a barbecue at our house," she said. "I just snapped. I began to punch and pummel Mick in front of everybody. I was screaming and hysterical. I looked up and saw that Mick had a helpless look on his face. He didn't know what was wrong because he didn't know how unhappy I was."

Jenny had reached her breaking point. The various conjugal woes she had tried for years to supress had surfaced in one frantic volley of blows. It was as if all her feelings of abandonment and resentment had taken on a life of their own, and there was no denying now that the marriage was in a state of crisis. Soon after this scene, the drummer was on his own. "I was stoned half the time," Mick told VH-1's *Behind the Music.* "I watched them walk down the garden path, just in slow motion, going 'Well, there's my wife and there's my two children walking out of my life.' It was all like a dream."

———

The Mac's newest members were not exempt from the general havoc that followed *Fleetwood Mac*'s release. As soon as the music critics got hold of the album, they immediately tore into Stevie, pummeling the quality of her voice from every conceivable angle. "They said my singing was 'callow,' and that really hurt my feelings," she later told *Rolling Stone*—referring to the magazine's own less-than-generous review of some years past. "Time after time I would read: '. . . the raucous voice of Stevie Nicks and the golden-throated voice of Christine McVie, who's the only saving grace of the band.' "

Suddenly, Stevie wasn't so sure that show business was the life for her. The old doubts returned. What if she *had* only been allowed into the band at Lindsey's insistence? While she loved to sing, dance, and perform, touring and recording was a lot of hard work. As it had been some time since the band had made any serious money for the record label, the travel accommodations were all but non-existent. Fleetwood Mac crossed the country in a pair of battered station wagons, lodged in fleabag motels, ate strictly on the go, and inhaled vast quantities of cocaine on a daily basis. The last thing Stevie wanted was to add to the band's problems. If all she was was a burden, she was prepared to take her leave.

One would think that the audiences' mass approval would have had the power to counterbalance the critics' harsh words. But to an insecure twenty-seven-year-old just stepping into the glare of the limelight, one truculent review was enough to make a world of praise disappear. Stevie would often express her willingness to leave, telling *Rolling Stone*, "If I'm not wanted, I'll get out." Of course, no one in the band would hear of it.

Unfortunately, Lindsey wasn't able to give his girlfriend the unconditional support she was after. The dynamic between the couple was bound to change now that they were part of a larger picture and no longer a duo. While Stevie was coming into her own and beginning to claim more space, both onstage and off, Lindsey remained as much in need of her attention as ever. Outwardly, he appeared headstrong and independent, but underneath this tough exterior was a person who had grown used to having a particular woman by his side, supportive of his interests. Instead of focusing on the alleviation of Stevie's self-doubts, Lindsey only added to her anxiety by finding fault with her performances. "It bothered him when the audience would go crazy about me," admitted Stevie. "He thought that I, being his girlfriend, was acting too sexy on stage, with my dancing and all that. But I like doing that. I've told him: I can't be your Stevie up there. I'm not telling him how to act up there."

Somehow, Stevie worked through her pain and emerged with a hard-won self-confidence. Whatever ambivalence and apprehension she may have been feeling offstage, she managed to cut a powerful figure in concert. "It's not like I just go onstage and sing every night, I SCREAM," she told *Crawdaddy*. "And crash [a] tambourine on my leg and dance around a lot. It's almost an athletic trip for me 'cause I've never been very strong. In fact, I'm like a snake all day, just grooving along slowly. Then for two hours onstage I have all that energy. Afterwards, I'm a basket case."

Considering the five-inch heels she wore to offset her diminutive stature, the eyeglasses she left backstage to present a glamorous image, and the fancy footwork she used to intrigue the audience, it's no wonder that on several occasions Stevie nearly toppled off the stage. Yet not even the threat of bodily harm could stop the fearless female. During each and every performance, she would throw herself headlong into "Rhiannon," a stirring number about a Welsh witch who controls the birdsong that relieves all pain and suffering. "That's what music is to me," she told *Rolling Stone*.

Contrary to popular belief, Stevie had no idea what the lyrics of "Rhiannon" would come to mean to her when she first wrote them. The song came from one of the characters' names in *Triad*, a book she had been given by a friend. "I just thought it was a really beautiful name," she told *Storytellers*. "I thought, 'If I ever have a little girl, maybe I'll name her Rhiannon.' And that's really what I took to the piano to write this song."

Eventually, Stevie would learn about the legend of the Celtic goddess. Armed with this knowledge, she would gain a deeper understanding of the words she herself had written months before. This new awareness would inform her stage act, making it all the more intense. Raised on Hans Christian Anderson and the Brothers Grimm, Stevie had a real flair for the fantastic. So instead of simply singing about Rhiannon, she became her. " 'Rhiannon' is the heavy-duty song to sing every night," she said. "Onstage it's really a mind tripper. Everybody, including me, is just blitzed by the end of it. And I put out so much in that song that I'm nearly down." But the result was always well worth the exertion. Every rendition would meet with the fans' boisterous applause, helping to ease the doubts that plagued Fleetwood Mac's newest rising star.

But once the show was over, the nagging fears would often return. It was only when "Over My Head," a song on which Stevie's voice figured prominently, became Fleetwood Mac's first-ever U.S. hit single that Stevie was finally able to put all her self-doubt to rest. Since the public had no objection with the way she sang, Stevie wasn't about to let the critics' poisoned pens bring her down again.

———

By December of 1975, it was all over. Emotionally disemboweling as the six-month tour had been, it was the one that brought Fleetwood Mac's five-year quest for reascendance to fruition. Their album had gone gold, the "Over My Head" single had reached Number Seven on the *Billboard* charts, and Fleetwood Mac was no longer an inconspicuous name known only to an initiated few. They were now the musical version of the awe-inspiring little engine that could.

Exactly one year had passed since Stevie and Lindsey joined the band. For them, 1975 had been both pivotal and bittersweet. "We were not famous. The record had just come out. We hit the road," Stevie told *Bam.* "Then, within three months, we were all famous and on our way with the hits." The holidays would bring a welcome respite from the laborious touring, but no amount of Christmas cheer could resuscitate the personal lives that had been sacrificed to the road.

6

BAND ON
THE BRINK

Many thought that the sudden success of Fleetwood Mac was doomed to end just as it had begun. After all, while the band might have garnered much recognition via their big single, the only venues in which they were headlining were still of the small, three- to five-thousand-seat variety. For the most part, the Mac had yet to break free of its opening-act image. But people entertaining notions of Fleetwood Mac's inevitable decline had cause to stop and reevaluate when "Rhiannon" came wailing out of their car radios—and not just once or twice a day, either, but enough times to permanently embed the lyrics in pop-listening America's collective gray matter.

Prior to this second coming, few would have predicted that the words "Fleetwood Mac" and "top forty" would ever peacefully coexist within the same sentence—much less that one day "Fleetwood Mac" would become a two-word synonym for the musical mainstream. While this day would dawn only one year after "Rhiannon" projected *Fleetwood Mac* into the platinum dimension, the climb to the pinnacle of white-hot stardom would be gradual. At least, that's how it would seem to the band members themselves.

Without actually going to anyone's head, several months of steady success had contrived to destroy all three of the long-term relationships involved in the band. John and Christine's had been the first union to bite the dust. Mick and Jenny had soon followed suit. Now Buckingham and Nicks were under twenty-four-hour breakup surveillance. "We had a lot of problems by the time we joined," Lindsey divulged to *Microsoft Music Central.* But although their troubles had started long before Fleetwood Mac came along, the change of pace certainly didn't help matters any. After seeing two marriages fold under pressure, there was little reason for anyone to expect that the Buckingham-Nicks union would last out another year.

The massive attention lavished upon Stevie was one of the factors contributing to the relationship's demise. "Rhiannon" was released as a single in January 1976. While it never made its way into the top ten, cresting only at Number Eleven on the U.S. charts, it was nonetheless a hugely popular rock number that made Stevie Nicks's transformation into Fleetwood Mac's ornate centerpiece a fait accompli. Suddenly, the previously nondescript ensemble had a readily identifiable grand dame within its ranks.

Since Fleetwood Mac had never put much stock in lead vocalists, the band's mutated image was better received by the fans than by Stevie's fellow musicians. Peter Green's ambivalence toward the role of frontman-as-rock-icon had set the precedent for the band's career, and for years the band was able to alter its personnel at will, without so much as a murmur from its core following. But Stevie's lovely face and larger-than-life persona had changed all that. Out of nowhere, people wanted to interview, photograph, and canonize her—and her alone.

This shift in perspective was not so much a product of Stevie's calculated manipulation as an organic outgrowth of Christine and Lindsey's onstage reserve. Still, the group's resentment was an inevitability. As she later told *Spin,* "My success was not easy for Lindsey, not easy for any of them. And I knew that, and I felt terrible about it. There's a part of me that would have said, 'Let's tell everybody to stop talking about Stevie. Stop giving Stevie all this attention, because, guess what, it's making Stevie miserable. Because I have to live with these four other people who know it's not my fault, but they can't help but blame me a little, and it's killing me.' "

———

Lindsey had good cause to feel somewhat indignant. Considering his key role in the formulation of *Fleetwood Mac,* the neglect he received at the hands of the public was especially irritating. As he himself told Timothy White, author of *Rock Lives,* "If I had to choose my main contributing factor to the band, it wouldn't be as a guitarist, a writer, or a singer. It would be as someone who knows how to take raw material from Christine and Stevie and forge that into something. That's a nice gift to have, and to be able to help people with."

To qualify Lindsey's contribution as tremendous is perhaps to understate the matter, and everyone in the studio knew it. But rarely do audiences demand an encore from the producer or the music arranger. The standing ovations, the fan mail, the on-sight recognition, and all the rest of stardom's trappings usually go to the squeakiest wheel of any vehicle. And on the Fleetwood Mac caravan, that wheel had Stevie written all over it.

Stevie has been remarkably candid about Lindsey's impact on her music. "I write my songs, but Lindsey puts the magic in," she plainly admitted to *Rolling Stone.* "If I were to play you a song the way I wrote it and gave it to them, and then play you the way it is on the album, you would see what Lindsey did." Yet there was nothing she could say to diminish her own mystique and loosen her hold over the audience.

According to the bewitching frontwoman, Lindsey was displeased with the way she began to assert herself as her confidence grew. While he may have accepted Stevie as a leading lady on the stage, he was uncomfortable with the mere possibility of any such shenanigans infiltrating their personal affairs. "We are talking about a man," she told *Bam,* "who was in love with a woman, and would just as soon she had faded out and just been his old lady or wife. Period."

In view of the couple's admittedly competitive relationship, Lindsey's rather negative reaction to his girlfriend's success was unavoidable. "Even when we were lovers, we never were really best friends," he said during a BBC radio interview. "We've always competed . . . ever since we started going together back in 1971. There was always tension on a musical level . . . even though we were excellent lovers, we were competitors as well." Stevie seconded Lindsey's sentiments, telling the *Record* that "when you go with somebody for six or seven years and you're a woman and the guy you're with is a man who is a guitarist/songwriter . . . and so are you, there's always going to be an ego problem just because of the relationship."

Such was the musical aspect of the foundation upon which Lindsey and Stevie's relationship was built. While the romance had also thrived on love, passion, and shared aspirations, fame was quickly expanding its influence over their lives. And as Stevie and Lindsey's competitive working relationship swallowed up everything that had once made the coupling viable, their personal relationship was left in a state of terminal dysfunction.

———

Meanwhile, John McVie was undergoing the brutal pangs of postseparation anxiety. Christine had never been much of a swinger. Prior to meeting John, she had been involved in a two-year relationship that ended with a broken engagement and a heart to match. ("I just ran around the house screaming when he left me," she has said.) Now that she and John were no longer one, Christine took up with Fleetwood Mac's lighting director, Curry Grant.

For some time, she managed to keep their affair a secret, but as the two became more serious about one another, that became increasingly difficult. As John's suspicions mounted, he became consumed with jealousy. "John can't handle Curry too well," Christine told *Rolling Stone*, "even though he's much more at ease with other women around me than I am with men in front of him. He's making an effort, but if I was the kind of girl who wandered in with a new boyfriend every week, enjoying my newfound freedom, I don't know how he could handle that."

Ever since the separation, John had been sullen and morose. His whole way of life had been turned upside down. Aside from the band, Christine had been his only constant. While he tried to summon up interest in other women, Christine's omnipresence within Fleetwood Mac made all distractions impossible. Unable to express his emotions through song, he sought salvation at the bottom of any bottle he came across. When Curry Grant entered the picture, there was no denying that John and Christine were now married in name only. His moods took a turn for the worse, and the band knew what had to be done. They would have to find themselves a new lighting director.

By all rights, Christine could very well have thrown a tantrum. Now that she was a free woman, she could date whomever she chose without interference. But she was not one to stand on principle when the feelings of the man she still loved were at stake. Curry Grant was dismissed, and the matter was settled without further ado.

———————

In January 1976, the band was in Los Angeles. Preparations for recording the sequel to *Fleetwood Mac* were underway. Since the album was still riding the charts, there was no apparent need to hurry. But the multimillion-dollar success of *Fleetwood Mac* had considerably upped the ante. When the band played now, people listened. Even the record company was rolling out the red carpet for their newest stars, as well as bearing down on the band to produce another money-maker. "Suddenly we had a definite reason for doing a great job," said the band's producer/engineer Richard Dashut. Everyone knew that it could all be over tomorrow if they failed to come up with an equally stellar follow-up. Like any other outfit, what Fleetwood Mac wanted most was staying power, and despite their own private hell, they were motivated to prove that it hadn't all been a fluke.

As usual, Mick was charged with the task of finding an appropriate studio. By this time, his trial separation from Jenny had ended in divorce. With all his professional responsibilities, there were simply not enough hours in the day to effect a mutually satisfying reconciliation. As he surveyed the recording studio scene in L.A., Mick was constantly being reminded of the band's many problems: Christine was living with Curry Grant; Stevie and Lindsey were going through a messy breakup; and he and John were both alone, and none too happy about it. "Mick was very insistent about taking everybody out of that environment," recalled Richard Dashut.

But it was exactly this state of turmoil that brought about some of the best songs ever to come out of Fleetwood Mac. Christine's relationship with Curry Grant was the impetus for the affecting "You Make

Loving Fun," just as her concern for John was poured into "Don't Stop." Lindsey and Stevie's knock-down-drag-out fights inspired such classic numbers as "Go Your Own Way" and "Dreams."

In February, Mick hit upon the idea to record the next album at the Record Plant in Sausalito. While the songwriters groused that they wanted to remain close to home, Mick and John were bent on skipping town. "I went, 'Great. We're out of Los Angeles. At least we'll be focused," recalled John. And since there was no dissuading Mick from his purpose, the band had no choice but to follow the leader to Sausalito. "I don't know why Mick wanted to do it there, but Sausalito was filled with freaks back then," Lindsey told *Guitar World*. To this day, it remains unclear why Mick decided on this particular site. The Northern California Record Plant did come equipped with offsite musicians' lodging, so perhaps his primary concern was simply to escape L.A. Nonetheless, located right across the Bay from San Francisco, Sausalito was hardly what one would have called a peaceful hideaway.

———

When the recording sessions for the as-yet-untitled *Rumours* album began in early February, *Fleetwood Mac* was still very much alive and kicking on the *Billboard* charts. The past six months had seen everyone in the band go from rags to riches and inconceivable fame. The whole idea was to strike while the iron was hot. The Mac had grown accustomed to a speedy recording process, and they were set on wrapping up their studio work in two months' time.

The deadlines were set as the band set out for San Francisco. The guys quickly laid claim to the Record Plant's proffered digs in nearby Berkeley Hills. "It was like a bordello, basically, with blacked-out rooms, thick shag carpets, and deprivation tanks," Mick recounted in the *Independent*. Meanwhile, the gals were left to fend for themselves in a condominium building where they had rented two apartments. Here, the Mac's female contingent bonded, becoming friends rather than just colleagues. "All we had was each other, really," Christine recalled. "We certainly weren't getting on with our respective husbands or boyfriends."

When Stevie and Lindsey had declared that they would not be living together, it was clear to all that their relationship was careening toward a deadlock. But as Stevie later told *Rolling Stone,* "Lindsey and I were still together enough that he would come up there and sleep every once in a while." Christine would also entertain her then-boyfriend, Curry Grant—who was not welcome in the studio—whenever he came to visit.

Although John and Mick were busy cultivating their own fleeting relationships at the Berkeley compound, neither was feeling any better about his suddenly single status. Their dwelling turned into an all-hours party house. According to John's description in *Rolling Stone,* the scene was "Amazing. Terrifying. Huge amounts of illicit materials, yards and yards of this wretched stuff. Days and nights would just go on and on." In fact, many a time, Christine was forced to hide out in Stevie's apartment when John showed up unannounced and stark raving drunk. "It was horrible," Stevie recalled with a shudder.

Most of the time, however, the band was tied up in the studio. "Lindsey took the point on the *Rumours* album," said Richard Dashut. "He was the one with the strongest opinion. He probably had more vision than any of us." After listening to the various songs his fellow writers brought to the table, Lindsey voiced his ideas and was quickly given a significant measure of creative control. From that point on, it was just a matter of recording, arranging, and polishing the tracks.

For everything to be done on time, the band had to spend excruciating eighteen-hour days at the windowless Record Plant, the studio that Sly Stone also called home at the time. The long hours had the musicians vacillating between abysmal boredom and mind-boggling frustration. Aside from Lindsey, whose musical problem-solving skills were in perpetual demand on the production front, the band members were often at a loss for activity while waiting for their turn to record.

The band's prodigious cocaine and alcohol consumption was attributable, at least in part, to the prevailing feeling of ennui. They had become so blasé about indulging their addictions on the job that when a "thousand-dollar" batch of hashish-laden cookies was presented to the busy band by some visiting friends, the musicians, along with their production staff, cast aside their differences and bonded by finishing off the entire lot.

The fact that the band members were scarcely on speaking terms for much of the time also fueled the drug abuse, which was often the sole link bringing the warring factions together. John and Christine were avoiding each other at all costs, while Lindsey and Stevie were acting like a couple of hellions intent on a rumble. Every silence was pregnant with ominous meaning, and all interaction was stunted and awkward, if not downright belligerent. It was no doubt this period to which Christine was referring when she told the *Los Angeles Times* that "there was a time when being in this band was no fun at all. What we did was stay out of each other's way and let the dust settle and let the wounds heal." It almost seemed as if the situation could not get any worse. Then Fleetwood Mac's last standing couple parted ways in what, today, has come to seem like a blaze of glory.

––––––

Although Stevie and Lindsey's breakup inspired a surplus of flowery lyrics, there was nothing poetic about the countless fights that led up to the final showdown. Now that the middle ground between work and sleep had been pulled out from under them, the relationship was at its weakest. Work had always wrought the most damage on their relationship, and the recording of *Rumours* proved to be the last straw.

The problems in the studio never failed follow the couple into the bedroom. Meeting the requirements of her dual role, as Lindsey's girlfriend and as his bandmate, was getting to be impossible for Stevie. "We'd go back to where we were staying and he would really need comfort from me, for me to say, 'It's all right. Who cares about them?' You know, be an old lady," she told *Rolling Stone*. "One problem. I was also pissed off because he hadn't gotten the guitar part on. So I'm trying to defend their point of view and at the same time trying to make him feel better. It doesn't work. I couldn't be all those things."

Other bones of contention included certain lyrics with which Stevie took issue. Born out of the pair's innumerable quarrels, the song "Go Your Own Way" included a line that sent Stevie through the roof. She couldn't reconcile herself to the words "shacking up is all you want to do," when, in fact, all she wanted was her freedom. "I very very much resented him telling the world that 'packing up, shacking up' with different men was all I wanted to do," she would later tell *Rolling Stone*.

"He knew it wasn't true. It was just an angry thing that he said. Every time those words would come onstage, I wanted to go over and kill him. He knew it, so he really pushed my buttons through that."

As Lindsey toiled under the weight of his self-imposed responsibility for bringing the album together, he was utterly wrapped up in the many ideas spinning around in his head. "All he wanted to do was fall asleep with that guitar," Stevie remarked in a subsequent interview. Yet what he didn't want was to end the relationship. Stevie had been the one looking for an escape. Having long since lost the bloom of youth, their romance was anything but romantic. "With Christine and John it was over really quick," Lindsey told *Guitar World.* "Whereas Stevie and I were more like, 'Well I don't know. . . .' There were times when we were sleeping together and times when we were officially something else. But there was definitely a moving apart." At this point, the only thing keeping the pair together was fear. Lindsey hadn't been without a girlfriend in nearly a decade and, furthermore, had grown comfortable with having Stevie for a partner, while Stevie simply dreaded the prospect of being hated by a person whom she would have to continue seeing every day and upon whom she relied to bring her songs together.

Finally, no matter how hard they tried to stick it out, the bottom line remained the same. The relationship was devoid of all pleasure. It drained both songwriters spiritually, emotionally, and creatively, and Stevie knew it had to be stopped. "I don't even remember what the issues were," she said. "I just remember that it got to the point where I wanted to be by myself. It just wasn't good anymore, wasn't fun anymore, wasn't good for either of us. I'm just the one who stopped it."

Much like John, Lindsey would need time to accept the termination of his long-standing union, especially because, as Stevie described to *Rolling Stone,* the relationship ended on a very abrupt note. "We had a terrible fight—I don't remember what about, but I remember him walking out and me saying, 'You take the car with all the stuff, and I'm flying back.' " To be sure, he was devastated by the separation, as there was never any doubt that he had truly loved Stevie. The passionate nature of this last confrontation left a lingering possibility of a rapprochement, but for the time being, neither party wanted to make a move in that direction.

In essence, Lindsey was left with no one to turn to. Despite his ex-girlfriend's daily attempts to keep the peace, the residual anger with which Lindsey suddenly found himself saddled had only one outlet—the Record Plant. No longer capable of influencing his private relationship with Stevie, Lindsey now directed his feelings of hostility toward sabotaging the onetime couple's professional interaction.

———

"We're your everyday soap opera," Christine told *Newsweek*. Truer words had never been spoken. Fleetwood Mac's romantic confusion was inescapable. Only by retiring to their respective homes after something like twenty hours in the studio could the bandmates evade seeing the pain they'd inflicted on the ones they loved. The situation was especially difficult for Christine and John. With a reserve typical of their English roots, the two spent much of their studio time perfecting the tactics of eye-contact evasion. Neither was able to speak an unnecessary word to the other.

Yet the whole while, Christine's songs were playing in the background. Their warm lyrics of hope and love everlasting, written for John, contrasted starkly to the chill wind blowing through the Record Plant's Studio B. But while Christine was finding solace in the arms of another man, John was alone. Seeing the impassive face of his one great love and listening to her songs everyday was an overwhelmingly depressing experience. "I'm sitting there in the studio and I get a little lump in my throat," John told *Rolling Stone,* "especially when you turn around and the writer's sitting right there."

To numb the heartache, he threw himself into a relationship with Peter Green's former consort, Sandra Elsdon. While back in 1970 Peter's drug use had forced her to break off the relationship, the studio's vats of cocaine, marijuana, and alcohol posed nary a problem for Sandra in 1976—drugs had become that implicit in the creative sphere. "In those days," Christine told *Rolling Stone,* "it was quite natural to walk around with a great old sack of cocaine in your pocket and do these huge rails, popping acid, making hash cookies." Stevie agreed, telling *Spin* that drugs were "just the friendly, fun thing to do. I swear to God, that's how it was."

All the while, Stevie and Lindsey's onsite relationship was fast on its way to becoming as stormy as their love affair had once been. Their collaboration had never been a simple matter of quid pro quo. Although Stevie's lyrics were always beautiful, poetic, and ethereal, her song construction was primitive. She needed Lindsey's special production talents to elaborate her simplistic instrumentals and bring out the magic of her tunes. Now that they were no longer together, Lindsey had the upper hand, and they both knew it.

They also knew that if they were going to act in the best interests of the band, they had better keep their professional relationship intact. But when the infighting reached fever pitch, Lindsey would understandably rebuff Stevie's requests for assistance. As Stevie explained her former flame's attitude to *Rolling Stone:* "So you don't want to be my wife, my girlfriend, but you want me to do all that magic stuff on your songs. Is there anything else that you want, just, like, in my spare time?"

Of course, Stevie could not help but view this as blatant emotional blackmail. "In the studio, if Lindsey said the wall was gray, I would be absolutely sure it was pink," she told *Bam* magazine. "In order to get one of my songs on a record I would have to say, 'Okay, the wall is gray, Lindsey.' Otherwise, it was the back of the bus." In light of the rupture she had so recently instigated, many of the ax man's unpleasant behaviors appeared to be motivated by revenge. For years, Stevie would rail against Lindsey's unprofessional conduct to any journalist who would listen. As recently as October 1997, *Spin* magazine quoted her as saying, "He could take my songs and do what I would do if I had his musical talent. When he wasn't angry with me, that is. That's why there's seven or eight great songs, and there's fifty more where he wasn't happy with me and didn't help me."

To be fair, Lindsey's efforts to remain supportive also bear mentioning. He was well aware that he could take full advantage of his position, and while it may have done his aching heart good to watch Stevie suffer, he abstained from indulging the hostile impulse and stuck to the high road. "I'd always been this kind of soulmate who always somehow knew what to do with her music—how to complement it and bring out its best," he explained in *Guitar World.* "But there were times when I really had the urge not to do that. . . . So I had to keep check-

ing myself—keep challenging myself to be a better person than I felt
like being at times."

————

Such were the times that tried Fleetwood Mac's souls and forced them
to extend their deadlines indefinitely. But love-induced traumas
weren't all to blame; the band was also beset by other difficulties from
the outset. First, the original engineer's delusions of grandeur caused
the band to turn on him, hiring Lindsey's old pal, Richard Dashut, in
his stead. "Deke Richards was originally scheduled to engineer
Rumours," Richard told *Modern Recording* magazine. "I remember
meeting him at a party shortly before recording was due to begin. The
band had asked me to second on the album, and I approached Deke
and told him how much I was looking forward to working with him."

"Oh, I guess you haven't heard, I've got my own engineer I work
with," Deke said.

"I thought you were the engineer," said Richard, confused.

"No, I'm producing."

When the band learned of Deke Richard's designs, Mick wasted no
time sending him on his way. "The thing is, Fleetwood Mac doesn't
hire producers," explained Richard. "They are capable on their own.
They don't need someone shouting in from the control room telling
them what to do." In retrospect, the addition of Richard was a stroke
of genius. As Christine explained to *Bam,* it was Richard, as well as
Lindsey, who was "at the fore, without question, when it came to the
ideas, and the sound and the production. And they were very good at
it."

Despite their talent, the two visionaries could do little to work past
the many travails of Christine's pianos. One out-of-tune piano didn't
necessarily signify a recording delay, but by the time the number of dis-
carded pianos reached a grand total of seven, thousands of dollars'
worth of studio time had gone to waste. "It was a very self-indulgent
time," recalled John in *Bassplayer.* "There was no limit, and no one
knew when to say, 'That's enough!'"

In the frenzy to complete the sessions on time, the band often remained in the studio way past the wee hours. Quitting times of five

A.M. were not uncommon as the musicians tried to nail the right sound irrespective of the clock and the fatigue. At an hour when farmhouse roosters were just beginning their song, innumerable directions such as "I think we should go for one more take to get a little brighter mood" or "This is really more of a cocaine song, than it is an alcohol song" would still be emanating from the Sausalito control room. "We'd work all night," John explained to *Bassplayer,* "and at ten o'clock in the morning, we'd be standing outside a pub waiting for it to open so we could have a nightcap, which would end at two in the afternoon."

On one such night, Stevie recorded her haunting "Gold Dust Woman." The weeks of sleep deprivation and overwork had weakened her immune system, but she was determined to persevere in spite of her cold. "She did her first take of 'Gold Dust Woman' in a fully lit studio," Mick told *Goldmine,* "and as take followed take, she began withdrawing into herself. So we dimmed the lights, brought her a chair, a supply of tissues, a Vicks inhaler, a box of lozenges for her sore throat, and a bottle of mineral water. And on the eighth take, at four in the morning, she sang the lyric straight through to perfection."

Her bandmates just looked on from the control room, in awe of the fragile young woman's hidden strength. But Stevie had known all along that she would have to nail the song right then and there. Since the conditions under which she was recording the song mirrored the circumstances that had first inspired the song itself, she understood that never again would her mental state so perfectly correspond to the lyrics of "Gold Dust Woman." As she explained in the *Rumours* rockumentary, "I don't think I had ever been so tired in my whole life as I was when we were doing that. The whole rock 'n' roll life was really heavy, and it was so much work, and it was so everyday intense, you know. Being in Fleetwood Mac was like being in the army. It was like you have to be there. You have to be there, and you have to be there as on time as you can be there. And even if there's nothing you have to do, you have to be there. So 'Gold Dust Woman' was really my kind of symbolic look at somebody going through a bad relationship, and doing a lot of drugs, and trying to just make it. Trying to live, you know, trying to get through it to the next thing."

———

Breaking new ground as a female rock icon has never been easy. But the task proved especially difficult for Stevie, as she was forced to witness the vivisection of her songs at the hands of her ex-boyfriend on a daily basis. Lindsey's often cutting comments in regard to her compositions did not fall on deaf ears. The criticism gradually ate away at Stevie's self-confidence to the point where she began to hesitate before bringing a song she'd written to the group.

But the day she wrote "Dreams," not even the threat of Lindsey's thinly veiled gibes could keep Stevie from showing off her handiwork to the rest of the band. Feeling useless, but stuck at the studio for the duration, Stevie had gone downstairs into Sly's luxurious pit. The band members often had occasion to use this room while it was unoccupied, and luckily, on this particular day, the room was empty. Her portable Fender Rhodes piano in hand, Stevie sat down on Sly's "fabulous" round bed and proceeded to write "Dreams." When she read over what she'd written, there wasn't a doubt in her mind as to whether the song was worthy of the album. "I knew when I wrote it that it was really special," she said during *The Making of Rumours.* "I was really not self-conscious or insecure about showing it to the rest of the band. I knew that they were gonna really like it."

The song would be one of the eleven tracks chosen to appear on the *Rumours* LP. Just like the others, "Dreams" laid bare the raw emotion behind the ubiquitous catchphrase "breaking up is hard to do." But while most of Lindsey and Stevie's songs had to do with one another, Christine's contributions were all inclusive. While she may have written "Don't Stop" with the expressed intention of lifting John's spirits, "Songbird" tried to do the same for the all her fellow bandmates. Then, with "Oh Daddy," it was Mick whom Christine singled out for recognition. The only actual daddy among the group, Mick was also the band's father figure, doing all he could to straighten out the priorities of his troubled children. In an interview with *Rolling Stone,* Christine invoked Mick's never-changing maxim, "We must carry on. . . . Let's be mature about this, sort it out."

"You Make Loving Fun" alone had nothing to do with the band, and everything to do with Christine. After the split from John, Christine hoped to find happiness with Curry Grant and expressed her longing in song. But as her own words would reveal, reality may not have fulfilled her most ardent dreams. " 'You Make Loving Fun' is an idealistic song about a point in my life when I was pretty unhappy with myself," she told the *New York Post.* "It's a fantasy, to be sure, but I love fantasy."

————

As April 1976 rounded the bend, so did the last days of Fleetwood Mac's Sausalito sessions. They had booked the Record Plant's studios for nine weeks, thinking this would be enough time both to record the album and to mend their broken hearts. Obviously, the plan had backfired. Not only was the finish line nowhere in sight, but the forced familiarity had bred contempt among the ranks.

Even Mick, whose personal life didn't seem to impinge upon the band, was in the midst of a gut-wrenching situation. "I was not spared at all," he said on *The Making of Rumours.* "My best friend was having an affair with my wife Jenny." After Jenny had moved back to England, she had begun dating Andy Silvester, Mick's good friend and a former member of the Chicken Shack. Now that the two were living together in Los Angeles, Mick's numerous second thoughts about the divorce were beginning to make him miserable.

While the band members often maintained that they were kept together by a prevailing sense of family, the Stevie Nicks statement that appeared in *HP de Tijd* rang the truest. "No one actually thought about leaving the band," she confided. "I thought: I'd be crazy to go and be on my own somewhere in Los Angeles and feel sorry for myself while the rest of the band is having success, stealing the show somewhere and having a little fun anyway. And everyone thought that. Everyone thought about the other: You leave, but I'm staying in."

All the while that love was having its way with the band, *Fleetwood Mac* was showing no signs of slowing down on *Billboard*'s Hot 100. Concentrating on their massive success proved an effective distraction for the musicians. "We thought it would go gold, but we didn't think it would sell four million," Christine told *Hit Parader.* "But then it became increasingly obvious, and then that delight developed into another feeling for each other—that we really pulled it off, and that was wonderful."

Finally, everyone in the band had good reason to anticipate headlining a large auditorium. Maybe they could sell out an arena yet. Even in the days of Peter Green, Fleetwood Mack had never had it quite this good where business was concerned. People were finally responding to their music, and as Mick Fleetwood told *Goldmine,* "to throw it away would have been a sin. And that's how we looked at it. And we got round all the other stuff . . . the bedroom stuff."

That said, Fleetwood Mac was ready to hightail it out of Sausalito without so much as a parting glance. Never had L.A. looked so welcoming as the day the musicians packed up their belongings and headed south. Despite its being the scene of their past struggles, Los Angeles really was la-la-land in comparison to San Francisco. And with *Fleetwood Mac* quickly growing into a hit of epic proportions, the band was about to experience the city's full star treatment at long last.

———

The prerequisites of fame and fortune would have to wait. Soon after arriving in Los Angeles, Fleetwood Mac found that the technical difficulties of Sausalito were hot on their trail. Back at the Record Plant, the band had used a tape player with a nasty penchant for mangling fresh takes. In a nod to Steven Spielberg's recently released blockbuster film, they had dubbed the machine "Jaws." But as in any scary movie, just when they thought they had outsmarted the tape-eating monster, the shark's fin began to encircle the band yet again.

When they played the tapes mixed at the Record Plant, the sound was muddled. As Mick recalled in *My Life and Times in Fleetwood Mac,* the band was "aghast at how awful they sounded." All the effort, all the time, all the emotion that had gone into the album—was it possible that it had all been for naught?

They tried everything from shifting studios to swapping equipment before admitting that the problem rested solely with their tapes, probably ruined by their exposure to Jaws. Luckily, they had recourse to one drastic measure that could save their Sausalito-based work from falling into the void of wasted time: a skin-flick-only movie theater with, of all things, a dubbing room. How they happened upon this remains a mystery, but for some reason, there the tapes sounded all right. However, as the Sausalito tracks had been very basic to begin with, this stroke of good fortune in no way signaled the end of Fleetwood Mac's hard labor.

The cramped makeshift studio and an adjacent office made up the whole of the group's new recording accommodations. Considering the alternative, it would have to do. For three months the band would assemble at this Hollywood Boulevard eyesore to mix and dub the new tracks. Everyone understood that the album would play like a public confessional, and they were willing to tell all. "I don't care that everybody knows me and Chris and John and Lindsey and Mick all broke up," Stevie told *Rolling Stone.* "Because we did. So that's fact."

But accepting the brutal truth didn't make working together any easier. To stay on track and keep distractions at bay, the band closed their recording sessions to all outsiders. In *Rock Lives* by Timothy White, Stevie remembered that "we were all trying to hold the foundation of Fleetwood Mac together, and trying to speak to each other in a civil tone, while sitting in a tiny room listening to each other's songs about our shattered relationships. It was very, very tense—a room full of divorced people who didn't dare bring anybody new into the same room, because nobody was gonna be nice to anybody brought into the circle."

At least in Los Angeles, the suffocating atmosphere of the studio was made more palatable by the comforts of home. This was the proverbial spoonful of sugar that considerably eased the strain of compiling the album. The band also found that there was no place like home for spending their newfound wealth. The suddenly rich members of Fleetwood Mac were now free to see exactly how it was that the other half lived. It was Stevie who summed up everybody's sentiments by declaring, "I can buy things I always wanted to have."

Of course, the greatest counterbalance to the members' personal distress was provided by the musical triumphs that sprang from these pressure-cooker recording sessions. The manner in which a few of Stevie's cryptic verses from the Buckingham Nicks period were turned into one of the band's best songs exemplifies the overall success of these sessions. Depending on how one wants to look at it, "The Chain" was created in one of two ways; Either Stevie had written some lyrics that were not initially intended for the album, or John McVie came up with a powerful bass line that immediately caught Mick's attention, inciting him to record a drum accompaniment. The bass and drum tracks were so stirring that Lindsey and Christine also recorded their own accompanying parts. After this tinkering was complete, Fleetwood Mac had a captivating musical arrangement, but they didn't have a song. That's when Stevie dug up the lyrics she had written back in the day, and voilà, "The Chain" was complete. It would go down in Mac history as the band's one and only group collaboration, as well as an emblem of their resolve never to break the chain binding their artistic union.

7

PICKING UP
THE PIECES

In the grand tradition of the British blues circuit, Fleetwood Mac had remained a touring band. Both John and Mick felt that nothing compared to the rush of connecting with an audience, and little had changed since the induction of Stevie and Lindsey turned Fleetwood Mac into the latter-day version of the Mamas and the Papas. But as the months of recording wore on, the band realized that nearly half a year had elapsed, during which time the live performances they had given could all be counted on one hand.

Held at the Oakland Coliseum on May 2 and 3, 1976, Bill Graham's "A Day on the Green" brought the band back to their roots. The two shows saw well over a hundred thousand fans rally in support of what the promoter touted as the British Invasion: Peter Frampton, Gary Wright, and Fleetwood Mac. These were by far the largest audiences Fleetwood Mac had ever seen. "I couldn't believe all those people were out there," recalled Stevie in *Bam*.

Despite the shock of a full arena, the concert critics agreed that Fleetwood Mac delivered the goods with panache. The exhilaration surrounding this event reminded the band members why they had turned to music in the first place. As Stevie told *Spin,* "When I walk with my band up to the stage, I feel like an astronaut. I feel like we should be in slow motion, and the wind should be blowing." No surprise, then, that less than a month later, in June, the band agreed that a concert tour was long overdue. With *Fleetwood Mac* gaining on the year's six-million-copy-selling chartbuster, *Frampton Comes Alive!,* and *Rumours* still in its formative stages, the time to dust off the amplifiers and round up the roadies had indeed arrived.

As expected, escaping the confines of their cloistered recording quarters turned out to be the best thing Fleetwood Mac had done in months. The nervous energy that had been percolating through the studio could finally be directed toward the greater good of riling up an audience. Displacing the pent-up anger and frustrations away from the bandmates who had done them harm and onto their performance made for a quality of sound and showmanship that was beyond reproach. Within days, they were ready to take their angst on the road—a warm-up act no longer, nor ever again.

———

Performing alongside the hot-ticket numbers of the day, such as Ted Nugent, Kenny Loggins, Jefferson Starship, the Steve Miller Band, and the Eagles, to name just a few, reacquainted veterans Mick and John with the ecstasy of success. And while Christine had also had her share of unconditional love from the masses back in England, the whole celebrity trip was uncharted territory for Stevie and Lindsey. "I really don't think we ever quite got over that," Stevie told VH-1's *Behind the Music.*

When Stevie noticed the hundreds of women who showed up at the concerts dressed exactly like her, she was able to let go of her past problems with self-confidence. Despite the persistent sniggering of certain virulent critics, there was no denying that she had become Fleetwood Mac's main attraction. This new self-awareness drove the vocalist to milk her fame for all it was worth. "She would always dress up as flamboyantly as possible when she went out, so she'd be noticed," Lindsey told *Bam.*

"She's a different kind of person than I am," he continued. "People are appreciating me for the reasons I want to be appreciated for, and not for my chiffon gown." Although the couple had split months ago, and Lindsey was sowing his wild oats with a vengeance, his ex-girlfriend's antics clearly remained a sore subject.

The real test of Lindsey's self-possession came when Stevie began a flirtation with rock's golden boy, the Eagles' lead vocalist, Don Henley. The two first connected when Henley called Stevie on a whim. Their teleconferencing continued until the Eagles and Fleetwood Mac were at last scheduled to play the same arena in July 1976. Stevie, a major Eagles fan, was waiting with bated breath until she could finally meet the band.

"We arrive and the Eagles are in the next dressing room, right?" Stevie recounted to *Crawdaddy.* "Now I would never go in there and say, 'Hi, I'm Stevie.' Never. I would DIE first. So I go into our dressing room and here's this huge bouquet of roses with a card in it. So I open up the card and it reads 'The best of my love, dot dot dot. Tonight, question mark, Don.' " It hardly sent Stevie head over heels. "I said, 'That's about the uncoolest thing I've ever seen in my whole life!' I mean how could he possibly preconceive something like that? And I'm DYING, right? My face is red and I'm FUMING. And then, finally, Christine grabs me and takes me aside and says, 'Don didn't send that. Mick and John did.' They were in hysterics."

It was lucky that Christine had been there, because Stevie was soon introduced to Don Henley and the rest of the Eagles. Had her fellow female in rock not intervened, Stevie's first encounter with the band could have turned out very differently. But as things stood, Stevie found Don to be just as attractive and charming in person as he was onstage. Since these sentiments seemed to be mutual, "we went out, off and on, for about two years," Stevie said. Don began sending his Lear jet for Stevie whenever the two could coordinate some free time. Soon, the pair was to the music industry what the head cheerleader and the football quarterback are to the run-of-the-mill high school. People didn't come much more beautiful than that.

While the gossipmongers were buoyed by the new alliance, everyone within Fleetwood Mac was stressing about Lindsey's reaction. How would he handle Stevie's choice of boyfriend? They needn't have worried. While he was initially concerned about how

Stevie's love life would affect him after they were no longer together, Lindsey found that, instead of driving him mad with jealous rage, the sight of Stevie and Don together was more proof that he had nothing to fear but fear itself. "It's strange," he explained to *Crawdaddy*, "it's one thing to accept not being with someone and it's another to see them with someone else, especially someone like Don, right? A big star in another group. I could see it coming and I really thought it was gonna bum me out, but it was really a good thing just to see her sitting with him. It actually made me happy. I thought there was something to fear but there wasn't. So the whole breakup has forced me to redefine my whole individuality—musically as well. I'm no longer thinking of Stevie and me as a duo. That thought used to freak me out but now it's made me come back stronger, to be Lindsey Buckingham."

To coincide with the beginning of the summer 1976 tour, the band had released yet a third single from *Fleetwood Mac*, Christine's enduring classic "Say You Love Me." Disc jockeys all over America were quick to pick up on the love song's infectious quality, and Fleetwood Mac was again thrown into the foreground. By now, the band's ubiquity was taken for granted; they were the new players on the music scene.

The beleaguered *Rumours* album, however, still hung over Fleetwood Mac's horizon like some ominous cloud. Thoughts of the record were never far from their minds. Even while crossing state lines, the writers busied themselves by thinking up still more ideas. One such evening, shortly after another argument with Lindsey, Stevie recalled that she was looking out the window of the tour bus as they passed "under a freeway sign that said 'Silver Springs, Maryland.'" The sign caught her attention, sparking a creative impulse. "Silver Springs sounded like a pretty fabulous place to me. And 'You can be my Silver Springs,' that's just a whole symbolic thing of what you could have been to me," she said on *The Making of Rumours*. The resulting song of the same name was also Stevie's way of telling Lindsey, "I'm so angry with you. You will listen to me on the radio for the rest of your life, and it will bug you. I hope it bugs you."

Despite the lingering problems between Fleetwood Mac's most quarrelsome former couple, and John's difficulty with no longer being half of "John and Christine" the band eventually had to return to working on *Rumours*. Miami was the chosen locale for the weeklong break from the road, as well as for Mick's valiant effort to reclaim his family.

Even in a cocaine-induced haze, Mick couldn't shake off the regret that accompanied his mishandling of his marriage. He'd been so clearly in the wrong, so obviously the absentee husband and father, that he felt another try could be enough to salvage the relationship. Without considering the many business responsibilities that would undoubtedly conspire against his plans for behaving better in the future, Mick entreated Jenny to join him in Miami. She agreed, and before the Mac returned to the tour, the Fleetwoods were back together.

As the Eagles were also recording in Miami, Stevie was able to continue her dalliance with Don Henley. While she by no means flaunted the relationship, for fear of aggravating the Lindsey situation and consequently jeopardizing the future of the band, Don had no such reservations. One morning he dispatched his limo driver to deliver a whole arsenal of presents—which included a stereo, records, fruit, and flowers—for Stevie. The driver found Stevie and the rest of the band enjoying a quiet breakfast together. He started "taking all this out onto the table and I'm going, 'Oh, please, please, this is not going to go down well.' And they want to know who it's from. And Lindsey is not happy," Stevie told *Spin*.

The possessive jealousy between Stevie and Lindsey wasn't always a one-way street. Back in Sausalito, Lindsey had already begun putting his unattached status to good use. "Lindsey was pretty down about it for a while," Christine told *Rolling Stone*, "then he just woke up one morning and said, 'Fuck this, I don't want to be unhappy,' and started getting some girlfriends together. Then Stevie couldn't handle it."

Of course, such mutual feelings of jealousy were only to be expected, for while the relationship had ended, the emotions that had fueled it still remained. The rest of the band was no different. Mick's reaction to his ex-wife's new boyfriend had brought out his residual affection for Jenny. As for John and Christine, there was no question but that the pair remained as much in love as ever. It's easy to see why the studio sessions—focused, as they were, on the band's romantic turmoil—had been so fraught with discomfort, and why—after months of incessant bickering, strained conversation, and awkward silences—the band was finally beginning to get past all the irascibility. Love was at the root of all the hotheaded accusations and recriminations. As time reined in the anger and misery that fed the flames of the ex-lovers' passion, the underlying warmth and devotion remained to continue keeping the band together.

After an eventful week of recording in Miami, Fleetwood Mac returned to the road. "Say You Love Me" had climbed the charts all the way to Number Eleven, and the band played to mammoth crowds wherever they went. Aside from the small percentage of concert critics and long-time fans in the audience, most of the people attending these shows thought of Fleetwood Mac as a groovy new band.

In fact, wherever this ten-year-old act went—be it to the fans, to the record label, or to settle the ongoing lawsuit with ex-manager Clifford Davis—they were treated with the care and delicacy befitting rock stars. Even the litigious Davis had backed down. "There's a chance it'll be settled out of court," Mick told *Crawdaddy*, "which is entirely at our discretion. Up to now the other side has been totally stubborn, but there's been a change of heart. Maybe it's because we've now got the money to continue paying lawyers."

The band's record company, Warner Bros. Records, had no complaints. Aside from a few subtle hints about how long it was taking to record *Rumours,* label executives were too busy raising their glasses to Fleetwood Mac the meal ticket to pay much attention to Fleetwood Mac the tardy recording artists. When *Fleetwood Mac* had been purchased by four million fans and reached Number One on *Billboard* early in September 1976, it became the best-selling album in Warner Bros. history. Every attempt was made to coddle the talent.

After winding down the tour, Fleetwood Mac returned to Los Angeles, where they were barraged by requests for interviews and special appearances. With their popularity still on the rise, and the worst of times decidedly behind them, the band could finally focus on their good fortune and the completion of *Rumours,* instead of ruminating on the decrepit state of their personal lives. In an interview with *Crawdaddy,* Mick attributed the change of attitude to the success of the summer tour. "After all the things that had gone down, it was doubly important. When we got back here we were all thinking, 'Shit, man, we did it! That's bloody good!' All the weirdness is gone." In the same article, Lindsey affirmed that he and the band "came back from this tour feeling really cleansed. All the things that had been happening between me and Stevie and between John and Chris mellowed into the situation they are now."

The band's lighthearted post-tour attitude was due, in no small part, to their being awash in success. The fame and power they now wielded within the music industry completely recompensed the price they'd had to pay. Those who remembered the earlier Mac couldn't believe what was happening. "Their success was grotesque," said Bob Welch in *People.* After making way for Stevie and Lindsey, Bob had gone on to form the short-lived rock trio Paris with ex–Jethro Tull bassist Glen Cornick. While he had remained friends with his former Mac colleagues, he was riddled with doubts. "For a year and a half I asked myself, 'What kind of schmuck am I?' Had I been holding back this miracle all those years? I felt like a demon."

Steeped in the bounty of fame, Bob's old bandmates could afford to adopt a more philosophical outlook. "There's a lot of good albums we've done," John told *Rolling Stone.* "It's just one of those things— the right album at the right time."

———

When Fleetwood Mac was nominated in the Best Album and Best Group categories for the Rock Music Awards, there could be no denying that their time had indeed come. The event itself amounted to little more than an ego stroking and a photo opportunity, but being suddenly singled out as one of the most popular bands of their era served to commemorate the breakneck pace of their progress.

The star-studded, televised ceremony would be Fleetwood Mac's first awards show, and everyone was duly thrilled. Even John, who was still nursing a broken heart, found something to smile about when he heard that Linda Ronstadt, on whom he had a crush, would be in attendance. While the bassist may have suffered a temporary setback upon learning that Ronstadt was a no-show, by evening's end all was forgotten. Fleetwood Mac had taken both the Best Album and the Best Group of the Year honors.

Although the victory was but a small sign of things to come, it had made one thing abundantly clear: Fleetwood Mac had arrived. The awards, the magazine articles, the international fan base, the hot-selling record—all combined, it was everything the group had ever worked toward, and more. But the realization of all their dreams came at a cost. "It really struck me, driving home in the back seat of a black limousine," Stevie recalled in *Rolling Stone*. "I was so lonely. I thought, 'Here I am, we just won these fantastic awards, we've just been on TV, everybody is singing our praises, and here I am driving home in my black limousine.' Terribly alone. Sort of knowing how it would feel to be Marilyn Monroe or something. It was a very strange feeling and I didn't like it at all. It scared me."

Even in the initial stages of stardom, Stevie had a sense of celebrity's dark side. With their crumbled relationships still fresh in their minds, the drawbacks of fame and fortune weren't all that hard for any of her fellow band members to notice either. None of this is to say that Fleetwood Mac wouldn't have done it all over again had they been given the chance. If the destruction of all things personal was what it took to succeed, then so be it.

Along with the acclaim came a financial windfall. No one was prepared for the vast sums of money that had begun to flow their way. One of the first things John had done was to buy a forty-one-foot schooner. For years, he'd been "going down to the bookstore and looking at boating magazines and drooling." So, after his split from Christine, John exchanged some of his money for a top-of-the-line sailboat, which would also serve as his home.

One of Stevie's first purchases was silicone breast implants. All the attention lavished upon her as pop music's newest sex symbol encouraged Stevie to enhance her look. While she would later have cause to regret her decision, "the whole world was getting them back then, and everyone was told they were safe," she told *People.* At the time, the plastic surgery seemed like a shrewd business investment. If it would bolster her confidence, Stevie thought, it was bound to improve her performance.

But it was Mick who proved to be the most profligate spender. With his deep-seated aspirations to being landed gentry and his cocaine habit simultaneously vying for attention, Mick embarked upon a routine of spending money as fast as he made it. This high-rolling pattern may have started out rather slowly—a Porsche here, an eight ball there—but the expenditures would eventually balloon to proportions dwarfing even a rock star's ransom. In a bit of foreshadowing, he would soon tell *Creem,* "There's enough money to go around for a while, and I have a feeling there'll always be more."

————

The longer the band took to record *Rumours* and the higher their budget soared, the more convinced everyone became that autonomous management was their only chance at staying together. In interview after interview, each of the five band members would profess a determination to remain independent.

Many a successful manager had tried to break down the band's reserve, and failed. Through her Eagles connection, Stevie had even become friendly with that band's übermanager, Irving Azoff, who also handled Dan Fogelberg and Boz Scaggs. In fact, the two were on such good terms that Stevie stayed at Azoff's deluxe Benedict Canyon ranch while looking for a house of her own. Despite the implied promise of this alliance, Fleetwood Mac was intent on going it alone. They simply didn't need another Clifford Davis fiasco to contend with.

"Before, people would come up to us and say, 'You won't make it without us.' Now they say, 'You *really* need our help now, you can't possibly keep it up without us,' " said Mick in a 1976 interview with *Crawdaddy.* "But take this band six months ago with all the heavy emotional stress that was occurring—I doubt seriously if we'd had a manager that we'd be here today. It would have been fatal, because the band was totally responsible to itself. No one could take sides. Besides, there was no way of anyone even beginning to understand how the people in this band work."

Professionally, it was an amazing time for the band. Even Europe and the U.K. wanted in on the Mac's action. The group's victorious visit to London in October 1976 was yet another reminder of how far they'd come. After years of being given up for dead by the Europeans, the interest of the overseas press agencies and news wires was all the more gratifying to the English band members. Making this turnabout all the more palpable was the reappearance of Peter Green.

The onetime frontman made his presence known as soon as the band arrived at their London hotel. "I heard this voice say, 'Hullo, Chris.' I turned around and saw this rotund little guy with a big beer gut and pint in his hand. I couldn't believe it," Chris recounted in *Rolling Stone*. "I said, 'Aren't you embarrassed?' 'Naw,' he says, 'fuck it, what the hell.' We gave him a room at the hotel for a few nights. He'd knock on your door, come in, and just sit there on your bed. He wouldn't volunteer anything."

Although Peter partook of his friends' generosity, he was hardly in need of charity. Still receiving large royalty checks for his work with Peter Green's Fleetwood Mac, he willingly disbursed most of these funds to any number of worthy causes. But the newfangled Mac wasn't aware of their founding father's selfless activities. To them, all Peter signified was the dissolution of talent. "Sadly enough, he wasn't the Peter Green anymore he must've been when writing 'The Green Manalishi,' " Stevie told *HP de Tijd*. "He was very far away when I saw him. I often tried talking to him. But he didn't want to talk the entire week. Especially not about music. And definitely not about Fleetwood Mac. He only wanted to watch. Everyone walked on tiptoe during those days."

The band saw only how low he'd been brought by his aimlessness and his inability to function within the music industry, and they couldn't help but reflect on the jarring contrast offered by their own against-all-odds success story. The experience was especially painful for the three Brits, who had started out with Peter and wished to preserve their memories of the Green God. Seeing the larger-than-life leader of the Mac reduced to this broken and slovenly man was almost too much to bear.

———

After their depressing run-in with Peter and successful European press tour, Fleetwood Mac returned to L.A. brimming with gratitude for their tremendous good fortune. Several months had passed since their Sausalito nightmare, and the feuding couples were now at peace. Mick and Jenny had even remarried, albeit under less than romantic circumstances.

Christine, John, and Mick were all in dire need of green cards if they were to remain in the States. As they easily fit into the Immigration and Naturalization Service's category of "aliens of extraordinary ability," the musicians' immigration process was rather swift. But since Jenny had no such claim to stake, she and Mick would have to be legally wed to remain together. They were already sharing a domicile, so there was no practical reason for the couple not to vow to make their second go-round last a lifetime.

The rest of the band had happily disentangled their private lives and their careers. John was living alone on his two-masted yacht at Marina Del Rey and had begun dating one of the secretaries working at Fleetwood Mac's management company, Seedy Management (now run by old pal Judy Wong). Lindsey was also playing the field, as well as happily sharing a comfortable Beverly Hills home with sound engineer Richard Dashut. Christine was still living with Curry Grant, but as she told *Rolling Stone,* "I don't think I'm in love." And Stevie had hit upon the perfect place to hang her top hat: the former abode of Velma Banky and Fatty Arbuckle, a couple who she'd learned had had "a passionate relationship, and when she happened to have another lover they went to him together and stabbed him." While Stevie was glad to know that the murder didn't actually occur in the house, she was equally excited about the prospect of owning a house with a torrid history. "You can tell the house once belonged to someone glamorous," she told *Creem.* "It has a real presence about it."

Ironically enough, while it had taken the combustible mixture of love and work to bring out the best of what the songwriters had to offer, it was the eventual separation of their public and private personas that helped the band complete *Rumours* without further incident. Of course, Fleetwood Mac was in no way immune to the technical difficulties that had plagued the recording process practically since day one.

After all the trouble they had gone through, dubbing and overdubbing the various album tracks, the quintet was faced with the realization that their master tapes were unacceptable. The damage had happened in such subtle increments that it had even eluded the circumspect ears of the sound professionals who'd been working on the album for months. Only when they listened to the rough tracks that had been recorded earlier did Lindsey and soundmen Richard Dashut and Ken Caillat realize how faded their masters had become. It was a full-scale disaster.

Sheer panic gripped the band as the engineers racked their brains trying to come up with a viable solution. Finally, it was decided that the master tapes would be replaced by the drum safeties, which sounded amazingly fresh and crisp in comparison. They would have to sync in all the other parts, the guitars, the vocals, and so forth. It was a grueling process. "It had to be done by hand," said Lindsey on *The Making of Rumours,* "which is really a task that I can't imagine having worked."

Despite his pivotal role in producing the album, Lindsey's name remained conspicuously absent from the production credits in the LP's liner notes. This being only his second album with the band, the guitarist didn't feel comfortable bringing the matter to the table. But, according to Lindsey, "If you were to ask Richard or any of those guys, 'Who produced *Rumours?*', they'd all say, 'Lindsey was the guy with the vision.' I didn't ask for a production credit on *Rumours,* and I didn't get it. Richard feels bad about that. There were band politics involved in that."

While upcoming albums would soon see Lindsey's efforts recognized, it would take much longer for one of Stevie's contributions to see the light of day. After Lindsey and the engineers restored the individual album tracks, it was time to organize them in sequence. Only at this late date, in December 1976, did the band realize that one of Stevie's songs would have to be pulled. As manager, Mick was again forced to be the bearer of bad tidings. " 'Silver Springs' was on *Rumours.* It was on the track list, it was gonna be on the record, but at the very last minute it was taken off, much to my disbelief. And the reason was because the song was way too long. It was really heartbreaking because it's such a wonderful song," Stevie told *Bam*. "The neat thing is that I had given this song to my mom—writing, publishing, everything. So when it was taken off the record, it was really a double disaster."

The disgruntled songwriter was somewhat appeased when her up-tempo "I Don't Want to Know" was chosen as the replacement track. While she would have preferred to see "Silver Springs" make it onto the album, on *The Making of Rumours* Stevie said that "if it was gonna be replaced by anything, that was a good replacement." At the time, no one could even begin to imagine the circumstances that would one day breathe new life into "Silver Springs."

————

Once all the last-minute changes were in place, the album was ready to be presented to the record label. At a time when most bands thought it extravagant to spend as much as six months in the studio, *Rumours* had been nearly a year in the making. Now the whole music industry and the community interested therein were hot on the trail of the band's encore performance. While eagerly awaited, the follow-up to *Fleetwood Mac* was also saddled with mass skepticism. In *Hit Parader*, Christine recalled that "people were saying, 'God, they'll never come up with another one as good as that.' "

True enough, 1976 had been a watershed year for Fleetwood Mac. Having sold an estimated four million albums that year alone, the band had become both the critics' darling and the media's target. Naturally, the public eye was focused squarely on their romantic trials and tra-vails. After being documented at length, the various ruptures within the group had become old news by year's end. Back in April 1976, *Rolling Stone* had already run a blurb that read, "We hear that Stevie Nicks and Lindsey Buckingham are the second couple within Fleetwood Mac to be treading choppy romantic waters; Christine and John McVie split up eight months ago." This explosive personal strife had kept the sensationalists' attention, giving them something to talk about all year long. At length, Stevie and Don Henley were prompted to write a joint letter to the editor of *Creem* magazine, stating, "NO-BODY gives a shit about Stevie Nicks and Don Henley."

While the media's impertinence may have been a nuisance for months, the band was now coming to terms with the inherent truth of the old adage "there's no such thing as bad publicity." The buzz surrounding their forthcoming album was deafening. The quintet knew they had a winner in the can and cared little that most of the attention was but a by-product of the cult of personality. Their nonchalance was evidenced by the title of the new album, which had been tentatively titled *Yesterday's Gone*. In the end, the group decided to take John McVie up on his suggestion to rename the album *Rumours*.

A none-too-subtle send-up of the madness encircling the band, the name was an indication of things to come. Soon enough, Fleetwood Mac would reevaluate their scruples and realize that if anyone was going to exploit their personal problems, it might as well be the group itself. "I think we rather enjoy being the center of gossip," Christine would later admit to *Us* magazine. "We enjoy other people enjoying it. People are actually fascinated to see if we really are fighting all the time, and we definitely get a perverted kick out of knowing that."

Fleetwood Mac was well aware of how interesting their lives were to music listeners nationwide. Instead of shying away from the invasion of privacy, the band members chose to embrace it. In a *Newsweek* article John stirred up anticipation by heralding the LP as "Mary Hartman on wax."

"That was part of the appeal of the album for the audience at the time," Lindsey told *Guitar World*. "It was clear that there was something going on beyond the music: the theater of interaction between these people making the record. Probably nine out of the eleven songs on that album were written specifically about other members of the band. It was a musical soap opera, if you will."

Not ones to disappoint their audience, Fleetwood Mac arranged the tracks on the album in a sequence that not only achieved optimum listening pleasure but displayed their behind-the-scenes trauma to greatest advantage. Every song was either a transparent message to another band member or a blatant retort to the previous song. "I don't think we realized back then quite how raw the songs were emotionally," said Lindsey. "They really were very direct messages to one another."

While they might not have known it at the time, Fleetwood Mac was about to learn that, in terms of record sales, honesty truly is the best policy. The domestic squabbles, the annoying rumors, the emotional devastation, and the album to which all of this had given rise were about to fuse into one history-making phenomenon that would change the tenor of their lives forever.

8

ALL THAT GLITTERS

Despite what appeared to be Fleetwood Mac's permanent residence on the *Billboard* 200—eighty weeks and counting—no one wanted the new LP to sit out the winter. Lindsey's "Go Your Own Way" was chosen to be the first single culled off *Rumours;* its B-side featured a rare early glimpse of "Silver Springs." As per standard practice, the song's December 1976 release predated that of the album by more than a month. Having been responsible for nary a hit single from his first album with the Mac, Lindsey was anxious to see his best efforts well received. "I just want it to be so good that I get paranoid," he told *Rolling Stone.* "I have to relax, get this whole time behind us."

Alas, hearing the song played on the radio for the first time would prove to be an experience more frazzling than it was gratifying. He had just finished mastering the album when he heard his handiwork coming over the car radio. Once the song had run its course, Lindsey was appalled to hear the influential deejay B. Mitchell Reed proclaim, "That was the new Fleetwood Mac single 'Go Your Own Way.' Well, I don't know about that one, folks."

Instead of chalking this reaction up to simple myopia, Lindsey turned the car around "and called the radio station. I was a little feistier then than I am now," he recounted in *Guitar World Acoustic.* "So they put me on the air, and I said, 'B, hey man, what are you talking about? What do you mean 'you don't know?' And he says, 'Man, I can't find the beat!' "

This was hardly the auspicious beginning the songwriter had been hoping for. Fortunately, audiences embraced the single. It soon rocked its way into the top ten, paving the way for the triumphant release of *Rumours.*

Never had Warner Bros. Records seen such a prodigious advance order. Due to the single's constant presence on the radio and the over-whelming demand it engendered, the LP actually shipped gold. An es-timated eight hundred thousand people wanted to purchase the record sight unseen.

———

Sweetening the taste of victory was a vast improvement in the musi-cians' rapport. By the time Fleetwood Mac was mixing the album in the fall of 1976, many past wrongs had become the proverbial water under the bridge. Even the McVies were once again on speaking terms, and relating better than ever. As Stevie told *Music Central,* it was generally understood that "there wouldn't have been a *Rumours* if everything had been fabulous. We couldn't have changed anything." Still, as the only band member wont to go against the grain, Lindsey had found himself in the unenviable position of being Fleetwood Mac's least sym-pathetic character.

"Lindsey is a very demanding person" was how Christine re-sponded when the *New York Daily News* asked her to describe the ax man. As popular as he was with the critics, his bandmates rarely in-dulged his artistic temperament. In *Rolling Stone,* he recounted an ex-change he had with Mick during the recording of *Rumours.* "I can re-member . . . saying to Mick, 'Well, things don't seem to be going exactly the way I would like them to go.' And he said, 'Well, maybe you don't want to be in a group.' "

Much of the tension emanating from such on-the-job dynamics was relieved when Lindsey fell in love. According to Carol Harris, the object of his affection, Cupid struck "right before *Rumours* broke." Lindsey had all but completed mixing the album when he met the twenty-three-year-old Tulsa native. A part-time model, she was also a receptionist at the recording studio where Lindsey was working. "I had been in Europe, and it was my first day back at work," she told *Rolling Stone*. "I walked in and saw Lindsey and that was it."

Taken with the beautiful blonde, the rock star was quick to begin wooing her. Nevertheless, recently separated from the love of his life, and the composer of such disillusioned lyrics as those found in "Never Going Back Again," Lindsey was no fool for love. Of course, one doesn't have to plan on falling head over heels to do exactly that. "At first, she was just another conquest," Lindsey told *Rolling Stone*. "And then later, obviously not."

"They were both very much in love," Richard Dashut affirmed. "In fact, I think that was one of the happiest times in his life." The band was thrilled to see Lindsey in better spirits with the possible exception of Stevie, whose idea of true romance precluded the plausibility of more than one real love. Her amorous exploits may have been keeping her from dwelling on the past, but she could never accept that Lindsey had moved on, so much so as to have fallen in love. In an interview with *Rolling Stone*, she explained the origin of the special bond she shared with her ex: "In Lindsey's mind, all the other women that came after me were all going after rich rock-and-roll star Lindsey. Nobody was looking into the heart I had looked into. Nobody was seeing the guy before he was famous. We knew each other before. That's what makes us unique to each other."

The truth was that the antagonism between the former duo had never fully dissipated. Since many of their working hours were still spent at loggerheads, Stevie attributed Lindsey's negative attitude to sour grapes. Furthermore, despite having been the one to put the ki-bosh on their romance, Stevie had yet to accept the finality of her decision. None of this is to imply that she wasn't indulging in her fair share of good times.

After ending her relationship with Don Henley, Stevie had taken up with Eagles songwriter J. D. Souther and was also rumored to be seeing Joe Walsh. "We had an incredible time. They were such good song-writers," she said of the Eagles in *Spin*. Yet Stevie remained unfulfilled by the rock 'n' roll lifestyle. "I definitely want to have a baby in the next four years," the twenty-eight-year-old revealed in *Rolling Stone.* "For sure, I want to have one or two children, and I don't want to wait any further than, say, thirty-four. This is all part of my plan. By that time I hope that I'll be living up in the mountains somewhere with a very pretty house and a piano and a tape recorder, just writing, and then going to New York every once in a while to shop."

The shopping trips were never hard to arrange. On the other hand, finding the time for a family life would prove an elusive goal even for this ambitious superwoman of the seventies. Indeed, Lindsey, who had always gravitated toward women who subscribed to the "behind every great man" theory, also saw the difficulty in mixing business with pleasure. As he summed up in *Rolling Stone,* "Being in this band really fucks up relationships with chicks. . . . Stevie and I have found that to be true."

———

With the success of *Rumours,* John and Christine remained philosophical, taking the change of fortune in stride. While Christine persevered with the divorce proceedings—intent on establishing a platonic friendship with the man for whom she still cared deeply—John was harboring feelings of love for his ex-wife intermingled with regret. He would often take his yacht-cum-dwelling miles offshore, both to flee the craziness of the Los Angeles music scene and to forget his personal problems. "There's no doubt about the fact that he hasn't really been a very happy man since I left him," the former Mrs. McVie confirmed.

As always, John chose to drown his sorrows in drink. At this time, one of his frequent binges landed him in an LAPD holding cell. Driving under the influence, John was in a two-car collision. When the police showed up, "they whisked me away to spend a night in the drunk tank," he told *Rolling Stone.* "My whole life passed in front of my eyes." Instead of using his near-death experience to turn his life around, John continued to pursue the same perilous course of action. Yet somehow the bassist managed to keep his ego in check. "People are always asking me, 'How does it feel to have made it?' " he griped to *Rolling Stone.* "If that's the case, what do I do now? Now that I've 'made it'? I hate that phrase."

Christine seconded this notion. "Everyone's just carrying on as normal," she assured *Hit Parader*. "We enjoy all this, but I don't think we're strutting around like peacocks." For Christine, a seasoned veteran of the music industry, there would be no vintage car collection, no sprawling Bel Air manse, and no $100,000 cocaine sprees. Notwithstanding the nagging fears for John's welfare, she would continue living with Curry Grant in her home overlooking the Sunset Strip, yielding only to one weakness—"jewelry, especially diamonds." But as the composer of most of her band's hit singles, this was an extravagance Christine could well afford.

Meanwhile, the band's future rested in Mick's hands—or, more likely, in the hands of his advisers. While his capacity for strategic thinking and keen insight had in no way diminished, neither had the dyslexia that had followed him since grade school. Thus, when time came to generate new and exciting ideas, Mick was all ears. Yet in matters of the pocketbook, the drummer was content to assume the executive's role, imposing either his veto or seal of approval according to the consultants' input. "He never read a contract agreement," an accountant friend of Mick's divulged to the *New York Times*.

However casual he might have been in handling the band's finances, Mick was a wiz at self-promotion. No sooner had *Rumours* been released than Mick rallied the troops to rehearse for an upcoming world tour. By the time they were ready for the road, the album had already secured the Number Ten slot on the *Billboard* 200. The band started at the beginning of March 1977 by canvassing the nation's ten- to fifteen-thousand-seat venues. For this tour, Mick spared no expense. It was jets, stretch limos, luxury hotel suites, and world-class catering, all the way. "We're just not that money-conscious," he told *Creem*. Fortunately, thanks in part to the publicity the Mac's members had received, many of the shows sold out, and all expenditures were recouped. "Audiences began flocking to our concerts out of curiosity," Christine told *US*. "They wanted to see if we would actually hit each other over the head with guitars. It was like people going to the motor races hoping to see a spectacular crash."

As the month-long U.S. tour came to an end, *Rumours* was locked in at Number Four on the charts and had been certified platinum. It seemed as though no one could resist the voyeuristic thrill of taking a gander at the band that had let all of America in on their secrets. Of course, this adulation had yet to extend to the U.K. But Fleetwood Mac was ready to go global and take Britain by storm.

———

While Fleetwood Mac was wandering the British countryside, the United States was falling under the spell of the band's second single, Stevie's seductive "Dreams." Suddenly, the song was the most requested single on radio stations nationwide. The first Fleetwood Mac single to top the charts and go gold, "Dreams" gave *Rumours* yet another push in the right direction. The album eased into *Billboard*'s coveted Number One position.

This happened despite a negative *Rolling Stone* review, part of which read: "Nicks has nothing on *Rumours* to compare with 'Rhiannon,' her smash from the last album. 'Dreams' is a nice but fairly lightweight tune, and her nasal singing is the only weak vocal on the record." Fortunately, the bewitching chanteuse no longer looked to critics for approval; the many fans she had won were validation enough. By this time, Stevie had become the object of much speculation. Her recondite lyrics and flowing black chiffon had some calling her rock's most fascinating woman, others imitating her look and sound, and still others wondering whether she was, in fact, a witch. While the latter reaction would one day drive Stevie to distraction, her less superstitious fan base was a great boost to her ever-burgeoning confidence.

Tired from touring, the band members were nonetheless elated with their success. Having set out to prove their longevity, Fleetwood Mac had outperformed even the greatest expectations.

Meanwhile, former bandmate Peter Green had managed to get himself into quite a bit of trouble. Not two months prior to Fleetwood Mac's transatlantic trek, Peter had threatened to shoot his former manager, Clifford Davis. Davis, who was now using the alias Clifford Adams, reported the threat to the police, and Peter was arrested when the police discovered that he had an unregistered gun in his house.

The British press had a field day, blowing the story all out of proportion and even misreporting vital facts. They painted Peter as a washed-up pop star turned gun-toting madman, and even mistakenly alleged that Peter had demanded that his thirty thousand pounds per year in royalty income be *withheld!* The press reported that Peter showed up at Clifford Davis's office with guns blazing, but Peter's own testimony tells a very different story.

According to Peter, an idle threat made over the phone became the basis for a media circus full of inaccuracies and unsubstantiated allegations. *Rolling Stone* had even opened its cover story on Fleetwood Mac by recounting the mixed-up Peter Green tale spun by the overseas press.

As it turned out, Peter couldn't even recall asking for the royalty funds to be withheld. In *Peter Green: Founder of Fleetwood Mac*, he told author Martin Celmins that "When I was talking to Clifford Davis on the phone, I wondered if he had any money for me because I didn't have any after the holiday. He told me he didn't. . . . On the telephone to Clifford, I forget how it came out, but I said, 'I'll shoot you.' "

The end result of this fiasco was the guitarist's temporary confinement to yet another mental institution. When Fleetwood Mac rolled into town a few months later, their old friend had already been released. Knowing only what they had read in *Rolling Stone*, the band could only reflect upon Peter's state with resigned disappointment. Of course, the musicians couldn't afford to lose sleep over Peter's problems when their own schedule permitted so few hours of shuteye. After their final U.K. performance, America's hottest act was whisked off to tour the rest of Europe.

According to Mick's description in *Goldmine*, the tour "was a very schizophrenic experience, because so many people remembered the Peter Green days, and for good reason. And now, whatever amount of time had lapsed, they were confronted with 'it's Fleetwood Mac, but it's not Fleetwood Mac.' "

———

When they returned to the States, Fleetwood Mac found their album bumped back to Number Two on the charts. The Eagles had nested in first place by virtue of their *Hotel California* LP. Still, *Rumours* had been Number One for two consecutive weeks, and the Mac had yet to become a band that would thumb its nose at Number Two. With two records riding high on the charts, three hit singles, and a ground-breaking tour schedule, 1977 was turning out even better than 1976.

Yet even as the Fleetwood Mac machine was gaining in every possible aspect of brand-name recognition, the various parts of that mechanism were at risk of losing sight of their own well-being. Stevie and Lindsey were especially put out by the extended touring and press frenzy that came with the job. Worse, Stevie's voice was beginning to falter. "The first time we played the Forum," Stevie divulged to *Rolling Stone*, "I went immediately to the doctor for all the preparations, and as I was leaving, he said, 'Good luck, my friend.' I said to myself, 'I am in big trouble.' At rehearsal, Lindsey started playing 'Landslide' and I couldn't sing it. I burst into tears."

Stevie's overzealous belting of songs such as "Rhiannon" had wreaked havoc upon her vocal chords. During the drawn-out *Rumours* tour, her voice would fail her so often, and the next day's reviews would be so cutting, that she began suffering from nightmares about losing her voice in concert. "My vocal muscles got so bad I would have to go to a throat specialist," she told *Rolling Stone*, "especially before the L.A. Forum or the Garden. They would give me shots that de-swell your [vocal] cords enough to allow you to sing. But it's not good to get those shots a lot with your cords in that shape. After two and a half hours of singing, you can shred them, truly blow them right out of your throat."

Despite insinuations to the contrary, Stevie was not so New Age as to entrust her million-dollar voice to faith healing. Since her best friend of thirteen years, Robin Anderson, happened to be an excellent vocal coach, Stevie brought her aboard the Fleetwood Mac express to learn proper vocal technique. Tour dates had to be canceled, but as Stevie told the *Arizona Republic*, "She taught me how to sing. She taught me how to use my voice."

While Lindsey's road-related problems would soon come to the fore, at the beginning of the Mac mania, much of his aggravation was rooted in chronic self-doubt. The idealistic guitarist very much resented all the publicity centered on his band's personal ordeals. The more albums were sold, the more he questioned the motives behind the public's interest. "It's not like *Rumours* was 'the best album ever made' because it sold the most copies," he told *Bam*. "It did well for a lot of different reasons, many, I'm sure, that had little or nothing to do with the music." This would have been easier to take had Lindsey's ultimate goal not been to actually record "the best album ever made."

The rest of the group agreed with Lindsey's assessment of the situation. As Christine told *Us,* "The melodrama and the fact that we were apparently such an interesting bunch of characters attracted a lot of attention. There really is nothing else that makes *Rumours* much more exceptional than anything else we've done."

Whatever the record buyers' rationale, it was compelling enough to make a huge number of people buy the new Fleetwood Mac album. After playing second fiddle to *Hotel California* for five weeks, *Rumours* resurfaced at Number One. Had they not been the hardest-working band in show business—without a moment to spare for interviews, much less for the extensive contemplation of their own success—the group would certainly have been nonplussed by this astounding response. Nothing—not the success of Peter Green's Fleetwood Mac, not the six million bought-and-paid-for copies of *Fleetwood Mac*, nothing whatsoever—could have prepared them for being where they suddenly were: at the epicenter of modern rock music.

———

Despite the unremitting fanfare, Fleetwood Mac didn't dawdle long before putting out their third single. Now was Christine's time to shine. "'You Make Loving Fun' is one of my choices from the album," she told the *New York Post.* "I wanted it to be our third single, but we put out 'Don't Stop' instead." Of course, while "You Make Loving Fun" was shelved, the tune was far from forgotten. It would have its day on the radio; in the meanwhile, summertime called for something with a little more punch. Considering that the soporific "Dreams" had been the band's last single, the new number had to be a rip-rocker.

The stratagem paid off when "Don't Stop" broke into the top five and the album went quadruple platinum in the States and double platinum in England. After sitting in the Number Three position for one week in July, during which Peter Frampton's and Barry Manilow's new albums battled for first place, the Mac returned to lead the pack. Bolstered by the autumn release and subsequent top-ten status of "You

Make Loving Fun," *Rumours* would remain the uncontested chart-topper for the next six months. It was the longest Number One run any album had ever seen. "I think we sort of took it for granted at the time. 'Oh, it's Number One again this week,' " Lindsey told *Bam*.

Throughout much of this time, the band toured on. They would cover the continental United States and even parts of Canada before finally taking a long-overdue breather. Keeping up with this schedule was no great feat for John and Mick, touring was in their blood by now. Christine was also used to dealing with the hardships of the road. But Lindsey and Stevie were not quite so inured. After waxing poetic about the road's many highlights to a *Creem* reporter, Mick was asked how the rest of the band felt about touring. "John adores it; he's the first on the plane," he replied. "Christine is a real trouper—she's adapted to all the rigors. Lindsey, on the other hand, can do without it. As for Stevie, she doesn't really like traveling, but she's an audience addict so she rises to the occasion."

Unfortunately, the effort Stevie had to exert to rise to the occasion was all but overwhelming. Always prone to exhaustion, she was driven to inhale enormous quantities of cocaine to keep up with the lightning pace of the *Rumours* tour. Eventually, her chronic fatigue would be attributed to the Epstein-Barr virus, but back in 1977 coke was the only cure for Stevie's malaise. While the other members would also indulge from time to time, she and Mick were, no doubt, the heaviest users in the band.

Lindsey preferred to spend his down time with his girlfriend Carol, who embodied everything he needed in a woman. The guitarist truly did want a partner who was serious and demure, someone who would take a backseat to his genius, as Stevie had before she evolved into an icon. Carol fit the bill, and the two would soon move in together. "We lived in seclusion a great deal of the time," she told *Rolling Stone*. "Even on the road, when everyone would be out partying, Lindsey and I would close ourselves off and stay together. He needs a lot of peace and quiet."

John and Christine were also not the cocaine type. While John was strictly old-school, choosing alcohol as his poison, Christine was too centered a person to let herself be carried away by the allure of drugs. "Basically, I spend all my spare time at home, I don't go raving around to clubs and parties," she told *Hit Parader.* "The rock and roll lifestyle doesn't really appeal to me."

————

For members of the band, success carried its share of responsibility. Within twelve months, *Rumours* had sold eight million albums, making Fleetwood Mac *the* power hitters of the music industry. The musicians were given free reign to do as they wished. For the ever-magnanimous Mick Fleetwood, the first order of business was to help out his steadfast pal Bob Welch, whose life savings had dwindled to a paltry eight thousand dollars. After Bob's post-Mac group, Paris, disbanded, Mick jumped at the chance to play the knight in shining armor by finagling a recording contract with Capitol Records for his former lead guitarist.

Around the time "Don't Stop" was being released, the product of Bob's recording sessions, *French Kiss,* was being put to bed. With the assistance of Mick, Christine, and Lindsey, the album was born with a platinum spoon in its mouth. Bob's first single, "Sentimental Lady"— which had appeared earlier on Fleetwood Mac's *Bare Trees*—got the kind of airplay that would have been unthinkable only three years earlier. The song eventually peaked at *Billboard*'s Number Eight, and the album at Number Twelve. Two additional hit singles later, Bob was the proud owner of his very own platinum record.

Other artists also stood to profit by the Mac's success. Lindsey and Stevie had made good on their promises to friends Walter Egan and Warren Zevon by collaborating with both on their forthcoming albums. Zevon's *Excitable Boy* album witnessed the release of his claim-to-enduring-fame single, "Werewolves of London." The song featured bass and drum tracks recorded by none other than John and Mick. Topping out at Number Twenty-four this single deserved much of the credit for catapulting its parent album to Number Eight. Walter Egan's album, *Not Shy,* was also destined to enjoy a warm reception.

While 1978 would see little recorded output from the Mac, their input would be unmistakable. The lapse in touring and recording amounted to no more than an unavoidable post-*Rumours* recovery period. But after word of Welch's, Zevon's, and Egan's Mac-assisted scores had spread, Kenny Loggins, Todd Rundgren, Leo Sayer, and John Stewart, of the defunct Kingston Trio, would all call upon the recuperating musicians, in hopes that some of their magic would rub off.

————

Fleetwood Mac had worn themselves out by charging ahead with a worldwide tour. Even the ten-day respite they enjoyed in October 1977 hardly sufficed as fortification for the remaining leg of the tour, which would take them to Australia, New Zealand, and Japan. Paying little heed to their bodies' demands for rest, Fleetwood Mac spent the last two months of the year playing to the notoriously fervid fans of the South Pacific.

Strung out from the effects of drugs and sleep deprivation, clear-eyed thinking was the first thing to bite the dust. With her then-boyfriend, record executive Paul Fishkin, thousands of miles away, Stevie naturally turned to Mick for support. As the group's most self-destructive members, the percussionist and the tambourine girl had always been drawn to one another, spending countless hours in each other's company. The last phase of the lengthy *Rumours* tour saw their resistance at its weakest. The two threw caution to the wind and consummated their long-in-the-brewing love affair. "Never in a million years could you have told me that would happen," Stevie told *Spin.* "That was the biggest surprise."

The direction their relationship had taken was no less surprising to Mick, who soon found himself enamored with his petite lead singer. Sensitive to their delicate situation, the pair decided to keep their romance under wraps. Mick was, after all, a married man, and it was less than two years since Stevie and Lindsey's breakup. Still, according to the drummer, Lindsey had sensed the chemistry between him and Stevie all along.

Back when the duo first joined Fleetwood Mac, Mick recalled being confronted with an odd question from his new guitarist. "You love Stevie, don't you?" Lindsey had asked matter-of-factly after a night of partying. "Through the mist I remember thinking, 'That's a heavy thing to say.' We'd all hardly been on the road," Mick told the *Independent.*

While there may not have been any truth to Lindsey's gut feeling at the time, three years had done a lot to prove the veracity of his premonition. Mick and Stevie were the Mac's newest couple, spending time together whenever they could slip away undetected. From this behavior, one might conclude that life's lessons had been wasted on the drummer. On the contrary, the memory of his own encounter with infidelity was still fresh in his mind. Mick dreaded what would happen should Lindsey learn of the affair from some tactless bystander, as Mick had found out about Jenny and Bob Weston about five years earlier.

After discussing the ramifications of remaining silent, Mick and Stevie decided to come clean with the affair as soon as the tour wound down. Stevie was less concerned about Lindsey's reaction—she knew he was getting on with his own love life—than about the sentiments of the band as a whole. The disastrous consequences the indiscretion could have for Mick's family were also a constant source of worry. Stevie had been a friend to Jenny Boyd; she'd even played with little Amy and Lucy Fleetwood. Betraying them pressed on her conscience. It would have been unbearable had Mick not been, as she told *Time*, one of "the three great loves in my life."

With the tour at an end and butterflies in his stomach, Mick prepared for a tête-à-tête with Lindsey. The conversation that ensued proved anticlimactic, as Lindsey "didn't feel betrayed by Mick." Although Stevie remembers that the bandmates' rapport was strained by her affair, Lindsey's testimony attests to the contrary. "Quite honestly, I'd have been surprised if it hadn't happened," he told the *Independent*. "I remember he came over, sat me down and told me, and I went, 'Oh, okay.' Stevie and I had long parted company and she'd had several boyfriends in between."

Nonetheless, with the affair out in the open, Stevie was left feeling like a pariah. Her acute sensitivity to Mick's family-man status may have been to blame for this discomfort. "Everybody was so angry, because Mick was married to a wonderful girl and he had two wonderful children, and I was horrified," she told *Spin*.

The strain caused by this relationship only fed the musicians' need for emotional strife. Having been surrounded by conflict for nearly three years, the band had become habituated to thriving within chaos. Thus, the potentially devastating affair turned out to be little more than a drop in the bucket of tears that Fleetwood Mac had already cried since embarking upon rock stardom's thrill ride.

———

The *Rumours* tour over, Fleetwood Mac once again settled into the comforts of home. With nine million sold records to their name, the band could indulge in lifestyles to which they had yet to become accustomed. Mick Fleetwood was the first to dispense with some of his fortune. Since Jenny was not aware of the affair between her husband and Stevie, separation was a nonissue, and Mick and Jenny moved their family act to Bel Air.

If there was one time that Fleetwood Mac could have been termed a happy group, this was it. They'd all been counting the days until they would no longer have to tolerate the presence of their bandmates, and the moment's long-awaited arrival came none too soon. John, Christine, and Lindsey were all enjoying their hours of leisure with significant others. Even Mick and Stevie had overcome their guilt and had fallen into an untroubled routine of secretive getaways and stolen moments.

Winter being the awards season, January 1978 capped off the band's era of good feeling. The star-studded American Music Awards gala, at which the industry leaders honor their colleagues, was the site of a Fleetwood Mac triumph. As the night wore on and the group won one award after another, the bejeweled quintet's flushed-with-joy countenances became the main focus of the camera's attention. A month later, Fleetwood Mac descended upon the Grammy Awards, taking home the trophy for Best Album.

Still in the top ten, *Rumours* was now the bestselling album in the history of pop. The ecstasy of victory was all the more pronounced because of the agony that had gone into the making of the album. Yet even as the band reveled in the feeling that the worst must certainly be behind them, they couldn't help suffering pangs of anxiety as the world looked to them for an equally brilliant encore. "I remember someone saying, 'God, you must be scared shitless! How are you going to follow up *Rumours?*' " Lindsey told *Bam*.

The multi-platinum album was indeed a hard act to follow. As the

LP's success grew, the band realized that with *Rumours* they had in effect created a monster. The five people at the center of the *Rumours* rage had no misconceptions about their own power. However talented and visionary, they were just musicians, with the same human frailties, needs, and desires as anybody else. When all was said and done, Lindsey, Stevie, Christine, John, and Mick knew that their chances of reproducing the *Rumours* phenomenon were no better than those of any other performer.

————

At the height of their influence, the band decided to take a break from both the road and the studio. They set aside five months to bask in their own glory. But for all their intentions, this hardworking act couldn't sit still for one month, much less several. As long as there were artists out there who needed their help, members of Fleetwood Mac would use their spare time as coproducers and session players on their albums.

Having worked up his confidence managing the career of Bob Welch, Mick felt ready to intervene on behalf of yet another former Mac member. Since Peter Green's last bout of troubles some nine months earlier, the guitarist had effected a complete about-face. He'd lost weight, become involved in a serious relationship, begun formulating plans for resuming his career in music, and, with the help of prescription drugs, even achieved emotional equilibrium. When he contacted Mick's Seedy Management as soon as Fleetwood Mac rolled off the *Rumours* tour in December 1977, it was clear that Peter had come to Los Angeles ready to play.

Mick was thrilled at the opportunity to extend some Southern California hospitality to his former mentor. The symmetry in this new arrangement was striking. In the beginning, it had been the Green God's clout that paved Mick's way; now Mick hoped that his *Rumours* pull would do the same for Peter. The drummer was so happy to have Peter back among the living, he all but gave him the keys to the Bel Air homestead. Even Peter's wedding was conducted at Mick's. With Jenny playing the matron of honor, Peter married his longtime pen pal, Jane Samuels. "We didn't know why he was doing it," Jenny told Peter

Green's biographer Martin Celmins, "but we sort of went along with him and supported him as friends."

Full of plans for Peter's solo album, and distracted by the ill health of his father, Mick chose to ignore the warning signs that indicated trouble ahead: Peter's cocaine consumption, his erratic behavior, and the early onset of marital discord. The label executives, especially the head of Warner Bros., Mo Ostin, did manage to elicit some concern over handing down a large sum to a person as famous for his unbalanced mental condition as for his febrile guitar playing. But Mick had no problem convincing himself and all involved that Peter was ready for a comeback. In short, he was able to parlay his *Rumours* cachet into a million-dollar, three-record deal for Peter Green.

Stevie was also using her mass appeal to leverage the efforts of fellow recording artists. Supporting the solo debut of Kenny Loggins, on the heels of his Loggins and Messina days, Stevie's role was much more than session harmonizing and background vocals. The song "Whenever I Call You 'Friend' " was a duet featuring her and Loggins exchanging lead vocals. During the summer of 1978, the track was released as a single from Loggins's *Nightwatch* album. Charting at *Billboard*'s Number Five, it performed as well as any Fleetwood Mac single ever had. This quasi-independent success also gave Stevie a much-needed dose of positive reinforcement, germinating her first thoughts of a viable solo career in the future.

———

As the months of repose sped by, visions of independent ventures amounted to barely a speck on a horizon that was completely overcast by the prospect of Fleetwood Mac's next album. The band made plans to reenter the studio in May. Inspired by Britain's punk rock movement—which was steadily infiltrating the U.S. music scene via new-wave rock bands—Lindsey, especially, was rearing to go. "All the new-wave stuff has been real healthy," Lindsey subsequently told *Bam*. "So much of it accomplished what its makers set out to do—give people a kick in the ass. It was influential to me in that it made it more tangible for me to proceed with experimentation itself. It wasn't a question of hearing a good song and then trying to emulate it. It instilled a sense of courageousness in me and solidified a lot of the ideas I had about my music."

Lindsey had given the follow-up to *Rumours* serious consideration. He wasn't out to recreate the chart-buster's commercial success. That album had been a creative success for all that it had expressed about the band's state of mind, and Lindsey was out to ensure that the next record remained just as true to the band's artistic development—whatever the commercial ramifications. His artistic integrity wouldn't allow a formulaic treatment of his craft; his goal "was to shake people up and make them think."

In convincing the rest of the Mac that groups like the Sex Pistols, the Clash, and the Pretenders were on to something, Lindsey would have his work cut out for him. "I'd bring in a record by the Clash, or even something like Talking Heads, and the others were just turned off by it," he told *Guitar World*. "I guess because it was young and enthusiastic, and maybe not at as high a level of musicianship. It wasn't as mature as the rest of the band saw themselves. But that music was so open to new ideas, and that's what got me."

Mick, for one, already had his plate full simply mourning the demise of his remarriage to Jenny. While the drummer had thought he was keeping the facade of a happy household intact for his loving wife, Jenny was growing weary of Mick's self-indulgent behavior and substance abuse. In April, Jenny had finally come to terms with the inevitability of divorce, taking the children back to their native England. Subsequent months would bring a couple of attempts at reconciliation, but in the end the separation would prove final.

His thinking clouded by marijuana smoke, Mick chose to repress the emotional impact of the rupture by stepping up his interludes with Stevie, investing additional time in Seedy Management, and snorting more lines of cocaine. John's mind was also elsewhere. His divorce from Christine had been finalized in February 1978, and he was already planning the imminent nuptials between himself and Julie Rubens.

Having moved off the yacht and into a land-locked domicile, at thirty-two years of age John was again ready to say "I do" and move on with his life. His wedding to his twenty-five-year-old former secretary took place just after the band began rehearsing for the album. The reception witnessed a jovial Mac cavorting into the small hours. Many of the problems that would soon beset their studio sessions had yet to be aired. As Lindsey naively told *Rolling Stone,* "We're overrun with new material and it all sounds really good. It's too easy—something must be wrong. People say *Rumours* was so great because of all the pain we were going through and so forth. Well, this time it's . . . hope you like us when we're happy."

Until this break, the band had spent nearly every waking moment in each other's presence since the beginning of 1975. Their first few months away from the band and each other lay at the root of their happy reunion. Despite the conspicuous absence of sexual tension, recording their next album, eventually titled *Tusk,* would prove as formidable a challenge as the production of *Rumours* had been.

9

SLOW GOING ON
THE FAST TRACK

The lion's share of the next thirteen months in the band's history would be spent in the studio. More than a million dollars would be spent on the recording of *Tusk*. Despite their deluxe, custom-built accommodations, Lindsey would set up a home studio, often using his bathroom to record entire tracks. As everyone in the band would say at one point or another, many of the quandaries hampering the proceedings were the direct result of Fleetwood Mac being "five people, with five big egos."

Without dirty laundry to air, the sensationalist faction of the media would then resort to trumpeting the band's amazing fiscal liberties, their divergent musical styles, and the experimental nature of the album itself. Yet most of the music critics would understand the Mac's rationale because, for all their excess, the group would emerge having accomplished exactly what they'd set out to do: record an album that resembled *Rumours* only in its vitality and relevance.

Even before the studio had been picked out, Lindsey was already at Mick's door with his suggestions. "I liked *Rumours*," he told the *Los Angeles Times*, "but to me there was a point where the focus became the sales, not the music. There is a lot of pressure to top yourself, to come up with a *Rumours II*, and that seemed like a trap. So I went to Mick and said, 'We've got to break out of this mold that is slowly closing in on us.' "

The most outlandish of Lindsey's demands was that he be given the leeway to work alone. He had set up a ministudio in the servant's quarters of his Beverly Hills home, fully intending to make use of it. "I have to be able to have a machine at home because it's home base and it's a very different relationship with your work," he explained to *Hit Parader*. "In the studio with four other strong-egoed people, plus all the mechanical units you have to go through, it can be limiting. By using all the state-of-the-art technology, it's easy to get away from what rock and roll has always been. The rawness of *Tusk* was a necessity, and I, in my own mind, had no choice in the matter."

Faced with the strength of Lindsey's conviction, Mick had no choice but to give in. According to Richard Dashut, the drummer could either acquiesce to Lindsey's requests or start headhunting. "Basically," Dashut told *Rolling Stone*, "if Lindsey hadn't been allowed to do what he did on *Tusk*, I think that you wouldn't have had a band. Or that they would have got another guitar player. I think that everybody else went along to save the band, as opposed to really agreeing with where his head was at."

However, while there may have been some bowing to pressure at the beginning, Mick was soon won over to the guitarist's vision, agreeing with Lindsey that *Tusk* would indeed have to be a radical departure from the big *R*. In an interview with *Bam*, Stevie confirmed that, in fact, "it was so important to Lindsey and Mick to do something that was nothing like *Rumours*."

Perhaps it was in reaction to the world's expectations, and as a testament to their own self-governance, that the band decided to turn the album into an expression of their own creative freedom. "I think that will probably be the signpost in terms of the band's continuing to feel good about making music and continuing on a creative level," Mick told the *Miami Herald*. "We could have become complacent or listened to all the people who were telling us what we should do to follow up *Rumours.* Instead we took some healthy artistic risks."

The decision to make *Tusk* a double album was one such risk. In fact, Mick told *Goldmine* that such a move was "unheard of, especially in those days when the whole record industry was about to die." Twice the price, twice the number of songs, and a mere fraction of the old Mac sound; was it asking too much from American shoppers? Mick thought not. "Making a double album is something I wanted very much to do," he told *Rolling Stone.* "We have three songwriters, and it is hard for them to develop their different aspects without room, they're artistically stifled. That's why people leave bands, you know."

The gambles taken on *Tusk* were not strictly of the musical variety. The amount of money the band shelled out on their studio alone was enough to dwarf the combined gross national product of several third world nations. "Our accountants couldn't believe the money we spent," Mick told *Creem.* "Before we started the album, I told the group we should just buy the entire studio."

Yet, instead of investing in a ready-made studio, and then renovating it to Mac specifications, the band decided to dispense with the expense of ownership and retool Studio D at L.A.'s Village Recorders. After the construction crews had finished, Fleetwood Mac had spent approximately a million dollars to become the proud tenants of a studio that included every innovation known to man, woman, and sound engineer.

————

The band spent nearly three months in the studio before heading out for an abbreviated summer tour in July 1978. While the call of the summer sun must have factored into the decision to hit the road, Mick felt that a short stint would do the studio-wan group a world of good. "I suppose we did it to feel like a band again," he explained to *Modern Recording* magazine. "We needed a short break from the studio, but not a complete break from playing. So, we picked up a very few dates just to tighten up. Communication onstage is almost like mental telepathy, and it was important to become attuned to one another before spending any more time in the studio."

The road trip would prove a study in contrasts for the recording-enamored Lindsey Buckingham. In the studio, the guitarist could tinker with his music ad infinitum without feeling the strain. "You have to allow yourself to get totally drawn into the music," he espoused in *Rolling Stone.* "Once you're there, the hardest thing to do is let yourself do anything outside that. I'd come out of my basement studio after about six hours, and Carol, my girlfriend, would be sitting in the living room watching TV or something, and I just wouldn't have much to say. My mind would be racing. I love it."

Yet the workaholism did take its toll. When time came to go on tour, the fatigue that had been so easy for Lindsey to deny in the studio surfaced. Just two weeks after the band had hit the road, Lindsey collapsed in his Philadelphia hotel room. The fainting spell occurred in the morning, and he was back onstage that very night.

After the show, Lindsey went to the hospital, where a spinal tap revealed that he suffered from a mild and easily controlled form of epilepsy. Lindsey had suffered a seizure. Doctors advised him to take it easy and even recommended that he sit on a stool during performances, but he did no such thing. Only a few shows had to be canceled before the guitarist was back in business, showing no sign of weakness.

Lindsey wasn't the only one plagued by show-stopping trauma during this tour. Mick had known for some months that his father was suffering from cancer, but when he was informed that Mike Fleetwood was in critical condition, he put the tour on hold to rush to his side. His father's subsequent passing devastated the Fleetwood family, but the tour required Mick's presence in the States. In no position to wallow in his grief, Mick returned to work forthwith.

By all accounts, Lindsey's illness and the death of Mick's father cast a pall over the frequently interrupted summer tour. So did Stevie's continuing struggle with her vocal problems, which evoked rapacious criticism from the concert reviewers. Save perhaps for the confirmed studiophobe, John McVie, the group welcomed their retreat into Village Recorders. It was agreed that *Tusk* would put the past behind them and cap off the decade by striking a blow for progress and musical integrity.

———

The million-dollar deal that Mick had negotiated for Peter Green came complete with a $400,000 advance. Peter had only to sign on the dotted line to start raking in the rest of his money. Earlier in the year, he'd sounded excited about recording his new album, joking with *Rolling Stone* that "it's going to be a lot of raw guitar rock. Are people still into that?"

But when the moment of truth rolled around, Peter's tune had changed substantially. In Peter Green's biography, Mick recalled how the guitarist had waited until all the participating record executives had been assembled, "and then in the office he suddenly turned and said, 'I can't do this. It's the work of the devil. This is not what music should be.' "

With his mentality still firmly rooted in the sixties counterculture, Peter believed that if he signed, he would become a company man. Even as Mick tried to assure his client that the record company would allow him the freedom he needed to create, he knew from experience that all efforts to dissuade Peter would prove futile. The meeting ended as a humbling experience for the manager. "I looked a bit stupid," Mick told *Trouser Press*. "After all, who would believe that he didn't want to sign a contract because he thought it was with the Devil?"

Mick not only lost face before the executives; he lost his commission and his most promising client as well. Yet despite having recently purchased a $400,000 plot of land in Hawaii and a property in Malibu, not to mention his house in Bel Air, when Peter informed him that he'd be returning to England, out of friendship Mick made no effort to detain him. "I was becoming the bad guy in his world," Mick told *Mojo*, "and I couldn't let that happen to myself."

Although both his partnership with Mick Fleetwood and his marriage to Jane Samuels had dissolved, Peter would at long last return to music. Within a year's time, Peter had recorded a fairly successful album, *In the Skies*. Oddly enough, the legendary guitarist allowed his name to grace an album that featured little if any of his own work. "A lot of the guitar is done by a friend of his," Mick lamented. "He told me that he'd handed over the guitar duties to someone else." Despite this reluctance to play, Peter would release four albums, with varying degrees of success, in the early eighties alone.

———

Peter would put in one final, albeit uncredited, performance with the Mac. After the band adjourned to the studio to work on *Tusk*, Peter agreed to play guitar on Christine's mystical song "Brown Eyes." "He plays literally about eight notes," Mick told *Trouser Press*. "He just wandered into the studio while the track was being done." Peter's input aside, the song differed from much of Christine's past material in that it wasn't what one would call a meat-and-potatoes love ballad. The spirit of innovation that informed the *Tusk* sessions inspired the songwriter to branch out in a different direction, to step away from songs that, as she herself told *Newsweek*, "don't bash away at your brain cells, but they're bouncy."

In so doing, Christine fulfilled the prediction she'd made in *Stage Life* a year prior. "We never seem to stop progressing," she had told the publication. "Once you slot yourself, there's only so far you can go in any one direction. I really don't want to stop experimenting in different directions, just to see what we can do."

Lindsey was enjoying the autonomy that came from working at home. To achieve the sound that he heard in his head, he recorded everywhere from his basement to his bathroom. At such times, he would eliminate all his bandmates from the recording process, laying down the instrumental tracks himself. "The *Tusk* album," he told the *Detroit Free Press*, "was the result of a certain process, the result of my songs being the radical departure and evolving into a different concept of recording, which was basically me at home recording all the instruments."

Working alone was nothing less than a slice of heaven for Lindsey. As he would go on to explain in a variety of interviews, the solitary working conditions allowed the artistry inherent in his production capabilities to reach a whole new level. "We had a twenty-four-track machine in my house that I was using to experiment with different sounds and ideas," he told *Bam*. "That approach, if used properly, can be really valid, I think. It becomes much more intimate. It's more like [being] a painter because you can respond to your intuitions, take an idea and just go with it. Sometimes it's hard to stop. It gets very, very exciting."

"The Ledge," "That's Enough for Me," and "Save Me a Place" were all recorded without a whit of help from his Fleetwood Mac cohorts. Yet despite his constant efforts on the home front, Lindsey was also a major presence in the studio. Holding tight to his producer's cap, he oversaw every move made in the control room, from cutting the tracks to overdubbing and putting on the vocals. Having gained the trust and admiration, if not always the sympathy, of his fellow musicians, he was always on call to arrange their compositions. "I have a lot of respect for this man," Christine told the *Record*. "I don't really imagine anybody else being able to do what he does with my songs."

A mandatory attendance policy had been strictly enforced by Fleetwood Mac during the *Rumours* sessions, but the recording of *Tusk* had a much looser feel about it. After John McVie finished cutting his bass parts, he sailed off to Maui, not to be heard from for weeks. "There's a point on that course, about a thousand miles out, where you are farther from land than at any other point on the planet," he told *Rolling Stone*. "I went out on the deck at that point and looked around, and all I could think was, 'Well John, this is how far you have to go to get away from being John McVie of Fleetwood Mac.'" However great his love of Fleetwood Mac's wine-women-and-song lifestyle, that atmosphere was not to be found in the studio but on the road.

With Lindsey doing much of his work in his lair, Stevie also gained the latitude to stay out of the studio when her presence was not absolutely necessary. Once she felt certain that she could, in fact, go her own way without any repercussions, Lindsey told *Bam*, "she'd come in to do her song once a week and that would be it."

Stevie remembered the *Tusk* sessions somewhat differently. "On *Tusk* I was in the studio every day for almost thirteen months," she told *Hit Parader*, "but I probably only worked for two months. The other eleven I did nothing, and you start to lose your mind after a while if you're not active. See, they all play instruments and I don't. So I'm looking at them through a window in the studio; five hours go by and they don't even remember I'm there. It's frustrating."

Unable either to jam with the band or arrange her own songs, she often felt left out of the proceedings. "There've been many times," Christine explained to the *Record*, "when she might come out in the studio and try and sing along, and we'd tend to say, 'Don't do that right now, let us work this out first.' "

The band's somewhat patronizing attitude toward their front-woman no doubt contributed to her growing reluctance to go into the studio. Sensing that Lindsey and the others didn't take her songs very seriously, trusting them with her material became doubly difficult. "She writes constantly, and all her songs are like babies to her, even though some of them are rubbish," Christine once told the *Record*. "When I write," she continued, "I sit down and work on an idea until it's finished, but Stevie cranks out songs all the time." In the same article, Lindsey called Stevie's songs "a little flaky."

While this interview took place three years after the *Tusk* sessions had ended, at a time when no one in the band was particularly pleased with their frontwoman's conduct, the group's air of condescension toward Stevie did not arise overnight. Chances are that Stevie felt her bandmates' disregard long before this public tongue-lashing took place.

———

Some of Stevie's reluctance to rush into the *Tusk* fray may have stemmed from her personal problems with Mick Fleetwood. While the passionate affair they'd carried on was marked by the total absence of promises and demands, the last thing Stevie expected was that Mick would go chasing after one of her close friends. By the time Mick started dating Sara Recor, he and the lead vocalist had already come to the understanding that their relationship had run its course.

Married to one of the band's better acquaintances, band manager Jim Recor, Sara had been the inspiration for Stevie's haunting song "Sara." Sara's relationship with Mick burst out of the closet when she joined him at his Bel Air home, leaving her husband in her wake. For Stevie, the perceived disloyalty of her friends was by no means easy to bear. While she would eventually forgive both parties, Mick's autobiography revealed that Stevie refused to leave her house for days after hearing the news and responded to her bandmate's reconciliatory overtures with a curt "Mick, I don't want to talk about it."

(*Above*) Stevie, Lindsey, and Mick reunited in January of 1993 to perform "Don't Stop" at President Clinton's Inaugural Gala (Reuters/Joe Giza/Archive)

(*Below*) Fleetwood Mac after their victory at the American Music Awards, 1978 (Frank Edwards/Fotos International/Archive)

(*Above*) *Left to right*: Christine, John, Mick, Stevie, and Lindsey reunited on May 22, 1997, to play their first full-length concert together since 1982 (Reuters/Fred Prouser/Archive)

(*Left*) Stevie, looking suitably festive at the Inaugural Gala, 1993 (Reuters/Joe Giza/Archive)

(*Above*) Frontwoman Stevie shows off her signature "witchy style" at the taping of Fleetwood Mac's 1997 MTV special (Reuters/Fred Prouser/Archive)

(*Below*) Stevie Nicks and Lindsey Buckingham were able to put aside their differences to perform at Fleetwood Mac's induction into the Rock and Roll Hall of Fame on January 12, 1998 (Reuters/Mike Sagar/Archive)

The legendary Fleetwood Mac (Archive)

But Mick and Sara were in love; and they weren't the only ones. Christine had also found a new inamorato. Although she had been living with Curry Grant for a few years now, she'd consistently maintained that she was not in love with him. Such a tenuous bond was sure to break sooner or later. If it hadn't been Beach Boy Dennis Wilson, it would have been some other infatuation.

Dennis was the first guy to come along and sweep Christine clear off her feet since John McVie. She met Dennis in November at the Village Recorders studios, where he was working on his solo album. In *Heroes and Villains: The True Story of the Beach Boys,* Dennis's secretary, Chris Kable, recounted how Christine "took one look at Dennis and knew that he was somebody she wanted to be with. The night they met, she went home with him and spent the night with him on the boat."

From then on, Christine spent most of her evenings with Dennis. Although still legally married, Dennis was in the process of a rather amicable divorce from his second wife, Karen Lamm. Soon, Curry Grant moved out of Christine's house, and Dennis became a permanent fixture, setting up shop in her poolhouse.

Besides providing him with shelter, Christine wound up supporting Dennis's expensive cocaine habit. His legal fees, alimonies, child support payments, and unrestrained spending had sapped his Beach Boys fortune. He was reduced to borrowing from Christine, which she tolerated, according to Dennis's business manager, "without any strings in a very nice manner." In an effort to please him, she also began tending to her fashion sense, parting with exorbitant sums to look the part of his girlfriend. Despite her home-court advantage and strong-minded nature, Christine was soon completely drawn into Dennis's crazy world. She would later describe their relationship, in *Us* magazine, as "the most bizarre two years of my life."

As her bandmates alternated their time between the recording of *Tusk* and the hot pursuit of romance, Stevie was busy forging a new alliance of her own. With the encouragement of her friends Paul Fishkin, Danny Goldberg, and Irving Azoff, the most engaging woman in rock was prepared to go solo. The plan was to launch a separate record company solely for Stevie's independent ventures. Fishkin, a music-industry insider and Stevie's onetime boyfriend, and Goldberg, an editor at *Circus* magazine, pooled their funds to start up Modern Records. "Paul Fishkin and I believed in her," Goldberg told *Circus*. "We both risked our careers on her, but we all had a dream."

Stevie's desire to branch out was fueled by her band's democratic recording process. To wit, she would bring in a piano-accompanied song and the rest of the band would proceed to "take it apart and put it back together," cutting the composer out of the equation completely. "Sometimes I don't mind my songs being changed around; sometimes it makes them better. But often I would rather they stayed real simple," she explained in *Playboy*.

The tremendous stockpile of songs she'd collected over the years was also a primary consideration. Knowing that they would never see the light of day if she didn't take matters into her own hands, Stevie felt that she would have to take her chances. "The only reason I had a solo career was so I could do more songs," she told *Music Central*. "You can't do many in Fleetwood Mac, doing an album every few years with three writers, so you get maybe three, four, or five songs at the most. I write all the time, and my songs get backlogged so much that I start to feel crummy if I can't record them."

Of course, all plans for the project had to remain strictly hush-hush for the time being. Stevie rightly believed that if she were to make her aims public, her commitment to the Mac would become suspect. The very real possibility of Stevie's solo debut winding up a bargain-bin disaster was perhaps of even more serious import. If the album tanked, the consequences could be ruinous not only for Stevie but for the band as a whole.

Fearing the worst, Stevie decided to weigh the pros and cons a while longer before taking any definitive step in the solo direction. "I was particularly nervous about making this album alone because I knew I wouldn't have four other people to blame if it didn't do well," she later told *Hit Parader*. "In Fleetwood Mac, I fail with four other people if I fail. Here, if I fail, I fail alone. And it's always scary to be alone."

Meanwhile, the painstaking recording process wore on at an excruciatingly slow pace. The first months of 1979 came and went, and the band had still not finished their elephantine double album. People were beginning to wonder. Rumors of a breakup again began to circulate. Yet there was a method to the Mac's madness. In the *Detroit Free Press,* Christine explained that "the albums take so long to make, largely because there are probably too many chiefs. It's not just the band members—there's also two engineers to work with. We tend to go back and forth and take a long time to decide on the final product. It's not push-and-shove in a bad way. That's part of the game, really; if you're going to do something you might as well make it the very best that you can, and if we ourselves like it, that's the best we can do."

It was just this sort of conglomerate decision making that led to the creation of "Tusk," the title cut widely regarded as the most exotic Fleetwood Mac song of all time. Much as *Rumours'* "The Chain" had started out as one piece only to morph into something altogether different, "Tusk" began as a warm-up sound-check riff that Lindsey and Mick would play onstage at the beginning of their concerts.

Not one to let a good riff go to waste, Lindsey wrote some accompanying lyrics and promptly forgot about them. Later, he realized that the riff corresponded well to another work in progress. After a lot of technical wizardry—not the least of which involved an engineer manually picking up the slack created by a thirty-foot-long loop of tape that Lindsey and Richard Dashut had suspended between two twenty-four-track machines on opposite sides of the control room—the song's rhythm track was completed to everyone's satisfaction.

Then Mick piped in with the wild idea of commissioning the USC Trojan marching band to play on the song. He'd been waiting for the opportunity to throw some winds into the mix, and "this was the perfect track," he told *Creem.* "I told everyone else, 'Whether you like it or not, we're going to have a brass band on this song.' I've even had visions of us on tour, with the local Salvation Army band coming up onstage and playing that part with us."

Mick's brainstorm initially had his bandmates rolling their eyes. Yet the drummer held his ground until everyone came around to his way of thinking. "It was a stroke of genius," Lindsey said in an interview with *Guitar World.* "I had the song 'Tusk,' and we had it all done. I don't know how he came up with the idea of adding a marching band to it, but it was brilliant. The challenge of that was getting the marching band on the existing track, in sync with the other instruments. Mick had this whole idea where he wanted to film it. We went to Dodger Stadium and got the band out on the infield. They had a remote truck there. Needless to say, it took a while."

———

The band would spend several additional months in the studio before handing *Tusk* over to the record company. In that time, Bob Welch's second solo album, *Three of Hearts,* unleashed a veritable inferno of disco rhythms upon the world. Released in February 1979, under the rubric of Seedy Management, the LP featured the production work of Richard Dashut, Mick Fleetwood on drums, and the backup vocal stylings of both Stevie and Christine. "Precious Love," the first single spawned by the record, was another feather in Bob's cap, catapulting this soon-to-be-gold album to Number Twenty on the *Billboard* chart.

If Lindsey contributed little to Bob's continued success, it was only because his spare time had already been spoken for by one of his childhood heroes. Having learned to play guitar by listening to many a Kingston Trio record, Lindsey didn't tarry when the Trio's John Stewart called him. Stewart had been struggling to carve out his niche in the solo realm ever since his folk outfit had disbanded in 1967. Despite having mastered the electric guitar by listening to Lindsey play on Fleetwood Mac records, he could not cut a hit single to save his life. Three successive record companies had dropped him from their rosters, and RSO, his current label, was threatening to do likewise if his next record didn't perform. This album, aptly titled *Bombs Away Dream Babies,* was Stewart's last hope.

After learning that he'd been one of Lindsey's seminal influences, Stewart figured he had nothing to lose by asking the impresario to produce *Bombs Away.* Lindsey listened to Stewart's demos and agreed to do what he could. "Lindsey would come in for fourteen hours at a time and then I wouldn't see him again for a month," Stewart told one interviewer. "As far as Lindsey went, it was just the way he would point the way to things, show me the direction in which to go, make me a

mix that was just mind-blowing, and play some guitars or do some vocals." In fact, Lindsey became so involved with the album that when
Stewart ran out of money, he ponied up the twenty thousand dollars
necessary to finish the album.

Stevie was also recruited to sing on the record. In an interview with
Capitol Radio, John Stewart recalled her well-timed words of encouragement. "She said, 'John, let's make hits. We've all made the other
kind of record. Let's make hits. They're more fun to make.' " Sure
enough, with her unmistakable voice filling out the harmonies on the
album's lead single, "Gold," the song sailed past the competition, all
the way into Number Five. The track was the first in a three-hit series
that was chiefly responsible for turning *Bombs Away Dream Babies*
into a top-ten platinum album, and John Stewart into the comeback of
the year. "Great relief has swept over my body," Stewart told *People*.
"This is a new breath of life. Lindsey's a genius, and there's no price
tag to put on that kind of support."

Although both Bob Welch and John Stewart would make disappointing follow-ups, Fleetwood Mac's generous assistance to these and
other artists helped shape the face of music in the late 1970s. Despite
the comings and goings of punk rockers, new wavers, and disco
dancers, the Mac's classic California sensibility would endure as pop-
dom's most entrenched aesthetic through the 1980s and beyond.

While the band's magnanimity was certainly to be admired, their auxiliary session playing and production work did manage to prolong
Tusk's cumbersome recording process. Consequently, the public's expectations, as well as those of the label executives, climbed a positive
slope for months. By the time the group's magnum opus was ready to
leave the studio, the general consensus seemed to be that Fleetwood
Mac's double album was, as Mick put it, "going to single-handedly rescue the record business."

At the time, the album's contents were still highly classified information. After the calming balm of *Rumours,* no one could have fore-
seen the audacity of *Tusk*. Even Stevie disagreed with the jolting shift
in direction. "I didn't understand *Tusk* when we were recording it," she

told *Bam.* "I really liked the idea, but I didn't really understand the concepts, like the dog biting the leg on the cover. Needless to say, I wasn't part of any of that."

Not only did Stevie decline to participate in planning the cover art, but she made sure that everyone heard her dissenting opinion by discussing it in a slew of publications. "I got attacked by a German shepherd about a year ago," she said in the April 1981 issue of *Hit Parader,* "and the picture reminds me of that dog. He really isn't a mean dog, but I don't like pictures of dogs that look like they're going to rip your face off. I simply had to learn to accept it. But I'll just never wear a T-shirt with that dog on the front of it."

The cover photo wasn't the last of Stevie's problems. Another unsavory tidbit that she'd be forced to swallow was the title of the album itself. Mick's idea to name the album *Tusk* was approved by all the other band members, most likely in Stevie's absence. When the group ran the title by their leading lady, her attitude took a turn for the livid. Mick would withhold the actual significance of the appellation from the press, saying only that "the title itself has no bearing on anything. We just liked the sound of the word in the abstract." Stevie was not amused by the truth, which Mick finally revealed to the public in his autobiography: The word was "a jocular term of affection for the Male Member."

Judging by the signature style of her contributions to the album, such as the upbeat "Angel" and the cryptic "Sisters of the Moon," Stevie also saw no reason to use *Tusk* as a means of trailblazing. "For me," she told *Bam,* "it was almost like we were trying way too hard. Like, it doesn't have to be this difficult. I mean, we were just making another record, for God's sake." In interviews, she had often attributed her sartorial flair to having found one style she liked and sticking to it. The same principle of timelessness may well be applied to her music; Stevie has never aspired to being of the moment.

While the rest of the band stayed true to the spirit of the seventies, Lindsey's dramatic change of image—from laissez-faire hippie chic to the cutting edge in minimalist fashion—led many to believe that he was in a hurry to join the new-wave revolution. The guitarist insisted that all such speculation was unfounded. "I decided to cut my hair long before anybody else did," he told *Musician Player and Listener* magazine. "It wasn't necessarily to look punk or anything. I was just tired of the beard, so I shaved it. Then the hair didn't look right without the beard, so I cut the hair. It's all been gradual. Found a couple of new clothes stores, started buying some new suits. . . ." Despite his aggressive deviation from the *Rumours* norm, Lindsey's motivation was not defined by the simple wish to remain *au courant*. His considerably more exalted purpose was to propel his music as far as his creativity and production skills allowed. The influx of fresh artists had opened up new vistas for Lindsey, and he meant to take full advantage by letting his imagination run free.

Although his bandmates had hoped to see his material assume a more commercial form in the control room, no one dared flout the ax man's dedication to keeping the tracks' rawness intact. His studio expertise had been the quintet's ticket to greatness, and they'd learned to trust his instincts. The result was a striking incongruity among the album cuts. Whereas *Rumours* had played like an extended conversation between the songwriters and their muses, on *Tusk*, as Lindsey told the *Los Angeles Times,* "if you pull my songs off, they sound like a first solo album. You've got these tracks by various members, which run toward the more conservative side, and you've got all my stuff that sounds real abrasive."

––––––––

When Fleetwood Mac brought the recording to a close in June 1979, Lindsey was satisfied that the final cut was a credit to the band. Equally enthusiastic, Mick decided that the demoralizing response of Warner Bros. personnel—who were warning the group against releasing *Tusk* as a double album—did not bear mentioning. In consequence, Lindsey had no way of knowing that the label executives were already dreaming up ways to counter worst-case scenarios.

Instead, as Lindsey told *Rolling Stone,* he was led to believe that when "Mick took the *Tusk* album down to Warner Bros., everyone was jumping up and down going, 'Oh, this is really one of the neatest things we ever heard.' " As the band's manager, Mick saw fit to shield his lead guitarist and production point man from outside detractors. But subsequent magazine articles revealed the record company's actual reaction, and Lindsey learned that "when a lot of those people at Warner Bros. heard that album, they saw their Christmas bonuses flying out the window."

Sure enough, the experts had been onto something. When "Tusk" was released as the album's lead single in September 1979, fourteen million *Rumours* albums had already been sold, and the ever-growing number of Mac watchers was bewildered. Where were the catchy lyrics? The melody? The Mac's signature style? This was not a tune to inspire traffic-jam sing-alongs or satisfy the fans' voracity for pop à la California. Despite the pangs of betrayal suffered by the band's following, the record buyers propelled the single to Number Eight on *Billboard*'s Hot 100. The promising response to the album's most left-of-center selection had Fleetwood Mac expecting another watershed.

They planned to promote the album through its October release date and begin touring shortly thereafter. Toward these ends, Fleetwood Mac installed their gear in a rehearsal hall and set the interview round in motion; *Rolling Stone, Creem, People,* and the like were clamoring for a crack at this long-sequestered outfit. When *Tusk* the album followed on the heels of "Tusk" the single, it found an eager audience aghast at the high price of music. Sparing themselves the sweet sorrow of parting with sixteen crisp dollar bills, thrifty fans nationwide stayed close to their tape recorders the night Westwood One broadcast the album in its entirety. The buzz of all those cassette recorders translated into nothing short of a great sucking sound for Fleetwood Mac and *Tusk,* as the radio transmission both stole the album's thunder and drained a good portion of the band's prospective profits.

As the follow-up to the most successful album of the century, *Tusk* should have debuted near the top of the charts. The largely rave reviews—calling the album everything from "the most spectacular event in records since Stevie Wonder's *Songs in the Key of Life*" to "the record that will overcome the basic critic presumption that records that sell a ton are automatically less worthy than those that don't sell at all"— stroked the artists' egos. Fleetwood Mac's brand-new star on the Hollywood Walk of Fame was also said to be a good omen.

Yet due to the Westwood One broadcast, the otherwise limited radio airplay, the economic slump, the prohibitive cost of the LP, its unorthodox content, or any combination of the above, buyers weren't biting—at least not with the same frequency as back in the *Rumours* heyday. Despite the Mac's efforts to keep mercantile concerns at arm's length, the dive in popularity ruffled feathers. The first few months in release saw a relatively modest two million double-record sets leave the shelves. "We all expected it to sell more," Lindsey told *Bam.* "Not sixteen million, certainly, but a couple of million more wouldn't have hurt."

———

In retrospect, Fleetwood Mac hardly needed to stage an exhaustive world tour to accelerate *Tusk*'s sluggish sales. The broad appeal of forthcoming singles such as Stevie's "Sara," which would peak at Number Seven, and Christine's top-twenty "Think About Me," might have sufficed to send four million people rushing for the record stores. Ten grueling months of road work later, various members of Fleetwood Mac would be thinking these very thoughts, wondering whether their longest concert tour yet had really been worth the superhuman effort.

Armed with neither extrasensory perception nor a reliable crystal ball, the Fleetwood Mac ensemble was bright-eyed and bushy-tailed at the prospect of filling the nation's arenas and amphitheaters. Over a year had passed since their last tour, and memories of the agonizing *Rumours* march had lost much of their impact. Since Lindsey's alt-rock-flavored cuts accounted for nearly half the LP, the radio deejays' unwillingness to foist them upon an indifferent public—interested mainly in the adult-oriented rock stylings of the "early" Mac—hurt the record's chances of measuring up to its predecessor. "A lot of Lindsey's tunes had trouble with airplay because people didn't know immediately who it was and a lot of people wanted another *Rumours* for their own good ends," Mick later told *Hit Parader.*

During a time of twenty-five-cent candy bars and buck-a-pack cigarettes, sixteen dollars was also a lot to ask of the fans. With the radio stations dead-set against giving *Tusk* its due air play, there was nothing the Mac could do for their album short of touring. By the time the band was road-worthy, *Tusk* was at Number Four, whereas the Eagles' much maligned *The Long Run* was Number One. With the critics all weighing in on the side of Fleetwood Mac, Mick decided that a lengthy concert tour was all the band needed to financially justify their studio experimentation. As he explained to reporters, the tour was a testament to the band's "commitment." "It's not that we just want to throw out an album and say, 'Oh, it'll do alright!' "

In exchange for his comrades' consent—some of them were none too keen on sacrificing yet another year to the road—the sovereign of Seedy Management vowed to provide the troupe with all the comforts of their million-dollar homes. The tour's expenditures overshadowed even those of the extravagant *Rumours* tour, as massage therapists were put on the payroll, private jets chartered, hotel rooms customized in advance, and Colombian drug cartels kept in business.

Salt Lake City, Albuquerque, St. Louis, New York City, Boston, Los Angeles . . . the first leg of the tour was slated to last two months and hit twenty-two U.S. cities. Yet trouble was afoot before the voyage had even begun.

———

Lindsey had suffered a seizure on the band's last go-round; this tour would see Mick's health fail. Back when *Tusk* was still in its infancy, the drummer had begun to experience strange symptoms. "I had been feeling burned-out," he told *People* magazine. "My eyes were going wild, I started drinking like a fish, I'd hyperventilate while talking. Manic-depressive one minute, eating a bowl of ice cream, quite happy, the next. I thought it was a brain tumor. I was afraid I was going to die. It was eighteen months of hell."

These problems were soon attributed to diabetes—bad news, considering that Mick had already been diagnosed with its polar opposite, hypoglycemia. With Sara Recor's help, Mick managed to pull himself together and adhere to the prescribed treatment. But even as he was telling *People* magazine that Sara had been "there to hold my hand and look after me," Mick was reverting to his old habits on the road. The excesses would catch up with him during a San Francisco press conference, under the glare of camera lights and the scrutiny of entertainment journalists.

Mick's credo had always been to put the shows before everything else, and he'd pushed himself to the edge trying to live up to it. In the blur of twenty-two cities darting past his limousine's tinted window, he barely noticed his woeful physical condition. The concerts at San Francisco's Cow Palace were to be Fleetwood Mac's last hoorah of the 1970s. Winded by the nonstop tour dates, the musicians were revitalized by the prospect of a month-long vacation. As they took the stage, Mick shouted out, "You know what this is? This is the last three gigs of the decade!" With New Year's Eve 1980 only two weeks away, the audience reciprocated the drummer's enthusiasm.

But when the time came to meet the press, Mick felt like a broken man. His body was telling him he should sit this one out and let his bandmates finesse the local news teams. Instead, he ignored the warning signs and joined the group. A half hour into the meeting, he was seized by convulsions, and the reporters' pens went wild. The Goliath of road warriors appeared to have gone down for the count. Of course, appearances can be misleading, and an attack of diabetes often looks worse than it feels. After Christine intervened, massaging Mick's shoulders and arms, he regained his composure, and the press conference was carried through to completion. Two concerts later, the band members had all scattered in different directions, not to reconvene for one blissful month.

The band members chose to devote their time off to following their hearts. While Fleetwood Mac was still their shared passion, the days of Benifold and bucolic communal living were but a distant memory for Mick, John, and Christine. Money and success had turned the band into a business, and working to maintain their megastar status had acquired the taint of necessary duty.

Since Sara had come along on the *Tusk* tour, Mick felt that he could in good conscience leave her side to spend time with his kids in England. Months had passed since they'd last spent quality time together, and he was eager to see how his daughters had grown. "I quite miss the fact that I can't be a father," he told *People*. "I happen to be one of those men who adores that thing of 'alright, kids let's go.'"

Still linked with the bête noir of rock, Dennis Wilson, Christine was planning to spend the month in the pursuit of pure relaxation. With the band and Dennis vying for her attention, in the past months she had been through the wringer. Although Christine's relationship was as intense as it was unstable—with Dennis constantly inventing new ways to disappoint her—the couple was talking of marrying in the near future. "Dennis has awakened things in me I'd have been scared to experience and made me feel the extremes of every emotion," Christine disclosed in *People*.

Having seen his family during the San Francisco concert dates, Lindsey adjourned to the home he shared with Carol Harris in Los Angeles. Despite Carol's absence from the tour, the couple's three-year relationship was still very much alive and well. A one-woman man, Lindsey didn't go in for the orgiastic groupie scene, saying that "getting crazy on a few drinks at the bar means nothing to me. I'm happier having time to myself in my room, doing my tunes, than looking for action."

While John was still prone to a good swig of ale, the march of time and his remarriage to Julie Rubens had turned him into a gentler version of his former self. The couple now divided their free hours between settling back in their Beverly Hills home and sailing into the majesty of L.A.'s smog-induced sunsets on John's upgraded sixty-three-foot sloop.

Oddly enough, the most romantic member of the Fleetwood Mac family had nothing but work on her mind. Stevie had been pouring her heart into her song lyrics for years and had been hoping to branch out on her own since the close of the *Rumours* tour back in 1978. She was recuperating in Hawaii when she spied a young local singer named Sharon Celani performing at a bar. In an interview with Jim Ladd, Stevie recounted how she introduced herself to the starstruck Sharon and said, "I know that you love being in Hawaii and everything, but if I ever have a band, if I ever do a record, will you consider coming and singing with me?"

An enduring friendship was born that day. Now, two years later, with the whole world falling at Stevie's platform-shod feet, the rather vague proposition she'd made to Sharon was about to pan out. Fleetwood Mac's beloved central character had at last attained enough confidence to helm her own project. Inundated with everything from

film offers to solo recordings, she decided to make public her new contract with Paul Fishkin and Danny Goldberg's Modern Records.

———

Stevie's restless stirrings, together with Lindsey's yen for artistic ex-
periments as evidenced on *Tusk*, marked the beginning of Fleetwood
Mac's ten-year process of disintegration. Although the breakups that
had characterized the *Rumours* era saw the musicians at their emotional nadir, the group had remained intent on keeping their musical
partnership alive. The pundits agreed that the collaboration couldn't
last forever, but years would pass before Fleetwood Mac would finally
prove them right.

The ensuing decade would find the rancor underlying Stevie and
Lindsey's relationship swelling to dangerous proportions. There would
be no winners in this clash of the egos; the battle would slowly wear
away at one of the greatest musical acts of the twentieth century. Solo
pursuits, bankruptcy, drug addiction, death, marriage, irreconcilable
differences, and, as always, tremendous musical success would combine to form the last years of Fleetwood Mac.

10

ENOUGH
ALREADY!

The Tusk world tour was meant to blow through a grand total of seventy-six cities. After Fleetwood Mac regrouped in February 1980, they were only a third of the way through. Despite their respective getaways into Mac-free zones, most of the band was still fried to a crisp. Mustering all the enthusiasm of underpaid assembly line workers, the celebrated quintet forged their attack on the Pacific Rim.

After allocating three weeks to the relentless wooing of their Japanese fan base, Fleetwood Mac was off to Australia. In order to sustain her voice for the tour's duration, Stevie had to center her life around a very strict regimen. "You give up everything so that that two hours is good onstage," Stevie explained on *Behind the Music.* "Every minute all day long . . . is all put toward that two hours onstage." Whereas the *Rumours* road trip had seen her take leave of her senses to join Mick in his fast-living element, she now restricted most of her spare hours to a myriad of hotel rooms. There, she would quietly document her thoughts in a journal, write songs, and, as the doctors had prescribed, nap with cotton plugging her ears.

Of course, hopping from town to town at the speed of light nullified even the best efforts at rest. The endless procession of trains, planes, and limousines coupled with a barrage of promotional appearances, sound checks, and concerts left little room for self-preservation. The fatigue began to seep out onstage. As the Mac's most performance-weary member, Lindsey gave vent to showtime antics that often exceeded the limits of good taste and professionalism. His first such display occurred during a concert in Australia. While Stevie was twirling off into her rendition of "Rhiannon," John, Christine, and Mick looked on in horror as Lindsey began to mimic her movements onstage. After the show, the band surrounded their guitarist and warned him against pulling any such stunts in the future.

Yet as soon as Fleetwood Mac arrived in New Zealand, Lindsey was up to his old tricks. One night in particular, right before the performance, Stevie and Lindsey had argued, then dutifully assumed their positions. Early in the show, Lindsey suddenly stopped playing. With thousands of people watching, Stevie recalled, he "came over—might have kicked me, did something to me, and we stopped the show." It was open season on Lindsey Buckingham. "He went off, and we all ran at breakneck speed back to the dressing room to see who could kill him first," Stevie told *Rolling Stone*. "Christine got to him first, and then I got to him second—the bodyguards were trying to get in the middle of all of us."

Desperately trying to impose some semblance of order upon her group's discombobulated lifestyle, Christine was on the warpath. Lindsey's senseless act tested the bounds of her British restraint. "I think he's the only person I ever, ever slapped," she told *Rolling Stone*. "I actually might have chucked a glass of wine, too. I just didn't think it was the way to treat a paying audience. I mean, aside from making a mockery of Stevie like that. Really unprofessional, over the top."

In Lindsey's defense, the predicament of working with Stevie could not have been easy to manage. In some respects, he resented her popularity with the fans. "It's not normal to tour with an ex-girlfriend," he'd told *People* at the beginning of the tour. "I don't really socialize with her, but things are fine." Stevie's was a different experience. As Christine recalled, "She cried. She cried a lot."

Lindsey's flare-up had not been the sole disaster of Fleetwood Mac's tour in the Pacific. On one excursion through the outback, Mick happened upon a sprawling farm, lyrically titled the Wendsley Dale. Although the two-million-dollar advance he'd received for *Tusk* had been consumed by his holdings in Maui, Malibu, and Bel Air, as well as by cocaine, child support, and alimony payments, his primary concern was to establish a home base outside Los Angeles. Mick's growing paranoia about life in the States was first evinced at the beginning of the *Tusk* tour, when he told the *Trouser Press* that "there is definitely going to be an earthquake. L.A. will be flattened. I'll have no regrets at all about moving."

As visions of imperialist grandeur and Los Angeles' inevitable doom danced in his head, he forgot all about his uncertain financial situation. Budgetary constraints had never limited Mick's aspirations to an aristocratic lifestyle. As he told the *New York Times,* "I was not into doing a major amount of bean counting." He blithely took out a loan of two million dollars, using the entirety of his assets as collateral. "I was finding a way to create a creative kingdom, a safe harbor from what was a very crazy world at that point," explained Mick, alluding to the hostage crisis, the threat of nuclear war, and his own turbulent ride with the Mac. "Australia was a very safe place."

At the end of March, this emotionally, physically, and financially draining leg of the tour sputtered to a halt in Honolulu. The band had been on the road for four solid months. *Tusk* had been in stores for half a year and sold three million copies—a respectable figure, but by no means the blowout for which the band had hoped. As the architect behind the Mac's new sound, Lindsey felt responsible for the less than spectacular showing. "Six months later," Lindsey told the *Los Angeles Times,* "Mick and several other people in the band turned around and said, 'You blew it.' "

Lindsey may well have overstated the matter, plagued as he was by his own culpability. While *Tusk* was a progressive album, and one in which the whole band took pride, he did tell the *Detroit Free Press* that he was "serious about selling records." Failing to replicate the success of *Rumours,* he was naturally sensitive to the slightest insinuation on the part of his bandmates, whom he believed to be harboring feelings of resentment. As Mick explained, "I did talk to him about how I thought his tracks could have gotten more radio exposure if he had made a few changes in them, but I was never trying to scold him. I was just trying to help him."

On a lighter note, having been fired from the Beach Boys, Dennis Wilson found ample time to join Christine in Honolulu. Here he made an elaborate production of presenting her with an unset ruby and asking for her hand in marriage. Although no date was set, the understanding was that the couple was officially engaged.

––––––––

After setting aside April 1980 for purposes of convalescence, Fleetwood Mac was ready to hit the concert trail in May. After covering Canada and the northernmost reaches of the United States, the band headed for Europe, where they spent another month in perpetual transit. Then it was back to the States for a short break and yet another month on the road. Fleetwood Mac's stage show developed a great deal during the *Tusk* tour. The wealth of material on their double album allowed Fleetwood Mac to let go of the past and center their concerts around the compositions of the current lineup.

Now that the band had discontinued their heavy reliance on selections from the Peter Green and Bob Welch eras, Lindsey's personal style came to the fore. Not only did he impress his own stamp onto oldies like "Oh Well," but his guitar solos, executed downstage center under a strategically placed spotlight, caused one *Rolling Stone* reviewer to rave that "he dominated the band as completely as any human being could ever dominate drummer Mick Fleetwood and bassist John McVie—one of the most cohesive and potent rhythm sections in rock." Clearly, the guitarist had finally come into his own in performance, becoming a force to be reckoned with. "I think we were playing like a really tight unit," Lindsey told *Bam.* "The shows got more rock and roll as we went along."

While some American concert reviewers derided Stevie's costume changes and fanciful ways, she had, by this time, learned to take all cheap shots at her sanity with a grain of salt. After all, the fans were the ones who really counted, and they couldn't get enough. If not sufficiently serious for the purist critics, Stevie's glitzy and thoroughly entertaining stage act had men and women alike queuing up at ticket counters. Christine, as always, was praised for her smooth-grooved vocals and chided for restricting herself to the background.

Toward the end of the tour, Lindsey's body gave out on him, and he collapsed just as he had a year earlier in Philadelphia. The diagnostic spinal tap left him in a state of agony for days, and a Cleveland concert date—for eighty thousand people, no less—had to be rescheduled. Barring this notable exception, the final month of Fleetwood Mac's last great stand went off without a hitch. Lindsey made a full and fast recovery, and the Mac played vigorously in anticipation of drawing the *Tusk* tour's final curtain.

This second wind aside, the musicians were tired and their future uncertain. "You just stop being emotional in a lot of ways," Stevie confided. "You become kind of hard and cold, because it's the only way you can exist and get through it."

At L.A.'s Hollywood Bowl, on August 31 and September 1, Fleetwood Mac played the last dates of the tour. After his recent brush with bodily pain, Lindsey, for one, couldn't wait to go his own way. "This is our last show," he told the audience. "For a very long time."

———

For all its inability to influence the record-buying public, the *Tusk* tour had managed to change the face of Fleetwood Mac forever. No one was willing to put up with any more kamikaze tour schedules, save perhaps John and Mick. And when the latter was relieved from his managerial duties, the band's new attitude was unmistakable. The quintet was no longer a band of musical outlaws, but a savvy business arrangement. If there was one thing that the members agreed upon, it was the need for increased control over their personal itineraries and funds.

Accused of lax management and gross overspending, Mick was found guilty and stripped of his manager's stripes at a meeting that included all the bandmates and their representatives. Solo projects crowned the new Mac order, and the group was temporarily put out of commission. The fact was that after a year on the road, playing to no fewer than twelve thousand people per show, the band had no profits to show for their efforts.

Crushed by his friends' insurgence, Mick threw up his hands and went with the flow. But now that the professionals were at the helm, he knew that Fleetwood Mac had lost an essential, grassroots quality. While they might very well continue to make beautiful music together, the energy would never be the same.

———

As if to underscore the band's new businesslike stance, a live album was released in time for the Christmas shopping season. Heretofore, Fleetwood Mac had been dead-set against putting out anything of the kind, but the pressure to recoup the losses of the tour and augment *Tusk*'s four-million-copy-selling revenue won out. "We will not do a 'live' album because we believe that 'live' music and studio sound are two different things," Richard Dashut had told *Modern Recording*. "I personally do not like 'live' albums. I would rather go to a concert and feel it rather than hear a recording of it. Editing in a studio is essentially the art of an album, and you can't very well do editing onstage."

For the most part, Fleetwood Mac shared their engineer's opinion. Mick's was the sole dissenting voice. He'd been thinking of recording a live album for some months, telling *Trouser Press* that when played live, "these songs are very different. Without all the overdubs they really kick ass. I think it'd be interesting to go in an empty hall and develop the number the same way you have to play it onstage." Not until the Mac's July break from the *Tusk* tour did his voice finally prevail.

Although he'd understood his bandmates' viewpoint, that a live record might take "the freshness away" from their presence on the cutting edge of pop rock, his belief in the project was undiminished. And after taking their financial prospects into consideration, the rest of the band finally yielded to Mick's strong convictions. Compiling the material for a live LP would take a matter of weeks. Since various concerts from the tour had already been recorded, the basis for the album was complete. "I really didn't spend much time in the studio," Lindsey told *Bam*. "It was more a question of assembling things that we already had, rather than building an album up from scratch."

Aside from the obvious concert favorites, hits such as "Rhiannon," "Say You Love Me," and "Go Your Own Way," the album included three new songs: Stevie's "Fireflies," Christine's "One More Night," and Lindsey's rendition of Brian Wilson's "Farmer's Daughter." As Mick had anticipated, all were performed live but without an audience at the Santa Monica Civic Auditorium. When the album was complete, even its staunchest opponent liked what he heard. "I'm really happy with it," said Lindsey. "I initially had some reservations about doing it, but now I'm glad we did."

While it failed to generate the sort of buzz the drummer had counted upon, the record served an ulterior purpose. "It sort of put a cap on the last five years of touring and recording," Lindsey told *Bam*. "Mick wanted us to go right into the studio to start work on the next studio record, but instead we're taking a break, probably until May, to relax a little, work on our own projects or whatever. It feels good to have a breather for a change. It'll allow us to be fresh when we start the next album."

Sure enough, when *Fleetwood Mac Live* came out in early December 1980, Stevie, Lindsey, and Mick were already into their own ventures. As for the McVies, "John went on a cruise," Lindsey told *People*. "Christine just [laid] out in the sun. But three weeks off and I go nuts. Working makes me happy."

―――――――

Although Stevie had been the first to announce her plans for solo recording, Lindsey had been quick to follow suit. He'd been writing songs throughout the *Tusk* tour and had amassed ample material for an album, which he would ultimately release toward the end of 1981. His contribution to *Fleetwood Mac Live*, Brian Wilson's "Farmer's Daughter," was significant in that it pointed to the reasons for his new-found independence. "I've always identified with Brian," he said in *Behind the Masks*, "because he has spent years attempting to take what was essentially a successful early sixties pop band into a more adventurous and challenging direction. Yet the pressure put upon him by the other members of the Beach Boys and even his own family because of the desire to experiment and change has been incredible."

Free from the coercion of his fellow Mac members, Lindsey re-treated to his garage, where he began to work on the first album ever to bear his own name, *Law and Order*. As late as December 1980, Lindsey was still unsure about his solo career. Not only was he nervous about shouldering all the responsibility for the album, but he wasn't even convinced of his material. "If, as a collective group of songs, it's not something I'm totally happy with, I'm not going to put it out," he told *Bam*. "I'm not in any particular rush to get 'my solo album' out. It has to be done right or I won't do it."

Finally, after compiling an array of satisfactory songs, Lindsey signed with Asylum Records in 1981. A veritable one-man band, he not only played guitar, wrote the songs, and produced for *Law and Order* but played drums and keyboards on most of the tracks. Eventually, he realized that he needed help. He called upon Richard Dashut to coproduce and incorporated Mick's and Christine's session playing because, as he explained to *People*, "doing all the production and playing nearly all the instruments, you begin to lose your objectivity as to what's good."

Mick's assistance on *Law and Order* left no doubt that he had revised his initial position on the solo routes taken by his bandmates. As a knee-jerk action, he had fought all such divisive steps since first hearing of Stevie's plans, taking them as omens of impending disbandment. Now that he'd accepted the inevitability of Stevie's and Lindsey's solo pursuits, his attitude executed a complete about-face. Since independent recording provided the songwriters with auxiliary creative outlets, Mick reasoned, it would serve as Fleetwood Mac's fountain of youth. Suddenly, he saw solo work as good for the band's life expectancy, and he was only too ready to play the rugged individualist.

Even before Lindsey had had a chance to sign with Asylum Records, Mick was already drumming up financial support for his own splinter project, *The Visitor*. He'd been toying with the idea of recording an album that would fuse his pop rock beat with African rhythms since before the *Tusk* tour began. Looking at the prospect of nine fallow months, he decided that the time was ripe to bring the African project to fruition. With RCA Records footing the bill, he hired Richard Dashut to produce, and the pair set out for Ghana by way of Australia and Singapore in January 1981.

While staying at his farm in Australia, Mick got a call from his accountant, Brian Adams, who had become convinced that the rock star was facing bankruptcy. According to Adams's testimony in the *New York Times,* when he arrived at Wendsley Dale to inform Mick of his dire straits, the drummer "told me it was not possible." Before he could be convinced otherwise, Mick was gone.

He had flown off to Singapore, where he continued his profligate spending by purchasing an eight-thousand-dollar Rolex President watch, which he deliberately shattered shortly after arriving in Ghana. In his autobiography, he wrote that "I looked around and thought, what am I doing wearing this big gold watch amidst such poverty and privation?" As he had yet to acknowledge his own money troubles, Mick "felt untouchable" as he embarked upon recording *The Visitor* with native drummers in a technologically barren part of Africa.

The album would be released to a largely indifferent audience in June 1981. Despite its interesting reworking of such old favorites as "Rattlesnake Shake" and "Not Fade Away," the LP climbed the charts to Number Forty-three, then disappeared from view. After the 1983 release of another commercial flop, *I'm Not Me,* Mick's three-record deal with RCA would come to a premature end.

———

The nine-month window of opportunity and the need for creative self-expression had been among Mick and Lindsey's reasons for branching out into solo recording, but Stevie Nicks's personal determination to chase after success independent of Fleetwood Mac had a hand in catalyzing the men's resolve. The past few years had not been easy for Stevie. The mammoth tour and her vocal problems aside, she'd had to fight an uphill battle to win the respect and admiration of her male contemporaries, whom she termed "pretty chauvinistic." As she confided to *People,* "They resent my success. I see it in their eyes: 'How did this dingbat manage to get everything she wants?' "

Stevie had also been slapped with a lawsuit. Not long after the release of *Tusk*'s second single, "Sara," a woman from Grand Rapids, Michigan, alleged that Stevie had stolen her song. Professing to have sent the lyrics to Warner Bros. in November 1978, she maintained her claim to the song despite unequivocal proof that Stevie had written the song in July of that very year. While the court would eventually rule in favor of the defendant, Stevie was deeply troubled by the event. "There were some great similarities in the lyrics," she admitted to *Rolling Stone,* "and I never said she didn't write the words she wrote. Just don't tell me I didn't write the words I wrote. Most people think that the other party will settle out of court, but she picked the wrong songwriter. To call me a thief about my first love, my songs, that's going too far."

For the most part, it was this passion for her music that led Stevie to become a solo artist. The extensive length of her compositions and the presence of two other songwriters in the band eliminated the possibility of including more than three Stevie songs per album. Even the twenty-track *Tusk* couldn't hold more than five of her four-minute-plus tracks and fell woefully short of satisfying one of the most prolific songwriters in rock. Stevie's legendary file cabinets brimmed with pages and pages of lyrics, and finding a venue for their release was her primary intention when she signed with Modern Records.

The long *Tusk* tour had also helped to convince Stevie that her attempts at a dual-career path were not unwarranted. In return for her overexertion, she needed something that guaranteed her longevity and was uniquely her own. "I just decided when I came off that tour that I was not going to give up my life and die a lonely, overdone, overused rock star," she explained to *Hit Parader.* "There's no glamour in that. I don't want to be written up in fifty years as a miserable old woman who never got to do anything but tour and be famous for ten years and then it was over. I'm far too intelligent to not know that there will be a time when I'm not thirty-three anymore, when I won't be that pretty anymore, and I'll be tired. I want to know that I can still have fun and function on my own and be part of the world. That's why I made this album alone. I can't give my life away anymore for Fleetwood Mac."

Turning thirty in May 1978 had forced Stevie to confront the passage of time, and she finalized her plans for a separate career during her thirty-first summer. She knew that after a certain point, she wasn't going to be a sex symbol anymore and would have to work twice as hard to make it as a solo rocker. In an effort to avoid the Norma Desmond syndrome, she disposed of her spacious home overlooking Sunset Boulevard. The purchase of a beachfront condo in Santa Monica affirmed her return to the roaming ways of her youth. "I want to get back to my old gypsy kind of lifestyle," she explained in *Hit Parader.* "I get tired of being a rock and roll star."

Rounding out the list of Stevie's motivations was her undeniable need to prove that she was a viable artist with or without Lindsey. Still unresolved were the problems that had emerged during the making of *Rumours,* a time when Lindsey's resentment of Stevie and her popularity impeded him from developing many of her songs to the best of his ability. Stevie felt that her ex lorded his power over her, making her feel less than adequate as a songwriter. Shortly after announcing her solo plans, she was interviewed for a *Rolling Stone* article on Fleetwood Mac. As she showed the reporter one photograph after another, she came upon one of her and Lindsey onstage. Pointing to it, she whispered, "This is the killer. And the pale shadow of Dragon Boy, always behind me, always behind me." In going solo, Stevie told *Bam,* "there was a part of me that was saying, 'See, I can do it myself. I do not need you every second to do everything for me.' "

Her friends, fans, and business associates agreed with her self-assessment. As co-owner of Modern Records, Paul Fishkin had no doubt that Stevie was the real deal. "She was the hottest female in the world at the time, albeit in a group, not as a solo artist, and had all these wonderful songs," he said. "I never had any doubt that she could sell millions of records."

To ensure the accuracy of such projections, Jimmy Iovine was recruited to produce Stevie's record, *Bella Donna.* The gist of his no-nonsense approach was that Stevie was not yet a proven solo artist, and if becoming one was indeed her goal, she would have to work hard to attain it. "This is not big rock and roll, this is something you've never done before," he told her. Although Stevie heeded Jimmy's warnings, the participation of her new friend Tom Petty, who both sang on and wrote "Stop Dragging My Heart Around," and her old friend Don Henley, who paired up with Stevie for "Leather and Lace," ensured her LP an edge in the marketplace.

Working in close quarters with Jimmy Iovine, Stevie soon found herself involved in another great romance. The producer's strong guiding hand and dedication to her success inspired her with feelings of loyalty and respect, and in no time the two were a couple. "This was everything," she recalled. "He said, 'I will be there with you to make you strong enough to do this.' "

————

While Stevie's hiatus went to sparking up a solo career and a new affair, Christine's time had been swallowed up by the mad capers of Dennis Wilson. Although many people expected her to follow Stevie's lead into solo terrain, Christine wasn't ready to take the risk. She'd had her brush with independent stardom back in the sixties when she half-heartedly released *Christine Perfect* to mixed reviews. She hadn't enjoyed the stressful experience then and doubted it would prove any more agreeable the second time around.

In fact, Christine might not have been able to find the time for the endeavor even had she wanted to. Dennis Wilson was a full-time job in himself. The extent of his randy antics was equaled only by his girlfriend's unwavering patience. His children and stepchildren from past marriages would often show up unannounced on Christine's doorstep looking for safe haven. Her poolhouse, where Dennis made his home, inexplicably burned to a cinder. Days would pass when Christine didn't see her fiancé at all.

"I came home one birthday to find he'd had my garden completely dug out in the shape of an enormous heart and filled with roses," Christine recalled in *US* magazine. "And although it was pouring, all our friends were standing round the edge of the heart holding lit candles. I had to run around in the rain blowing them out. There were things like that nearly every day—it was too much." In the commotion of the party that followed, Dennis managed to bed his stepson's girlfriend. The bill for the landscaping was also delivered to Christine.

Vacillating between charming magic man and strung-out alcoholic, Dennis Wilson tried Christine's good nature at every turn, until she could take it no more. Despite the lengthy periods of separation, which no doubt made the relationship easier for Christine to bear, the fact that she endured Dennis's philandering and drug abuse for two years makes a good case for the veracity of her Mother Earth image. However, with the *Tusk* tour at an end, Christine had the chance to spend four solid months in her lover's company. In so doing, she realized her mistake in trying to take care of Dennis. The couple argued incessantly, upsetting Christine's neighbors with their angry screaming. Soon even Christine's lawyers were counseling her against persisting with the liaison. So, in December of 1980, after repeated attempts to cut Dennis out of her life, Christine braced herself and brought an end to the relationship once and for all.

———

Amid the clamorous buzz of rumors detailing the reasons behind Fleetwood Mac's impending split, the band quietly reconvened to record their next album, *Mirage*. The time was May 1981, and the place was Le Chateau, a castle turned studio-to-the-stars located in Herouville, France, sixty miles from Paris. Having whiled away his months with his wife Julie, his homes in Maui and L.A., his sixty-three-foot yacht, and his potent potables, John was the picture of somnolent placidity. While the same could not be said of his frazzled fellow musicians, all were present and ready to work.

With Ken Caillat and Richard Dashut comprising the engineering department, the band began to lay down the basic tracks to Stevie's "Gypsy," Christine's "Hold Me," and Lindsey's "Oh Diane." The group seemed to fall right back into the old groove, but much had changed to make the recording of *Mirage* unlike anything Fleetwood Mac had done in the past. *Tusk* had seen the band following their instincts just as they had with *Rumours, Fleetwood Mac,* and *Then Play On*. Failing to rack up the astronomical numbers of *Rumours, Tusk* was an example of what not to do, and they set about correcting the faux pas.

Surprisingly, Lindsey didn't balk at the band's insistence that he restrict his recording to the studio and steer clear of taping in his bathroom. He attributed his acquiescence to the lackluster performance of *Tusk,* telling *Bam* that it had become "clear that there was either a little bit of a backlash, or maybe I'd just overestimated what the public wants to hear. And that's when it started for me. I was sort of left not knowing exactly what course to chart. I was kind of drifting through a mirage, and it was pretty much like that until the end with me."

For the time being, Lindsey's experimental tendencies had been exorcised on both *Tusk* and *Law and Order*. The maestro of pop was ready to play team ball. Shortly before his arrival in France, Lindsey told *Musician Player and Listener* magazine that "the next Fleetwood Mac studio album will be more group-oriented—it certainly won't be less."

With the musicians isolated at the French studio, the first stage of recording was completed in the space of a few months. The considerably longer process of additional recording, mixing, and mastering would have to take place back in Los Angeles. With Stevie's debut album scheduled for release in July 1981, and *Law and Order* slated to hit the stores in the fall of that year, Lindsey and Stevie were both expected to take some time away from *Mirage*. Because of the increased demands on the band members' time, the public would have to wait until the summer of 1982 to hear what the 1980s Fleetwood Mac was all about.

———

When Stevie's "Stop Draggin' My Heart Around" first rocked the airwaves, the single left little doubt that its parent album, *Bella Donna*, was going to be a smash hit. The duet between Stevie and Tom Petty caught on fast, peaking at *Billboard*'s Number Three position by the beginning of September 1981. The track would hang on to third place for six consecutive weeks, at the end of which time most people would know the song's lyrics better than the opening lines of the Gettysburg Address.

Despite Tom Petty's writing credit, the song was Stevie's first triumph as a soloist, and the fans were ready for more. The second single released from *Bella Donna* would be Stevie's "Leather and Lace," which was sung as a duet with Don Henley. Again, the single nestled comfortably into the top ten, hanging tough at Number Six for three weeks running. The success dispelled Stevie's worst fear, that she was nothing without Fleetwood Mac. As she explained in an interview with *Playboy*, "On *Bella Donna*, the producer Jimmy Iovine left the songs as close to the demos as possible, so it was really just me—which is what I've always wanted."

To hedge their bets, Stevie and her team released the brand-name duets as *Bella Donna*'s first singles. Her fairylike signature style, so prevalent in "Edge of Seventeen," was relegated to the status of third single. If Stevie's advisers feared that her Rapunzelesque image would detract from the success of *Bella Donna,* they were mistaken. "Edge of Seventeen" held on at Number Eleven for two weeks and is still remembered as one of the most beautiful of Stevie's compositions.

Despite apocryphal tales to the contrary, Stevie's home run as a soloist was hardly due to a covert deal with the devil. Of course, the gossip didn't spring from a vacuum, as Stevie paid a steep price for her glory. First came the problems with the rest of Fleetwood Mac. After *Bella Donna* became America's top-selling album in September 1981, promotional appearances, interviews, and the abridged White Winged Dove tour left her with little time for the group. As the band worked on completing *Mirage,* Stevie was off in her own world. "She's flexing some kind of emotional muscles that she feels she can flex now that she's in a more powerful position," Lindsey surmised in the *Record.* "There's a certain amount of leeway in how you can interpret Stevie's behavior, I'd say, but at the same time there's no denying that her success is making her feel that she can pull things that she wouldn't have felt comfortable pulling before. And most of them aren't particularly worthwhile, but she's venting something—loneliness, unhappiness, or something."

Stevie was certainly deeply troubled at this time: Her best friend, Robin Anderson, had terminal leukemia. Stevie learned of the illness on the day *Bella Donna* went to Number One. Two days later Robin called her with the tragic news that she only had two months left to live. Suddenly, being designated *Rolling Stone*'s "Reigning Queen of Rock and Roll" was of little consequence. If she was powerless to save her friend, of what use was her Number One album? "It's the only friendship that I've ever had," Stevie explained to the *Arizona Republic.* "We just started out together at fifteen years old. She kind of walked me through life. And, as I questioned would there be life after Fleetwood Mac, I certainly questioned would there be life after Robin."

In all the time he had known her, Lindsey told the *Record,* "Stevie's never been happy, and I don't think the success of her album has made her any happier. In fact, it may have made her less happy." Doubtless, the release of *Bella Donna* had not been to blame for Stevie's unhappiness. Lindsey's misattribution made clear that even Stevie's bandmates, who also knew and loved Robin Anderson, failed to appreciate the depths of despair into which her friend's death sentence had plunged their frontwoman. "People ask, 'Wasn't it incredible when *Bella Donna* was Number One and sold three million albums?' " she told *Bam.* "Yeah, it was totally wonderful except that I was watching one thing go up while I was watching another thing go down. It was really, really hard."

———

While Stevie was coming to terms with Robin's illness and her own newfound status as a platinum-selling recording artist, Lindsey's solo career was giving the critics, if not the listening public, something to rave about. Released in October 1981, *Law and Order* elicited cries of jubilation from music reviewers. "Buckingham writes songs that seem both effortless and encyclopedic," proclaimed *Rolling Stone,* while the *Philadelphia Daily News* called the LP "a perfectly wonderful collection of good old-fashioned pop fun."

Despite the overwhelming critical support and its top-ten single, "Trouble," the album sold only three hundred thousand copies and peaked at a modest Number Thirty-four on the *Billboard* charts. The lack of commercial success did not dissuade Lindsey from plowing on with his satisfying sideline. In fact, he so enjoyed his creative freedom that—while all questioning eyes turned to Stevie, wondering when she was going to leave the band for good—he was already looking forward to his retirement from Fleetwood Mac.

But while *Law and Order* led to a multialbum deal with Elektra, Lindsey was content to anticipate his emancipation from the Mac. Unbeknownst to the band, he was now biding his time until the moment most opportune to his departure presented itself. "I initially had thought about leaving after *Tusk,*" he later admitted. "I don't think it would have been a good idea, because it was important to do it at a time that was not just good for yourself but maybe wasn't going to be too hurtful to everybody else involved."

His musical ideals weren't the only thing to be sublimated for the greater good of the band. To continue his association with Fleetwood Mac, he was forced to repress the morass of unresolved issues stemming from his romantic rupture with Stevie. "You can feel the sparks between Stevie and Lindsey because they're both sparky, wiry people together," Mick explained in *Hit Parader*. "I daresay, if they had to work together now without the influence of the band, it'd probably be a potential horror show."

Due to the unpleasantness in the studio, Stevie's contribution to the completion of *Mirage* was negligible. While she was singled out for her want of commitment, however, Stevie wasn't the only one eschewing the studio's danger zone. John was also prone to using evasive tactics when it came down to working in cloistered quarters with Christine. As Lindsey described to *Bam*, there was a "very unhealthy emotional situation going on between two couples who had broken up, and were trying to say, 'Okay, we don't want to see each other, but we're going to have to do this anyway. You stay way over there, and I'll stay way over here.' So it was kind of a mess from the beginning, at least emotionally."

———

Against all odds, Fleetwood Mac did manage to finish *Mirage*. Despite songs like "Hold Me" and "Gypsy," today's general concensus has it that the album was an act of contrition for *Tusk*'s excess. At the time, however, most fans were just pleased to hear the Mac harmonizing and working as a band again. Released in June 1982 and buoyed by the enduring top-five success of the first single, "Hold Me," the album was in first place on the charts by August. Never before had a Fleetwood Mac album risen to the top so fast; the climb had taken *Fleetwood Mac* a year to accomplish. Even *Rumours* took two months, and *Tusk* never made it at all.

Busy putting together her sophomore solo album, *Wild Heart*, Stevie had to suspend recording to go on the road with Fleetwood Mac in support of *Mirage*. According to a miffed Christine McVie, her efforts weren't vigorous enough. "She phones her part in," Christine told the *Record*. "She asks what songs we plan on doing and what songs we want her to do. The rest of it will be decided between Mick, Lindsey, and me."

The *Mirage* tour kicked off early in September 1982 and lasted a mere two months. The Number One status of the Mac's new album was equally ephemeral, lasting for only five weeks despite the chart success of Stevie's "Gypsy." A year after its release, *Mirage* had "only" gone triple platinum. Even with all the band's efforts to re-create the *Rumours* sound, the uninspiring sales volume cemented the reality of Fleetwood Mac as an empire whose power was on the wane.

When the tour ended, the members took their leave without making any plans for the future of the band. Although no one mentioned disbanding, the ensuing months found the five musicians pursuing their separate lives with all the energy formerly reserved for Fleetwood Mac. The group was still together, but only in the most tenuous sense of the word. Many onlookers chose to blame the unproductive period on Stevie's thriving solo career, but the separation was the long-overdue result of years of contention, excessive touring, and minimal rest periods. Five years would pass before Mick, John, Christine, Lindsey, and Stevie finally released what many billed a "comeback" album— and it would be another fifteen years before Fleetwood Mac saw another Number One.

11

BAND IN FLUX

The frenzy of speculation that had surrounded Fleetwood Mac in its late 1970s heyday had died down considerably since the emergence of MTV and "eighties music." The Police, Michael Jackson, Madonna, Cyndi Lauper, Culture Club, Prince, and Duran Duran were among the bevy of young faces ruling the media and the pop charts. The drama and intrigue that had made Fleetwood Mac so popular during *Rumours* was now old news, and the group was left to stay together or split apart without the impertinent interference of the press.

Of course, no mention of the eighties is complete without Stevie Nicks, whose ubiquitous music and over-the-top sartorial style helped set the tone for the entire decade. She put out one top ten album after another, and her loyal and enamored following turned her into a rock 'n' roll icon. The rest of the band, however, was largely dismissed as having gone the way of the Eagles and Steely Dan. Their five-year hiatus was simply too long for audiences to accept as anything but a terminal rupture.

Circumstances had conspired to keep the band members apart, since everyone was busy with solo projects and the trials and tribulations of life. However, the Mac had not broken up. As Christine explained to the *Los Angeles Times,* "we all expected to get back together, but no one ever set a date when we would get back together and the time just slipped by."

—————

With the *Mirage* tour over and Fleetwood Mac on an indefinite break, Christine was left without official employment. The crazy hours she'd been keeping with the band had her yearning for rest. "I was busy redecorating my house, fixing up the garden, being around my dogs," she said. "It was the first time I ever had to indulge the domestic side of me."

Eventually, she grew bored with the household chores and began laying the groundwork for her own solo outing. She had long since wanted to explore new territory as an artist, telling *Joepie* that "when I'm with Fleetwood Mac I'm the romantic lady. Once in a while it's annoying that I always have to bring the romantic ballads, while the boys can do the heavy stuff."

Getting a contract out of Warner Bros. posed no problem for the proven hit writer. The only obstacle had been her own uncertainty. "People have constantly been saying, 'When is Christine going to do her album, when, when, when?' " she told the *Philadelphia Daily News.* "But I wasn't ready when everybody else was doing it. I didn't want that kind of pressure or responsibility. Also, I'm always insecure about material."

With the success of her fellow Fleetwood Mac songwriters to look to for inspiration, she had finally overcome her doubts. Hiring a manager and a backup band, she settled down to the task of planning *Christine McVie* a year after her last tour date with Fleetwood Mac. After cowriting a few songs with her new lead guitarist, Todd Sharp, and securing the participation of the producer she wanted, Christine was ready to enter the studio. In June 1983, she and her new entourage flew to Montreux, Switzerland, where Christine was surprised to find the atmosphere "peaceful and quiet in the studio. Quite different from the walking madhouse which calls itself Fleetwood Mac."

Established rock stars who wanted to work with Christine started coming out of the woodwork, just as they had for Stevie. During a telephone conversation with old friend Steve Winwood, Christine proposed that he collaborate on one of the album tracks. She only had to ask once, and Winwood showed up to cowrite "Ask Anybody," a tune on which his voice is featured prominently. Eric Clapton joined up as a guest guitarist as well. Once the recording moved to Gloucester, England, Lindsey and Mick also made cameo appearances.

Christine McVie was released to an expectant audience in February 1984. The first single, "Got a Hold on Me," quickly slid into *Billboard*'s top ten. Christine would have preferred to reenter the studio with Fleetwood Mac, but key forces within the band were delaying the regrouping process. Overcoming her reluctance to stand alone in the spotlight, she mounted a tour to support her top-thirty album.

Eddy Quintela was the keyboard player in Christine's new band, and in classic Fleetwood Mac fashion, the two soon began dating. This relationship, however, suffered from none of the turmoil that had characterized Christine's union with Dennis Wilson, whose drinking eventually led to his drowning in the Marina Del Rey on December 28, 1983. Christine and Eddy's relationship progressed without impediment, and the couple married in October 1986.

———

Mick's shocking reversal of fortune was about to make headline news. The drummer had been on the road to financial ruin for years, but it was only after *Mirage* that his spending finally caught up with him. Coming off that tour was in itself a hardship for Mick. "I felt sick when we stopped touring," he told *Goldmine*. "I wanted to be on the move, touring until the cows came home. But the others were less enthusiastic."

With no choice but to fend for himself, Mick returned to his new home, a $2.4 million Malibu mansion. Booze, cocaine, and the constant comings and goings of his musician pals served as his substitute for Fleetwood Mac. The immense pleasure he derived from the all-hours jam sessions soon had Mick toying with the notion of an adjunct band. Finally, it was this band, entitled Mick Fleetwood's Zoo, that recorded *I'm Not Me*, the misconceived follow-up to *The Visitor*.

Released in 1983, the album marked the end of Mick's solo career. After the disastrous *I'm Not Me* tour, he kept busy in his role as guest session player for Christine's and Lindsey's albums. With no money coming in, Mick had to live on what he'd saved, namely nothing. Hoping that his band would reassemble before he was left in penury, Mick soon realized that it was not to be. He declared bankruptcy in the spring of 1984.

Selling off his prized automobile collection, recording equipment, houses, and land was a humbling experience for the rocker who had once told a friend that he would never need to work another day in his life. "Everything about him became little," Christine recalled in *Rolling Stone*. "He wasn't walking with his shoulders straight like he always used to. It was sad to see that. He didn't seem happy, didn't know how to function unless he was high. He would just sleep the whole time— just hooked on drugs, about as low as he could get. I remember him telling me he was living in somebody's basement with a damp carpet. The carpet was soaking wet, and the bed was damp, and he used to lie in bed watching soap operas all day long."

Sadly, Mick's relationship with Sara Recor did not survive this demoralizing time. The couple broke up, and Mick went ahead with the business of putting his life back together the only way he knew how: by coaxing his bandmates back into the studio.

———

Despite her accelerating solo career, Stevie wasn't against cutting another Fleetwood Mac record. Working herself to the bone, she had completed her second album, *Wild Heart*, soon after the band came off the *Mirage* tour. Even before she'd left for that two-month trek, Stevie had already begun recording. But no sooner had she repaired to the studio than she was thrown into a tailspin by the news of Robin Anderson's death. "I didn't even have the time, or the luxury, to sit around and be sad," she lamented in *Bam*.

With professional responsibilities pulling Stevie in every direction and the passing of her best friend weighing on her heart, she lost all control. The horror of her situation was intensified by the fact that Robin had died less than one week after giving birth by an emergency cesarean section. As the baby's godmother, Stevie tried to do what she could. On January 29, 1983, in one of the most misguided moves of her life, Stevie married her best friend's grieving widower, Kim Anderson. "I went crazy. I just went insane," Stevie later explained to the *L.A. Report.* "And so did her husband. And we were the only two that could really understand the depth of the grief that we were going through. I was determined to take care of that baby, so I said to Kim, 'I don't know, I guess we should just get married.' And so we got married and no one, no one understood. It was a terrible, terrible mistake. We didn't get married because we were in love, we got married because we were grieving and it was the only way that we could feel like we were doing the right thing."

A few months into the marriage the couple filed for divorce. In the meantime, she would see *Wild Heart* through to completion. Dedicated to Robin, the album held special meaning for Stevie. "It set me free," she told the *Arizona Republic.* "This is two records now. So the first record wasn't just a fluke accident. And I can go and write and dance and do children's stories and do whatever I want now and no one is going to be saying to me: 'You still aren't a proven solo artist.' "

Released in June 1983, Stevie's follow-up album was another platinum hit. "Stand Back," the album's lead single, had been written on the day of her marriage to Kim Anderson. The two were driving to Santa Barbara for their honeymoon when "Little Red Corvette" came on the radio. The song gave Stevie an idea, but she needed to go to the source to bring it to fruition. "I phoned Prince out of the blue, hummed a melody, and he listened," she explained in *Rock Lives* by Timothy White. "I hung up, and he came over within the hour. He listened again, and I said, 'Do you hate it?' He said, 'No,' and walked over to the synthesizers that were set up, was absolutely brilliant for about twenty-five minutes, and then left."

The resultant song would become a top-five hit and an enduring showstopper for both Stevie and Fleetwood Mac. After the top-twenty success of the second single, "If Anyone Falls," Stevie had indeed showed the world that she was much more than the Mac's dancing tambourine girl.

At this point, it had been about a year since she'd last played with her Fleetwood Mac associates, but Stevie had too much on her mind to go rounding up her bandmates. Aside from her flourishing solo career, she had yet to redress the grave mistake she'd made by marrying Kim and would need a while longer to make her peace with Robin's death. Also, her alcoholism and cocaine addiction were becoming more of a problem with each passing day. Stevie spun into a downward spiral, leading Christine to make this comment in *Joepie:* "Stevie is making herself crazy. It's not only those mystic situations in which she's involved, like magic and astrology, but also her excesses like alcohol, drugs, and one boyfriend after another. A normal human being can't keep that up."

By the time Stevie began recording her third album, *Rock a Little,* the hard living had begun to affect her work. Whether because of the success of her past albums or the pernicious effects of her drug and alcohol abuse, she wasn't cooperating with her longtime producer, Jimmy Iovine, the man she'd once trusted to mold her songs into hits. When Jimmy brought her "Reconsider Me," a song penned by Warren Zevon and a perfect match for Stevie's voice, she flew into a rage. "I was pretty crazy at that point in my life, and you couldn't tell me anything," she later admitted to the *San Jose Mercury News,* "and I said to him, 'I would never say the words "reconsider me" to somebody. I would never ask somebody to reconsider loving me.' Well, he thought that was the biggest bunch of crap he'd ever heard; so we had a big fight about it, and that's just about the last time Jimmy and I ever worked together."

To take Jimmy Iovine's place, she hired another industry heavyweight, Rick Nowels, and joined him in the production of *Rock a Little.* As she'd said, she was a proven solo artist with enough experience to know what went into the making of a hit record. Now that she'd freed herself from Lindsey and the Mac, she wasn't about to bend for anyone. Sure enough, she'd been right. Released in November 1985, *Rock a Little* and its first single, "Talk to Me," were both top-ten hits.

That's when the call finally came. Fleetwood Mac wanted their singer/songwriter back.

———

John McVie was only too ready when the band decided to regroup. For all his proficiency on the bass guitar, his three-year separation from the band had shown him to be something less than resourceful. After he hooked up with former Rolling Stone and fellow Bluesbreakers alumnus, Mick Taylor, the two called upon their old bandleader, John Mayall, to reform the Bluesbreakers posse. John played a few weeks of gigs with the band before joining Fleetwood Mac on the *Mirage* tour.

Once the Mac fell into a state of dormancy, John found himself with absolutely nothing to do. He figured he'd lead a life of leisure and sail the seven seas until his bandmates were ready to resume, unaware that the waiting period would extend to well over a year. "I sat around, and it didn't help my alcohol problem," he said in *Rock Lives.* "I sat in St. Thomas for a long time, and it being a duty-free island, for $2.98 you can get right twisted."

If John had been something of a barfly ever since his early years with the Bluesbreakers, the three-year hiatus saw him descend into full-blown alcoholism. As the months of unemployment turned to years, he often wondered when, if ever, his band would reconvene.

———

With John, Mick, Christine, and even Stevie ready to regroup at a moment's notice, the prolonged procrastination could not be attributed to simple inertia. Indeed, a strong countercurrent was working to keep Fleetwood Mac in seclusion. At its source was none other than Lindsey Buckingham.

After agreeing to take some time away from the band to record another solo album or two, Lindsey "just kind of sat, tinkering around, letting the emotional dust settle." Then he withdrew into his studio and set up camp. In his zeal for production work, he built a complete recording studio right across the hall from his bedroom. He could work for hours without once looking at a clock. Much as he'd done on his last album, Lindsey would take responsibility for nearly every instrument and every vocal track. He had once told *People* that *"Law and Order* is about the sense of personal order in your life. If there are songs about a special, stable relationship, it's because that's what I have." His follow-up LP, *Go Insane,* was diametrically opposed.

"The lyrics were to some extent inspired, if that's the right word, by the slow disintegration of a six-year relationship I had with a young lady," Lindsey explained. "I tried everything I could to maintain a commitment to this person, but she began to display nonconstructive behaviorial patterns, and I just reached a stage where no more allowances could be made. So a lot of the songs on *Go Insane* have something to do with various aspects of what happened."

The aptly titled album was a musical deconstruction of his failed relationship with Carol Ann Harris, the woman who had been his girlfriend ever since the *Rumours* era. At the time, Lindsey's brother Jeff told *Rolling Stone,* she'd been "a sweet young girl, very pleasant. But she changed to a music [scene]-hardened, drug-hardened person. It just wasn't the same."

While most songs openly alluded to the various problems undermining the relationship, the album track "DW Suite," a memorial to the late Dennis Wilson, appeared unrelated. Lindsey's comment to *Bam* revealed that there was more to this story: "I knew him pretty well, he even had an affair with my girlfriend." Without a trace of irony, he went on to add that "he was a good guy. He was kind of lost, but I thought he had a big heart. I always liked him."

To paraphrase Stevie Nicks, tragedy makes for great art, and *Go Insane* was no exception. When the album came out in August 1984, the critics were agog at the mere mention of the artist's name. In their eyes, Lindsey was the best thing to come out of Fleetwood Mac since the early Peter Green. In stark contrast to Stevie, whose audiences clamored for a piece of her chiffon even as the critics dismissed her talent as marginal, Lindsey's work was touted as triumphant even though commercial success continued to elude him. While the single "Go Insane" did manage to chart in the top thirty, the album itself would climb no further than Number Forty-five.

Lindsey's aversion to touring may have had something to do with this poor showing. He had always held fast to the belief that an album should speak for itself, so he wasn't tempted to support *Go Insane* on the road. Neither did he wish to put on a show that relied heavily on Fleetwood Mac classics. "I've seen Stevie's show, I've seen Christine's show," he told *Rolling Stone.* "To me, they both bordered on being lounge acts, simply because they were resting so heavily on Fleetwood Mac's laurels."

By the time 1985 rolled around, Lindsey had geared up for another solo album. While he'd been unable to convince Richard Dashut to lend his production capabilities to *Go Insane*—as Richard had felt completely burnt out from working on Mick's *I'm Not Me*—the two could now resume the process of collaboration they'd begun on *Law and Order*. Lindsey had no intention of returning to the Mac, telling *Rock* magazine and anyone else who cared to listen that "I've always been fairly altruistic about my duties with Fleetwood Mac. Right now, I'm being a little less altruistic."

———

Christine's appeal to Richard Dashut managed to break down Lindsey's resistance. On the surface, the proposal seemed unlikely to impede Lindsey's solo work for long. Christine had been asked to record Elvis Presley's "Can't Help Falling in Love" for the *A Fine Mess* soundtrack, and she requested that Richard come in to produce. Lindsey, a long-time fan of the King, and no stranger to motion picture soundtracks—having written "Holiday Road" for *National Lampoon's Vacation* and "Time Bomb Town" for *Back to the Future*—followed Richard into Christine's studio.

Seven years would pass before the album Lindsey had been so loath to put off for the sake of Fleetwood Mac would finally see the light of day. Working with Christine, he soon found himself surrounded by Mick and John as well. The three made no secret of their wish to reenter the studio as a band. Of course, now that Fleetwood Mac had its own bureaucracy to deal with, wishing alone wasn't going to make their next album, *Tango in the Night*, a reality. According to Lindsey in *Rolling Stone*, "The problems really kicked in when you started adding five managers and five lawyers to the equation. Once Stevie was singled out and selected as the star of the band, the machinery of the rock business kicked in, and things really got stupid. By the time of *Tango*, you could hardly fit all these people in one room for a band meeting. It was a heartbreaking thing to watch, until it became almost comical."

The mountain of red tape notwithstanding, the fact that the band members' representatives were finally in contact signaled that the time to record was near. Soon, Lindsey was installed in the producer's chair, and the seventeen-month process of recording *Tango in the Night* had begun. Although he'd appeared to be dead-set against returning to Fleetwood Mac, the thought of *Mirage* cast the deciding ballot. "[*Mirage*] was an ambiguous piece of work in my mind," Lindsey told the *Orange County Register.* "It wasn't too visionary. There were a lot of things hanging out on a limb at the end of the *Mirage* tour that we wanted to tie up with *Tango in the Night.*"

Originally, Lindsey had thought that he would be able to work on his own album while someone else produced *Tango.* Struck in the last months of 1985, the initial agreement had been that an outside producer would be brought in and that the individual band members would record their parts separately. This method was completely foreign to Fleetwood Mac's group-think process. In fact, according to Lindsey, "it reeked of being a business arrangement."

Finally, Lindsey and Richard agreed to postpone the former's solo album in order to produce the Mac's latest opus. But the guitarist didn't accept the responsibility without setting forth certain stipulations. If he was going to arrange, produce, and discontinue his solo work for the good of the group, then the least they could do would be to accommodate him by working out of his home studio. After positioning a Winnebago in front of Lindsey's Bel Air house, the musicians were ready to rock and roll. Lindsey remembers this time as "trying to get things done in an atmosphere where there was just a lot of crazy stuff going on and not a lot of focus, and not a lot of unity and certainty. And no sense of us wanting to do this for . . . the reasons we originally got into it for."

Without any sense of camaraderie or even the shared musical vision that had once made their studio work bearable, the sessions were "a mess." Consequently, these seventeen months of playing with the band would be Lindsey's last.

————

Despite her formidable contribution to the lyrics of *Tango in the Night*, Stevie's appearances in the studio were few and far between. Only too willing to regroup, she had first to finish the *Rock a Little* tour. As the rest of the band recorded in Bel Air, Stevie's struggle with cocaine addiction was coming to a head on the road. Her nasal passages were giving way, and she was referred to a plastic surgeon. The meeting was not one she would soon forget. "He said to me, 'The next line that you do could be your last. The tissue in your nose is very delicate. It could go straight up to your head, and then you could drop to the floor and die a lousy, two-hour death.' "

The warning sounded a wake-up call, and Stevie decided to quit cocaine cold turkey. A habitual user for nearly a decade, still surrounded by the drug everywhere she went, Stevie needed serious help. Yet the tour remained her first priority. "I didn't feel I was strong enough to go to Betty Ford for a month in the middle of a tour," she explained in the *Los Angeles Times*, "because anybody in the world will tell you that if you are going to do something that serious, you shouldn't be stupid and turn around and go right back onstage in front of seventy-five thousand people, where you are going to be terribly nervous and probably want to go back to whatever it was you gave up."

Instead of canceling the remaining shows, Stevie soldiered on until there was a break in her schedule. When she tried to quit cocaine on her own, she was directed to a psychiatrist for some additional assistance. She left the doctor's office with a prescription for an antidepressant called Klonopin. It was supposed to keep her off cocaine, but the drug would slowly come to consume her life, nearly destroying her career.

Stevie was unaware of the deterimental side effects when she began her Klonopin regimen in 1986, and she was still drinking heavily. The mental and physical effects of her substance abuse were becoming readily apparent in her performances. She began to feel overburdened by her schedules; as she told the *Orange County Register:* "I'd be out on the road for a month. Then I'd come straight home to Los Angeles, get a hotel room, and go into the studio with Fleetwood Mac for two weeks. It was difficult; I'll make sure it never happens again."

Ultimately, the strain was less a result of Stevie's multifarious responsibilities than of her drug-riddled lifestyle. According to Lindsey, she "was probably around for something like ten days for that whole record." Granted, some of her truancy was brought about by the obvious tension still dividing the former couple. "I would have to say that by the time of *Tango in the Night,* I didn't recognize her at all," Lindsey told *Rolling Stone.* "She wasn't the person I had known and had moved to Los Angeles with."

Lindsey's disdain, however, was the least of Stevie's problems. When the album was nearly finished, and Stevie's part recorded, her friends and colleagues arranged an intervention. In the spring of 1987, she checked into the Betty Ford Center for a comprehensive, twenty-eight-day chemical dependency treatment. She told *Rolling Stone:* "They are hard-nosed. They're harder on you if you're famous—'Oh, if it isn't Miss Special.' It's awful. But it works. Now, I don't do things that make me feel bad, 'cause I have way too much work to do." She hasn't touched cocaine since.

———

Stevie wasn't the only one hitting rock bottom that spring. The season also saw John McVie pay a price for his own life of excess. After laying down his bass tracks for *Tango in the Night,* John repaired to the St. Thomas hideaway he shared with his wife. Despite the vocal concern of his family and bandmates, he showed no signs of limiting his daily alcohol intake.

Only when his own body cried foul did John finally address his problem. "I woke up on the bathroom floor," he said in *Rock Lives.* "I had a seizure, an alcohol-induced seizure, which scared me and scared my wife. It was time to stop because it was destroying everything. There's nothing constructive [that] comes out of being an alcoholic."

With the help of a therapist, John began to gradually wean himself off the bottle. Seeking professional help was, in itself, a daring move for the Brit, who, like most of his countrymen, believed that seeing a psychotherapist went hand in hand with donning a straitjacket.

Although John and Stevie had been in varying degrees of disrepair throughout the making of *Tango,* both were roadworthy by the time the album was ready for public consumption. When *Tango in the Night* was released in April 1987, it soon became obvious that the album was going to be a monster hit. The first single, Lindsey's "Big Love," was already in the top ten and enjoying a sizable chunk of airplay on radio stations across America, while the accompanying video was in heavy rotation on youth-dominated MTV. After sitting out five years, the band was back with a vengeance.

Stevie's "Seven Wonders" (cowritten by Sandy Stewart) and Christine's "Little Lies" and "Everywhere" would follow "Big Love" straight into the pantheon of unforgettable pop singles of the eighties. A top-ten seller in the States, the U.K., Canada, and Australia, *Tango in the Night* looked to be Fleetwood Mac's great comeback album. In fact, the band had already begun to gear up for an eight-month tour when news of Lindsey's alternate plans broke. Suddenly, the comeback was being depicted as a last will and testament.

———

The press mobilized to grill the members of Fleetwood Mac as soon as their album hit the stores and the charts. Articles about the band revealed that all was not well with the comeback kids. Comments from Lindsey, such as "We didn't want to leave on the note struck by *Mirage*," and "This band has done some remarkable things and *Mirage* was no way for it to say goodbye . . . it now feels like the time," left little doubt as to his true intentions.

Called to task by his tour-bound bandmates, Lindsey "kind of agreed to go." In *Bam* he recalled that during one group meeting, in July of 1987, the rest of the group somehow "smoothed things over and coerced me." By consenting to limit the tour to ten weeks, Mick, Stevie, Christine, and John thought they had secured Lindsey's participation. Summing up the situation as she perceived it, Stevie described Lindsey's fluctuating moods as "kind of like a romance, when someone is always saying 'I'm going to leave you,' and never does."

Only a few weeks later, Lindsey would make good on his threats. As hard as he'd tried, he couldn't reconcile his personal needs with those of the band. Figuring that he'd done enough for the Mac just by abandoning his solo work to produce *Tango in the Night* and funneling his favorite solo tracks into the Fleetwood Mac album, he informed the rest of the group that he would not be going out on tour.

The change of heart couldn't have come at a worse time. Ever since Lindsey had agreed to take to the road, the booking and logistics people had not stepped away from the phones. Most of the arrangements had been made, and the band didn't want to accept that everything would have to be canceled due to one of Lindsey's whims. In a last effort to salvage the group, the whole of Fleetwood Mac descended upon Christine's Coldwater Canyon home on August 5, 1987. Despite his bandmates' repeated supplications, Lindsey flat-out refused to tour. He sensed that he was at a creative peak, and his only aim was to finish his solo album.

Watching Lindsey trying to explain and apologize for his actions, Stevie began to lose her composure. Angry and disappointed, she asked Lindsey to step outside, where she bore into him with the full force of her bottled-up resentment. Lindsey was quick to rally with his own volley of verbal abuse. For years, the two had been biting their tongues to hold back the venom for the sake of the band, but no more. "We said too much to each other," Stevie recalled in *Rock Lives*. "We said all the things that we had wanted to say for the last ten years, and we screamed at each other. Those things in a relationship that you try to never say just in case you do get back together, we said those things. Lindsey and I had been together from about 1971 to around 1976. But we never really broke up until that moment."

After all was said and done, Lindsey made a dramatic exit, leaving his former bandmates at loose ends. The four remaining musicians could hardly believe what had just transpired; after all, it had been twelve years since they'd last lost a band member. Yet believe it they would, for Lindsey's management would soon make public the following statement: "In 1985, I was working on my third solo album when the band came to me and asked me to produce the next Fleetwood Mac project. At that point, I put aside my solo work, which was half-finished, and committed myself for the next seventeen months to produce *Tango in the Night*. It was always our understanding that upon completion of the *Tango* album I would return to my solo work. Of course I wish them all the success in the world on the road."

———

With no time to mourn the passing of their lead guitarist and visionary, the band had to think fast and act without hesitation if they wanted to satisfy their hunger for the road and their promises to concert promoters nationwide. "A lot of people probably expected us to do the old roll-over-on-your-back trick," Mick told *Bam*. "Rather than shut down, we decided to press on and get out on the road."

In classic Fleetwood Mac style, the band held no auditions to assemble their new lineup. Yet within two weeks, two new singer/guitarists were officially inducted into the band. Both Billy Burnette and Rick Vito were longtime music-industry insiders. The former had been immersed in rock 'n' roll all of his life as the son of rockabilly hero Dorsey Burnette. Having put out several solo records and written songs for the likes of Jerry Lee Lewis and the Everly Brothers, Billy had impeccable qualifications. But it was his enduring friendship and working relationship with Mick Fleetwood that clinched the deal. Billy had been a part of Mick Fleetwood's Zoo for some five years when he got the call to join Fleetwood Mac. He'd already collaborated on songs with both Christine and Stevie, and his addition to the band seemed entirely organic.

Billy was slated to work the rhythm angle; Rick Vito would pick up the lead. As a young boy, Rick had taught himself to play the guitar by listening to Chuck Berry and the Rolling Stones, yet not until his college days did he finally decide to make music his business. His calling came to him during a December 1968 Fleetwood Mac concert. "I went with some friends and we sat in the second row, right in front of Peter Green," Rick told *Guitar World*. "They were really tremendous. . . . I immediately started writing songs, although listening back now, they were pale imitations of Peter Green songs."

Beginning with Delaney and Bonnie Bramlett, who gave him his start as a professional sideman, Rick went on to play lead guitar for such hot-ticket acts as Little Richard, Bonnie Raitt, Jackson Browne, and Bob Seger. He too knew Mick long before the Lindsey debacle had the drummer racking his brain for hot guitarists. In fact, Rick had met Mick through none other than Billy Burnette. After asking Billy to join, Mick naturally thought to call Rick Vito.

Within days of Lindsey's flight, Mick arranged a group rehearsal with Billy and Rick on guitars. On August 18, the two were publicly proclaimed to be Fleetwood Mac's newest members. Every effort was made to convey the appearance of a band that was moving on as if nothing ever happened. Despite the practiced show of bravado,

Lindsey's departure signaled the end of the Fleetwood Mac that fans
had come to know and love.

————

Although there were only a few weeks left to rehearse for the Shake the
Cage tour, the band was going to make good on their concert bookings
after all. "It was a little scary before we played that first show in Kansas
City. I'd wake up at night sweating, going, 'Oh mannnn . . . ,' " Billy recalled in *Guitar World*. "I could just see Rick and I getting jousted
about the arena by fans. And I'd hear stuff secondhand from people,
saying, 'I'd hate to be in his shoes. The critics are just going to rip him
apart.' But it was just the opposite. When we played a lot of people said
we'd never sounded so good. That made it a lot easier on me and Rick.
We knew we had a killer band."

Originally slated to span the world and several months, the Shake
the Cage tour wound down after just three months of playing in the
United States. While Billy and Rick did a fine job of simulating
Lindsey's vocal and instrumental stylings, it was Stevie's health that ultimately brought down the curtain. Diagnosed with the Epstein-Barr
virus and in the throes of pneumonia, Stevie struggled to make it
through. The steroid shots administered to keep her vocal chords from
swelling had the reverse effect on her figure, and Stevie began gaining
the weight that would one day cause her to renounce touring altogether. "And I was on antibiotics the whole time," she told *USA Today*,
"in addition to serious asthma treatments."

The tour broke for the Christmas holidays and would not resume until May. The idle months witnessed a reconciliation between Lindsey and the band. While he did not intend to reenter
Fleetwood Mac's fold under any circumstances, Mick's wedding ceremony managed to bring everyone together. Mick and Sara Recor
had reconciled after their breakup during Mick's earlier depression.
The guest list of their April wedding included the many members of
Fleetwood Mac past and present; a jovial Lindsey Buckingham
proved no exception.

Not a month after his wedding, Mick was back on the road.
Stevie's health had put the kibosh on the Australian leg of the tour, but

the plans for a European trek were still on for May. This time around, there was no more emotional trauma and very little in the way of drugs and drinking. The band's following still showed up to hear the songs they loved, but no one came expecting to behold the kind of fireworks that only Stevie and Lindsey could deliver.

12

TOGETHER WE STAND, DIVIDED WE FALL

Aptly enough, the departure of Lindsey Buckingham marked the twentieth anniversary of a band that had elevated losing its lead guitarists and central creative forces to an art form. Jeremy Spencer, Danny Kirwan, Bob Welch, and now Lindsey had all gone the way of Fleetwood Mac's founder, Peter Green. To steadfast Fleetwood Mac fans, the response to Lindsey's departure came as little surprise. Rick Vito and Billy Burnette were more than touring stand-ins; they were vital parts of the new Fleetwood Mac.

In stark contrast to the fresh start promised by the new lineup, the band's first order of business after wrapping up their world tour was to put out a greatest hits album. Nearly ten years earlier, Mick had discussed such a project with *Trouser Press*, saying that it would take the "freshness away of what we're trying to do. Of course, there'll be a 'Greatest Hits' sometime. One day. As a final curtain, perhaps."

While the band would go on to record two more albums, their subpar quality would prove Mick's early pronouncement right. In a way, the November 1988 release of *Fleetwood Mac Greatest Hits*, dedicated to Lindsey Buckingham, was a statement that their best material had all been recorded. With Mick already thinking of writing his tell-all autobiography, the group's first post-Buckingham album, *Behind the Mask,* seemed destined for failure.

————

Although her band may have been on its last legs, there was nothing perfunctory about Stevie's approach to her solo career. Soon after the Shake the Cage tour ended, she began to record her fourth solo effort, *The Other Side of the Mirror.* To this end, she rented a vast castle in Los Angeles and turned it into a studio. "It cost twenty-five thousand dollars a month. It was like, forget it, nobody should rent this house," she admitted on VH-1's *Behind the Music.* "We changed the formal dining room into a recording studio and recorded the whole record there. So it was my magic album."

Never staying far from her ethereal style and subject matter, in June 1989 Stevie delivered an LP that critics found predictable and fans satisfying. While its sales would ultimately prove slower than those of Stevie's previous albums, the unforgettable first single, "Rooms on Fire," was a top-twenty hit that helped *The Other Side of the Mirror* peak at an impressive Number Ten and sell over a million copies. Sadly, the year that brought Stevie her fourth platinum album would also bring a temporary end to her prolific songwriting.

The songstress was only half lucid for the duration of the tour that followed the album. The antidepressant she'd been prescribed three years before had sapped rock's once vibrant lady of all her joie de vivre. The effects had been so gradual that Stevie hardly noticed the change in herself and would no sooner attribute her lethargy to Klonopin than to her morning coffee. "By 1989, it wasn't that I didn't write well, I just stopped writing. Just too blasé to care," she explained to *Entertainment Weekly.* "It almost killed me, this stuff. I fared way better on the cocaine and coffee than I did on the Klonopin. . . . It's like you aren't there. So if you're not there you can't possibly be writing anything that's very good."

In the end, the drug would dominate years of Stevie's life and rob Fleetwood Mac's next studio album of her distinctive songwriting.

Without Lindsey Buckingham's tortured artistry, Fleetwood Mac's current forays into the studio harked back to the early days, when the band members were still able to enjoy their time together. "In the last few years, it's been more of a band than it's ever been," Christine told the *Los Angeles Times.* "I think we spent more time laughing in the last few years than in prior years. That's one thing that's held us together."

Unfortunately, those words were spoken in November 1990, mere days before Christine was scheduled to give her last live performance with Fleetwood Mac. Joining Christine in the farewell was Stevie, who had also agreed to record with Fleetwood Mac as long as she was exempted from any more concert tours.

However pleasant, the mutual regard that had bound the sextet together during the making of *Behind the Mask* was powerless when it came to reinventing the group for a new generation of listeners. Released in April 1990, the eagerly awaited album was both a commercial and artistic disappointment. Mick and John had always believed in sticking to the basic formula: five minus one, plus one (or two), still equals a band. But international fame had changed all the rules. Even Peter Green's demoralizing exit had nothing on Lindsey's departure. After twelve years in the spotlight, the singer/songwriter/guitarist had become irrevocably linked with Fleetwood Mac in the minds and hearts of American audiences. And the group knew it.

While the United Kingdom remained loyal to the flourishing expatriates, boosting *Behind the Mask* to Number One, the States were plainly bored with the new band. On the *Billboard* charts, the album rose no higher than Number Eighteen, and the first single died at Number Thirty-three. The public's disinterest only contributed to the unspoken concensus that Fleetwood Mac's thrill ride was grinding to a halt.

Of course, one uninspired album would not have sent Fleetwood Mac stalwart Christine McVie running for cover. Had her father not passed away shortly after the release of *Behind the Mask,* her participation in the lineup with John, Mick, Stevie, Billy, and Rick might have survived the twentieth century. As it was, the death of Cyril Perfect in the summer of 1990 helped Christine realize that "when time comes for change, you know it, you feel it. Things can't go on the same as always."

Christine's decision left Stevie with no choice but to begrudgingly follow in her wake. Ironically, while both the world at large and Fleetwood Mac had pegged Stevie as the most likely to defect, she was the last of the songwriting triumvirate to say goodbye. As the date of her last concert approached, there was no mistaking Stevie's reluctance to part with the band. As she told the *Los Angeles Times,* "until three years go by and I see the whole thing with no chance of getting back together, I'll never believe it's over."

On December 10, 1990, at the Great Western Forum in Inglewood, California, Christine and Stevie retired their act with the Mac. Many of the group's old friends had come out for the emotion-steeped event. Even Lindsey joined his old band onstage for a few numbers. "I know that maybe someday he will find it in his heart to spend some time with me, and maybe do some music," Stevie told the audience.

Since both Stevie and Christine were still attached to Fleetwood Mac's next album, the Inglewood show by no means indicated the band's dissolution. In retrospect, though, the evening was one of those anticlimactic partings whose true significance can take years to sink in.

––––––––

Lindsey, Stevie, John, Christine, and Mick would not appear onstage together for another two years. Of course, when this performance did finally roll around, all of Western civilization took notice. President Bill Clinton's Inaugural Gala revived the band members, who had, for the most part, spent 1991 and 1992 embroiled in both professional and personal frustrations.

Mick's telltale autobiography, *My Life and Adventures in Fleetwood Mac,* was the first aggravation to hit the group after the frontwomen's departure. While the members had known of Mick's collaboration with a writer, they were displeased with the final outcome. In *Bam,* Lindsey recalled: "Everyone was very hurt by that. Not by any facts in particular, which I definitely was hurt by, but just the tone of it in general. Just the fact that it was so trashy. Fleetwood Mac may have wound down, but it's a shame to have things come out that sort of add a lack of dignity to it. It doesn't have to be that way. I was very unhappy with a couple of very specific incidents described in there, which were totally untrue. I never responded to it. I didn't think there was any reason to dignify it."

Although Lindsey disliked the dismissive manner with which Mick treated his contribution to Fleetwood Mac's success, one glaring untruth proved more upsetting than anything else. "There was one story that had me slapping Stevie when I said I was leaving the band," Lindsey explained. "The next time I saw Stevie after that, she came up to me, and said, 'God, I'm really sorry he wrote that.' She was apologizing to me for something he wrote. So, I don't know. I think that was the product of a lot of late nights Mick spent with a writer, and maybe not keeping as much control over what was said, or certainly what was edited, as should have been. I'm fairly sure that he's sorry he did that. It was unfortunate."

Mick's book also revealed his *Rumours*-era affair with Stevie Nicks. While Stevie didn't take issue with this disclosure, she and Mick quarreled over an unrelated issue. In 1991, Stevie was planning to release *Timespace: The Best of Stevie Nicks*. Hoping to take this opportunity to let her fans hear "Silver Springs," the song that had fallen into oblivion as the B-side to Lindsey's "Go Your Own Way" single, she asked Mick for the rights to the song. Stevie had been angry and upset when her song about Lindsey was cut from the album and used as backup to Lindsey's song about her. Yet that anger paled in comparison to the exasperation she felt when Mick denied her request.

The drummer had good reasons for his negative response. Recent years had seen a groundswell of interest in "Silver Springs" from Fleetwood Mac's followers. With the band's silver anniversary coming up in 1992, Mick was planning to release *25 Years: The Chain*, a four-CD boxed set spanning the whole of Fleetwood Mac's eclectic career. Since the record that featured "Silver Springs" on its flip side had by now become a rare collector's item, the song's inclusion in the set would be a major selling point. Stevie and Mick were at an impasse, so Stevie was forced to release *Timespace* without "Silver Springs." Shortly thereafter, she told *USA Today* that she would never record with Mick again.

Meanwhile, Mick, Richard Dashut, and Ken Caillat were working long hours to get the compilation CDs ready in time for the Christmas shopping season. Rick Vito had left Fleetwood Mac in the fall of 1991, and Stevie was "not speaking" to Mick. Consequently, the drummer told CNN, this boxed set would represent Fleetwood Mac's "swan song, so it's put to bed really. I have just the best wonderful memories of that whole experience."

———

Bill Clinton's adoption of "Don't Stop" as his campaign anthem during the summer of 1992 took the members of Fleetwood Mac completely unaware. At the time, all plans for the Mac's future were on hold. Even though Stevie was back on board to record (the band members' squabbles never seem to last for long), her songwriting was still paralyzed by the Klonopin addiction. *Behind the Mask*'s lackluster sales also provided little impetus for rushing back into the studio.

Mick's life had changed drastically in the time between the recording of Fleetwood Mac's last album and the moment he heard "Don't Stop" emanating from his TV set. Within three years of his 1988 marriage to Sara Recor, Mick was divorced and on the verge of a new relationship with his investment adviser's daughter, Lynn Frankel. The forty-four-year-old drummer needed to preserve his health to keep up with his twenty-eight-year-old girlfriend, so he was inspired to quit drinking and snorting cocaine altogether. Immersed in the romance and in his musical side projects, Mick recalled his initial reaction to the presidential candidate's campaign song in the *Washington Post:* "The first thing I thought was 'Someone has ripped off one of our songs.' And then I realized it was us."

Christine, the writer of the number, was no less astonished. It had been a long time since anyone other than classic-rock deejays had spun "Don't Stop." She was feeling far removed from Fleetwood Mac and enjoying her quiet home life with her husband of eight years, Eddy Quintela. Christine recalled, "I was at my home in Los Angeles watching television but not paying that much attention. But of course my ears pricked up immediately when I heard that song. I couldn't believe it."

All the members of Fleetwood Mac were flattered to learn that they had fans in such high places. All, that is, save one. As Lindsey told the *San Francisco Chronicle,* "My reaction wasn't as strong as [that of] other people in the band."

After leaving the Mac to return to his solo album, Lindsey found that he needed a year just to collect his thoughts. His newfound freedom was instrumental in his personal growth. In the ten-odd years since his separation from Stevie, Lindsey had never had the luxury of analyzing or working through the issues germane to that relationship. Finally, he was able to examine his own shortcomings with the same probing eye that he turned toward his music. Having begun the process of self-realization, he was able to reenter his home studio, not to emerge for three years. In *Rolling Stone,* he said, "People might think I've been off on some island getting my ya-yas out. The truth is, I've basically been here twelve hours a day. I've been goofing off only in the most productive sense."

By the time Lindsey found out that the former Arkansas governor was using his band's song, his third solo album, *Out of the Cradle,* was already in the stores and being heralded as the Second Coming by swooning rock critics nationwide. Despite the industry-watchers' genuflection, *Out of the Cradle* was not music to laypeople's ears. Released on June 16, 1992, the album didn't even break into *Billboard*'s Top 100. While Lindsey had not seen the need to tour in support of his previous albums, this one was different. "My other solo records were made quickly as sidebars to a more mainstream situation," he says. "This is no longer the sideshow, this is the main event, and I hope there are hits on there somewhere."

To spread the word, Lindsey agreed to appear on VH-1's *Center Stage* program. Since the show would televise his solo concert, he needed to audition a group of musicians. The process took over a month. Then rehearsal began; another two months. An unadvertised trial-run performance at a small club outside Los Angeles saw people showing up in droves. With the backing of Warner Bros., Lindsey was already planning his first solo tour when the Inaugural Gala Committee began rounding up the five incomparable musicians who had made Fleetwood Mac a household name back in the seventies.

———

When Bill Clinton triumphed in the presidential race of 1992, Fleetwood Mac's opus was suddenly as ubiquitous as it had been during the band's chart-topping prime. To the tune of the Mac's "Don't Stop," Clinton had managed to get the inside track on MTV's "Rock the Vote" movement and sent millions of young first-time voters scurrying for the nearest ballot box.

The newly-elected president's greatest wish was for Fleetwood Mac to perform at his Inaugural Ball. Stevie, Mick, Christine, and John wanted nothing more than to oblige; Lindsey was the wild card. "It was a tough thing," he recalled. "The [Inaugural Gala Committee] was asking for the five people that had been involved with that song, and I just felt that if everyone else in the band wanted to do it, I didn't really have anything against doing it. I would not have done it if it had been a major commitment to rehearsing, or if we were going to do a whole set."

What with the President of the United States of America calling for a performance, and his whole band intent on grabbing this final moment in the spotlight, Lindsey found himself in no position to refuse. As much as Stevie hated to ask her old bandmate for anything, she swallowed her pride, telephoned Lindsey, and begged him to play just this once, for old time's sake. As she recounted in the *Island Ear*, "I called him and said, 'If you cheat me out of this honoring moment, I'll never speak to you again.' So he did it."

For a brief moment, Fleetwood Mac was again the center of the universe. On January 19, 1993, they rocked the Capital Center as a beatific first family and most of America looked on. "It was great," Stevie told the *Miami Herald*. "It was something I don't think any of us will ever, ever forget. Walking out and knowing that we were walking out because Bill Clinton wanted us. That was the most incredible thing. You couldn't feel more special than we did that night."

During their performance of the song, complete with thirteen choruses, Fleetwood Mac proved that they had not lost any of the electricity that had charged their early concerts. In context, "Don't Stop" helped to infuse the entire audience with hope for the country's future.

To onlookers, Fleetwood Mac's prospects appeared equally bright. The quintet's tight stage act had many wondering if they would reunite. Of course, Lindsey had no intention of sacrificing his solo tour to the needs of Fleetwood Mac, as he told every reporter who ventured to ask. Within a month, Stevie also handed in her resignation—this despite Mick's plans to record another Fleetwood Mac album with the studio lineup of Christine, John, Stevie, and Billy.

For Stevie, the exit was long overdue. In the *Boston Herald*, she said: "It was very hard to leave. I just couldn't leave them after Lindsey left. I couldn't do that to them. I just couldn't. But after Lindsey came and played the inauguration with us, I realized I could never deal with Fleetwood Mac again unless it would be the five of us. And it never will be that way again. So I decided my part in that particular Shakespearean drama is over."

———

After quitting her band of eighteen years, Stevie went straight to work on her fifth solo album, *Street Angel*. Although her Klonopin dependency had made her lose touch with her body and her feelings, her strong sense of responsibility to her fans prevailed. Among the old friends she contacted to collaborate on the record were Waddy Wachtel and Mike Campbell, who had been instrumental in Stevie's previous projects. Even Bob Dylan joined in for Stevie's cover of his "Just Like a Woman."

But by the end of 1993, Stevie could no longer deny that something had gone horribly wrong. While hosting a bridal shower for one of her friends, she had a head-on collision with a fireplace. The impact would have sent most people reeling, but not Stevie. She felt nothing at all. No longer on cocaine and hardly drinking, she suddenly realized that it was the Klonopin that had changed her "from a tormented, productive artist to an indifferent woman."

Having already beaten cocaine, she decided to do the same with the prescription drug. She never imagined how arduous this process would be. "In those forty-five days [of rehab] my hair turned gray, my skin molted, I had a headache from the second I got in there until the day I left, I didn't sleep, and I couldn't go to any of the therapy things, I was so sick. It was awful," she recalled in *Entertainment Weekly*. "It was so much worse than getting off cocaine."

Weakened but drug-free, Stevie returned to her home in Scottsdale,

Arizona—and to writing. Although she added another ten pounds to her already zaftig frame during her month-long convalescence, she felt healthier than she had in years. Responding to her fans' outpouring of support, she embarked on a tour to promote *Street Angel,* which had been given a relatively tepid reception upon its release in May 1994. Stevie had learned to avoid all concert reviews, but she would be unable to ignore the slap-in-the-face treatment she would be dealt during this particular tour.

As one concert critic after another leveled a potshot at her size, Stevie's stoic resolve began to crumble. If the pressures of staying clean and sober and of having to please the audience with her music had not been enough to send her into seclusion, the added strain of trying to maintain the girlish figure that had won millions of hearts back in the day was truly overwhelming for the forty-six-year-old woman. Feeling that her looks were disappointing her fans, Stevie finished the tour determined either to lose weight or never perform again.

———

Fleetwood Mac's remaining members were also at a loss. After Stevie and Rick Vito left the band, there was only John, Mick, Billy, and Christine. Since Christine wouldn't tour and Billy didn't play lead guitar, the band was in dire need of new recruits. Mick's efforts to sustain his lifelong passion and meal ticket now took on a desperate tone. For talent, he plundered his side band, the Zoo, and emerged with young Bekka Bramlett, the daughter of rock 'n' roll heavies Delaney and Bonnie Bramlett. With her on vocals, the only thing standing between Mick and the beloved road was a lead guitarist. That's when Mick hit upon the idea of inviting his friend and former Traffic member Dave Mason into the band.

Aside from a negligible number of dogged fans, most of the concert-going public assumed that the Mac had broken up. To trumpet their existence, the new version of Fleetwood Mac toured and recorded another album, *Time.* Even Christine's in-studio contribution couldn't save the album from falling into a vat of mediocrity. In terms of sales, the album got exactly what it deserved: not much. Released on October 10, 1995, *Time* was the album that Fleetwood Mac fans preferred to forget. Lindsey told the *San Francisco Chronicle* that "by the time it got down to being no Stevie and Bekka Bramlett and Dave Mason . . . a lot of people were not too happy with that because it really did bastardize the good name."

If the album was unworthy of Fleetwood Mac, their tours were even more so. On *Music Central,* Lindsey remembered how the fall from grace demoralized Mick. "This may not be exactly right, but it's my take on where Mick was: Even though he was personally in a really good place, that last incarnation of Fleetwood Mac in the studio and on the road, with Dave Mason and Bekka Bramlett, had gone out basically as a nostalgia package. It was with Pat Benatar and REO Speedwagon, stuff you don't like to see the name Fleetwood Mac associated with. I think it was very hard on him. The making of that album was hard on Mick, and his confidence as a player had gone down."

Finally, even Billy Burnette and Bekka Bramlett deserted Fleetwood and McVie to record an album as a duo. For Mick and John, there was nothing left to do but face the facts: Fleetwood Mac was over, and had been over for years. "At the end," Mick told *Goldmine,* "it was starting to be too much hard work. We'd made an album that was a total failure, and I just couldn't see myself starting all over. So we stopped."

————

Ironically, it was the end of Fleetwood Mac that inspired the band's jubilant revival. Audiences across the nation had long since given the Mac up for dead, and now that the group members themselves were ready to accept the inevitable, serenity reigned supreme. John resumed his familial responsibilities to wife Julie and seven-year-old daughter Molly. Christine continued restoring her four-hundred-year-old home in Kent, England, with Eddy Quintela, her husband and songwriting partner. Even Mick accomplished the unbelievable by turning his attention to his third wife, Lynn, whom he'd married while on tour in the summer of 1995.

By 1996, John, Christine, Stevie, Mick, and Lindsey were no longer bound by ties of resentment. They were just five people with tremendous memories of having lived life to the fullest as a group. With the surrender of Fleetwood Mac, the cold war between Lindsey, Stevie, and the rest of the group had been resolved. And since the old undercurrent of animosity had effectively been quelled, there was nothing to keep Mick from calling his old friend Lindsey to catch up.

Mick could not have picked a more opportune moment to reach out. Lindsey had only recently begun trying to record another solo album with his touring band of 1993. He was in the process of looking for a new drummer when the phone rang. Mick's familiar voice came over the receiver, and according to Lindsey's recollection in *Rolling Stone*, "over the course of the conversation, I could tell that he had gone through a lot of changes. I had done a solo album and gone through my own period of reinvention, so I was in a much better place than when I left the band back in 1987."

The next thing either of them knew, Mick and Lindsey were in the infamous Bel Air garage-studio relating, jamming, and generally having a good time working on Lindsey's solo album. "Initially, I thought it would just be two weeks in the studio as two players, two guys. It turned out to be over a year," Mick told the *Independent*. "That was the beginning of a whole new relationship for me and Lindsey. We'd go out and have meals and talk about things that had worried him in the past."

The collaboration stretched on for several months, during which Mick regained all the assurance he'd lost while toiling to sustain the Mac through its innumerable permutations. During the summer of 1996, Lindsey recalled that "it came time to do some bass parts. I asked Mick who he thought we should use. I should have known what his answer would be."

Reenter John McVie. Well rested and all sailed out, John had no problems overcoming his aversion to the studio. He and Mick were musicians, and as such, they needed a band. It was John's recruitment that really started the reunion ball rolling. According to Lindsey, "John came in and it was great. What he had to offer was kind of eye-opening. So at that point I think there was this implication—gee, there's three of these guys working together—and I think a lightbulb went off over at Warner Bros."

With Mick, John, and Lindsey getting on famously, no one but Christine would do when the keyboard tracks needed to be cut. If the male contingent of Fleetwood Mac had been enough to give the record company some rather big ideas, Christine's return to the cadre galvanized the execs. From the moment she walked into the studio, a sense of impending greatness filled the room. "It was an odd feeling, being back together," she said, "but it was obvious we were having fun."

While all four components of the illustrious lineup were ostensibly working on Lindsey's solo project, Mick began plotting the supergroup's restoration and "lobbying for it behind the scenes." Thanks to the Eagles' When Hell Freezes Over reunion tour, the market research was over and done with. There was much to gain if Fleetwood Mac could only regroup.

———

For most fans, a Fleetwood Mac reunion without Stevie Nicks would have been no reunion at all. The tension between Stevie and Lindsey had only increased with the years. Shortly after renouncing her life as a performer in 1994, Stevie had described their relationship in *Rolling Stone*, saying "We're really not friends. We're really not anything. We did not break up friends, and we have never been friends since. He is not really able to have any kind of relationship with me. I just bug him to death. Everything I do is abrasive to him."

Lindsey would have expressed similar sentiments. At the time, it would have taken a lot more than hell freezing over for him to consider touring with Stevie again. What a difference two years make.

By 1996, Stevie was a new woman. Gone were the breast implants she'd been so quick to purchase after the *Rumours* windfall. Just like the sudden fame that the album had brought, the silicone had gone from enhancing her life to marring her health. The Epstein-Barr virus had not been wholly to blame for Stevie's chronic fatigue; when the doctors removed the implants, "it turned out they were totally broken." As Stevie later told *People*, "I'm living proof that they aren't safe."

Having conquered the listlessness that had plagued her for years, Stevie resolved to shed the excess pounds. By the time she was asked to contribute to the *Twister* soundtrack, she had reclaimed her beauty, vigor, and peace of mind. By calling in her old flame to produce "Twisted," Stevie managed to affect a reconciliation. Lindsey's curios-

ity coupled with the modest commitment required by the project sufficed to bring the scorching duo back into contact. Since neither had
anything left to prove to the other, Lindsey and Stevie were suddenly
transported to the days of both for one and one for both. "Ironically,"
Lindsey told *Music Central*, "because of where I'm at and where she's
at, it's almost like I'm seeing the Stevie I used to live with."

Mick needed a reunion, Lindsey's record label wanted a reunion,
and Lindsey could find no valid answer to the big question: Why not a
reunion? "For my part," Lindsey told *Salon* magazine, "I had made a
lot of changes in my life. I was done with my girlfriend after twelve
years, the last few being especially difficult. I had new management
and new lawyers. And I had gotten past all the things I'd seen as bag-
gage with Fleetwood Mac. So there was this pitch to do the band
again."

———

The added exposure that a Fleetwood Mac tour would bring to his solo
work was not lost on Lindsey. His album, *Gift of Screws*, could wait,
but Fleetwood Mac's time had come. By 1996, *Rumours* had sold over
twenty-five million copies worldwide, making it the third highest-
selling album of all time—as well as the supreme accomplishment that
allowed Lindsey, Stevie, and Christine as much creative and personal
freedom as three human beings could ever hope to achieve. The year
1997 would mark the album's twentieth anniversary, and as the five
musicians responsible for its creation were once again seeing eye to
eye, there was every reason to celebrate.

Mick, John, and Lindsey were the first to recognize the opportunity
and repledge their allegiance to the Mac. Christine's stipulations had
also been fulfilled during her session work for *Gift of Screws*. "I said to
my manager the requirement I had was that we were going to get on,
and it would have to be fun," she told the *Orlando Sentinel*. "We sat
around and talked, sang a little bit, and it was pretty clear, I think, that
everyone was performing well, singing well, and there was a good
chemistry there."

When the record label called Stevie to check where she stood on
the reunion tour, she was just about to record her next solo album. In

Rolling Stone, she said: "I was truly starting on a record of my own when the whole world changed. . . . All of a sudden this thing about Fleetwood Mac happened, and as the days went by there was more talk, then somebody from Warner Bros. actually came up and said, 'Lindsey Buckingham really is going to put his record on the shelf to do this.' I said, 'Well, I don't believe that, because he said that a million times before.' So I called him and I said, 'Lindsey, I need you to tell me what's happening, because if we really are going to do this . . . I'm not even going to start my record and have to stop it.' And he said, 'No, I'm going to do it.' I said, 'You're sure. You promise?' "

A simple yes was all it took to send Stevie running back to her band. The five points of the Fleetwood Mac pentacle had at last connected, and the star power was tremendous, bringing whole cable networks, record companies, and media syndicates to their knees. " 'Fleetwood Mac'—they're magic words that just open doors," Lindsey told *Salon.* "As soon as the word gets out that this Fleetwood Mac is back, MTV wants to do a special, the Hollywood Bowl is calling for a concert date, and so on."

————

A feverishly anticipated MTV special, a platinum-selling video of the whole affair, a quadruple-platinum live album entitled *The Dance,* and a sold-out forty-city U.S. tour were to be the fruits of the reunion that reestablished the band as rock's most passionate act. But it was their unrelenting love for the music and each other, more than any financial rewards, that had drawn the group together.

While no one knew whether the band would, in fact, survive all six weeks of rehearsal, the joy of playing music together soon supplanted all doubts and memories of troubles past. Of course, the rehearsals weren't all about sweet nothings and the sound of laughter. But the egos were quiet, and reason had its way. Finally, the quintet had all the glory of their best days, with none of the pain.

Two shows had been scheduled to take place in Burbank, California; the second would be videotaped for MTV. The old friends and the new, the famous and the unknown, all mingled in the audience with the same feeling of nervous expectation that the five realigned personalities were experiencing backstage. The first night was a test run, Fleetwood Mac's first live performance in nearly fifteen years. In an unprecedented mishap, Stevie flubbed the opening lines to "Dreams," the band's only Number One single.

No matter. The next night's main event would make up for any mistakes. Among seventeen chill-inspiring selections, including the power of "The Chain," the virulence of "Go Your Own Way," and the lively elegance of "Everywhere," Stevie's heartrending "Silver Springs" was the song of the night. Tears sprang to every eye as the blonde rock goddess turned to Lindsey and lamented the end of their relationship and the death of the group's innocence in song.

Cloaked in azure stage lights and an aura of timeless romance, Stevie, Lindsey, Mick, John, and Christine sparkled their way through the performance, letting a new generation of fans in on the secret of their success. From the meaningful looks to the conciliatory hugs, every uncensored gesture served to fuel the fire of imagination raging in the hearts of viewers. Was the scorching dynamic between Stevie and Lindsey real, or was it showbiz? Could *The Dance* really be Fleetwood Mac's final statement of closure—or might this be just the beginning?

Only time will tell. Meanwhile, the memory of Fleetwood Mac's sweeping career leaves little room for regrets. As Stevie affirmed: "However much fun you think it was, it was more. It was a grand ride, a great trip. Fleetwood Mac was one of the great glamour rock groups, and we had the best of the best. . . . If I was going to do it again, I don't think I could do any better than that."

EPILOGUE

Amazed by the unexpected harmony charging *The Dance* concert tour, Fleetwood Mac was all set to take on Europe when Christine's exhaustion put a stop to the festivities. Shortly thereafter, on January 12, 1998, Fleetwood Mac was inducted into the Rock and Roll Hall of Fame. Of the sixteen musicians who have had occasion to call the band their own, only eight were invited into the hallowed hall: Peter Green, Mick Fleetwood, John McVie, Jeremy Spencer, Danny Kirwan, Christine McVie, Lindsey Buckingham, and Stevie Nicks.

Only six were present. The whereabouts of Danny Kirwan could not be established; recent reports have had him in and out of institutions and living on the streets of London without a permanent address. Jeremy Spencer could also not be prevailed upon to attend, preferring to play his slide guitar solely with the Children of God.

Of the six in attendance, only five performed under the moniker of Fleetwood Mac. Instead of joining John and Mick, a clear-eyed Peter Green played "Black Magic Woman" with another of the evening's legendary inductees, Carlos Santana. Peter had embraced his blues roots and musical ability and returned to the road with his new band, the Splinter Group.

"Say You Love Me," "Big Love," and "Landslide" were performed by the superlative Fleetwood Mac lineup. Their illusions had been dispelled and their vices shed, but otherwise the five had not changed much since their early days as a group. Looking forward to the birth of his first son, as well as the release of his postponed solo album, Lindsey remained enamored with the studio. Stevie's priorities also had not changed, and *Enchanted,* a boxed set of her solo work, was scheduled to hit the stores in a few months' time, to be followed by a tour and another solo album. Mick had started his own record company and was busy producing and overseeing *Legacy: A Tribute to Fleetwood Mac's Rumours,* while John and Christine continued to find as much satisfaction in their self-made Arcadias of sailing, cooking, and gardening as they ever had in years gone by.

INDEX

219